MODERN WEDDING

MODERN WEDDING

Creating a Celebration
That Looks & Feels Like You

KELSEY McKINNON

Principal photography by
Abby & Lauren Ross

ARTISAN | NEW YORK

Library of Congress Cataloging-in-Publication Data
Names: McKinnon, Kelsey, author. | Ross, Abby, photographer. | Ross, Lauren, photographer.
Title: Modern wedding : creating a celebration that looks and feels like you / Kelsey McKinnon ; principal photography by Abby and Lauren Ross.
Description: New York : Artisan, a division of Workman Publishing Co., Inc. [2018]
Identifiers: LCCN 2018014191 | ISBN 9781579657758 (hardcover : alk. paper)
Subjects: LCSH: Weddings—Planning. | Weddings—History—21st century.
Classification: LCC HQ745 .M396 2018 | DDC 392.5—dc23
LC record available at https://lccn.loc.gov/2018014191

Published by Artisan
A division of Workman Publishing Co., Inc.
225 Varick Street
New York, NY 10014-4381
artisanbooks.com

Artisan is a registered trademark of Workman Publishing Co., Inc.

Published simultaneously in Canada by Thomas Allen & Son, Limited

Design by Jennifer K. Beal Davis

Front cover photographs: Abby and Lauren Ross
Back cover photographs, clockwise from top left: Olivia Rae James, Hannah Thompson, Joel Serrato, Donna Newman, Abby and Lauren Ross, Abby and Lauren Ross, Joel Serrato, Abby and Lauren Ross, Joel Serrato, Abby and Lauren Ross

Printed in China
First printing, November 2018

10 9 8 7 6 5 4 3 2 1

FOR JOSH

CONTENTS

INTRODUCTION

It's hard to say exactly when the wedding industry erupted into the prodigious enterprise that it's become, peddling mass-produced gowns and lavish parties that people can barely afford, but attitudes have thankfully begun to shift. Couples today want a carefully cultivated celebration that's unpretentious, beautifully designed, and reflective of their unique partnership—but what exactly does that look like, and how do you pull it off?

As an editor at a wedding magazine, I am always on the lookout for examples of weddings that embody this forward-thinking ethos, and have been lucky enough to get to know the people behind them and learn about their creative processes. In the course of my work (and in preparation for my own wedding), I have reviewed thousands of celebrations from across the country (and farther afield), and this exhaustive search eventually culminated in this book.

One of the most important things I've learned is that a couple's budget does *not* determine whether they have a beautiful and meaningful wedding. The key to planning a memorable event isn't how much you spend, how grand it appears, or how fancy your planner is; it's about finding special ways to convey your core values. In this book, you are given the tools to reclaim your wedding day as something you can design (and actually pull off) in a way that is truly authentic. This means embracing your natural surroundings; celebrating timeless ideas and traditions; and focusing on the emotional qualities of the day, not just how it will look in pictures.

Each chapter unpacks an element of a wedding—from stationery and gifts to flowers and tablescapes—with examples that will appeal to couples who care about how things are made, who are conscious of how the choices they make impact the world around

them, and who are not influenced by trends. Modern dresses, minimalist ceremony structures, naked cakes, and frameworthy invitation suites are all illustrated with photos from real weddings. Interspersed between these chapters are "case studies" featuring couples who were able to translate what is most important to them and their relationships into weddings that were totally unique. There's a destination fete in the Tuscan countryside, an artful "house party" in Brooklyn, a same-sex wedding in Big Sur, a new age celebration in Kauai, and more. While the examples range in style, budget, and location and represent various cultures and religious traditions, the couples behind them all share the belief that authenticity on this day matters above all else.

There are many ways to throw a modern wedding. Let these pages give you the freedom to design a wedding that is wholly you, whatever that may look like, by taking a closer look at the things that add meaning to your life and finding ways to incorporate them into your celebration. If it comes from the heart, it will be beautiful.

THE COLOR STORY

One of the first things you'll be asked after you get engaged is "What are your colors?" (Translation: "What's the color scheme of your wedding?") Before you can answer that question, you'll need to determine what kind of feeling you want your wedding to evoke (think "modern and eccentric" or "traditional and feminine").

Creating a mood board, whether it's a physical bulletin board or a digital one, such as a Pinterest board, is the best way to help you establish a general tone and feeling for your wedding.

As you cull pictures for your board, don't limit yourself to wedding images. A wedding represents the confluence of so many different lifestyle categories (fashion, music, design, food and wine, travel), and pulling references from a wide range of nonwedding sources will help make your day more unique. Include pictures of anything that inspires you, be it a favorite flower, a piece of artwork you love, a page from a fashion magazine or a book on interior design, a family heirloom, or a swatch of fabric. Try to incorporate images that are meaningful to your relationship—something you purchased on a trip, the menu from your favorite restaurant.

As this mosaic comes together, take a step back and look at the big picture: Does everything feel minimalist? Rustic? Edgy? More or less traditional? Once you extrapolate a few key words to define your mood board, you will be ready to focus on the actual color palette (or, the "color story").

Traditionally, couples pick two or three hues to make up their color story (the most classic combination being white, blush, and green), but a newer approach is to select a wider range of tones to create a more nuanced palette (for example, a moody autumnal story of olive, maroon, cream, pumpkin, and navy). More relaxed

This new spin on the classic blue-and-white palette features a soft velvet runner, mismatched vintage plating, a faded blue linen napkin, and a blue-and-white deckle-edged menu with the couple's custom heraldry.

couples may even be open to letting their color story naturally reveal itself as they go through the process of designing their wedding instead of pre-selecting hues.

The colors that you choose should obviously be ones that you love (these are usually apparent on your mood board), but they should also be reflective of the season (What flowers will be in bloom when you get married? Will the surrounding landscape be lush or dry?) and the colors of your venue (if it's a dark, wood-paneled room, you may need to use light colors). And, of course, they should complement one another. If you aren't sure which colors work well together, order a Pantone book or use paint samples from a hardware store to try out different combinations. Pin these colors to your mood board so you have one centralized reference point.

Establishing a color story early and being mindful of it as you move through the design process will make each individual decision you face much easier (as you'll have essentially narrowed down the options for yourself in advance) and will leave you with a wedding that feels considered the whole way through.

For a citrus-themed wedding in the California desert, shades of yellow and orange were woven into elements used throughout the day, from the bridesmaids' gowns and kumquat-laden flower crowns to the ceremonial garland and the ikebana centerpieces.

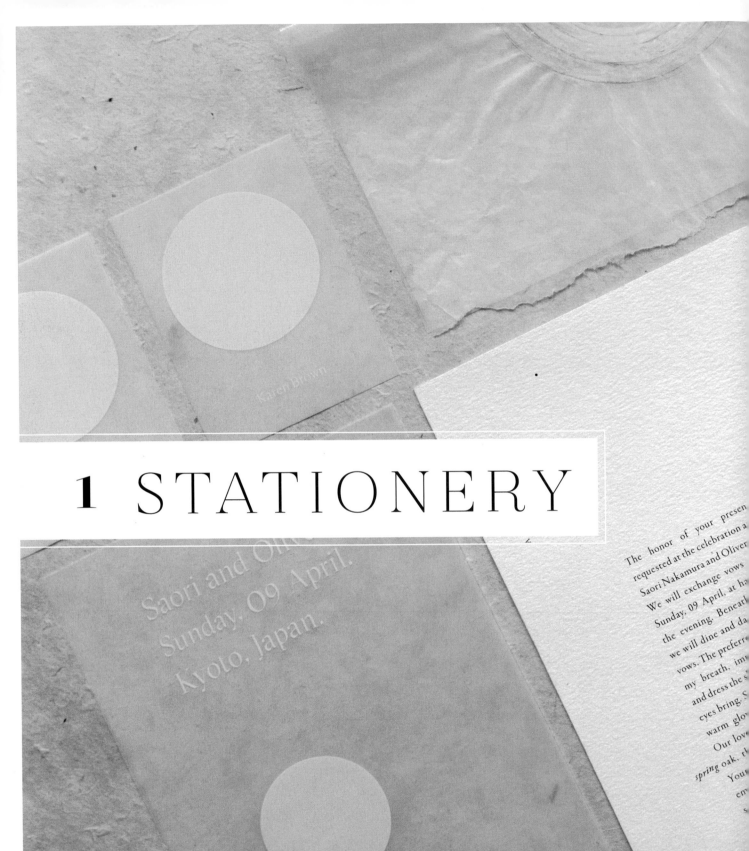

1 STATIONERY

In this speed-obsessed age of email and Evites, the process of designing an invitation suite forces us to slow down and think carefully about how we communicate with one another. The subtleties of how this information is presented—including details like wax seals, custom icons, and printing techniques—are often just as telling as what's written inside.

Think about your invitation suite (and save-the-date) as a preview of your wedding, with hints of your color story (see page 17), details that evoke the event's level of formality, and language that's uniquely reflective of your personalities. And here, perhaps more than any other part of wedding planning, there are etiquette rules that you should be aware of (whether or not you decide to actually follow them).

CREATING A GUEST LIST

One of the first things you'll need to do after becoming engaged is create a guest list, because deciding how many people to invite will inform almost every other decision you make. This is of course easier said than done! Start by organizing the names in a spreadsheet (Google Sheets allows for easy updating and sharing, though Excel works, too) or on a planning site (such as AppyCouple.com, WeddingWire.com, or AllSeated.com). More than just an invitation tracker, this spreadsheet will be a central place for you to chart lodging information and gifts. Include columns for the following categories.

- Titles and full names (written exactly as the invitation should be addressed—see page 51)

- Names for the inner envelope (if using)

- Street address

- City

- State

- Zip code

- Country (if you have a large number of international invitees)

- Other events guests are invited to (the rehearsal dinner, for example)

- RSVP status (and RSVP card number—see page 42)

- Entrée choice (if applicable)

- Food sensitivities

- Hotel and room number (if you are delivering welcome bags and itineraries)

- Off-registry gifts (most registries offer a tracking service)

- Email address (if you are doing an Evite or for emergency correspondence)

GETTING HITCHED ON A HOLIDAY While you might be planning to take a week or two off from work to get married, chances are your guests won't be able to allot more than a couple of days to your wedding (if that), so choosing a date over a long holiday weekend might be a practical choice, especially if your wedding events extend over multiple days or if you are having a destination wedding. Try to avoid major holidays, when guests may have family or religious obligations. Presidents' Day, Memorial Day, and Labor Day weekends, as well as Halloween and New Year's Eve, are acceptable options—just be sure to mail the save-the-dates well in advance (closer to eight months before the wedding), as people often make plans for these holidays, and hotels and flights are in higher demand during these times.

THE B-LIST

Many couples choose to send out a second round of invitations (i.e., to the "B-list") as they receive regrets from their first round of invitees. (Note: There's no way to accurately determine the number of regrets to anticipate, but it's usually 20 to 25 percent of invitees for local weddings and up to 35 percent for destination events.) Obviously, you don't want people to know they are on the B-list, so if you are planning to mail invitations in stages, consider mailing the first round earlier than you normally would (see page 26)—that way, the second round won't encroach too closely on the wedding date (though you may still need to print a later reply-by date on second-round invites). If you are still worried that the turnaround time will be too short, consider asking all guests to reply via email instead of mailing back a reply card to expedite the process.

TIMELINE & BUDGET

Designing and ordering the different components of your wedding suite and any additional paper goods will require some organization. Break down the process into three general stages: first designing the invitation (and all the enclosure cards with it), then the save-the-date, and finally the day-of stationery (such as ceremony programs and table numbers). Then, based on your initial preferences for paper stock and printing method, your stationer will give you itemized quotes for each component, which will help you decide how to allocate your budget. For example, you may not be happy with splurging on the invitation if it means having to skimp on your program. As you go through the process, ask your stationer for updated quotes for any changes that will influence the cost— the little details can quickly add up, so if you have a firm budget, be sure to give your stationer a number not to exceed.

EXTRA INVITATIONS
It can be costly to print more invitations after placing your initial order, so get at minimum an extra 10 percent up front. There will always be invitations that don't arrive and will need to be re-sent. You also need to anticipate guests you may want to invite off the B-list. And you will want extras to frame and for your wedding album.

This suite features a Picasso-inspired dove and the motto for the weekend, "Laissez les bons temps rouler!" ("Let the good times roll!")

STATIONERY TIMELINE

TIME BEFORE WEDDING	TASK
9 MONTHS*	Interview and hire a stationer
6 MONTHS**	Send out save-the-dates
4 MONTHS	Order invitations (be sure to build in time to proof/edit them)
2½ MONTHS	Assemble and address invitations (if hiring a calligrapher, build in their turnaround time)
8 WEEKS	Send out first round of invitations
6 WEEKS***	Send out B-list invitations (if applicable)

*OR AT LEAST 3 MONTHS PRIOR TO YOUR TARGET SAVE-THE-DATE MAILING
**OR UP TO A YEAR IN ADVANCE IF YOU ARE HAVING A DESTINATION WEDDING OR HAVE MANY INTERNATIONAL INVITEES
***OR AS YOU RECEIVE REGRETS

THE HONOR OF YOUR PRESENCE IS REQUESTED
TO CELEBRATE THE HOLY MATRIMONY OF

KOURTNEY NICOLE JACKSON

&

NATHANIEL KYUNG SMITH

SATURDAY THE ELEVENTH OF MARCH
TWO THOUSAND SEVENTEEN
AT TWO-THIRTY IN THE AFTERNOON

PARADISE VALLEY RANCH

HEMET, CALIFORNIA

RECEPTION TO FOLLOW IMMEDIATELY

FORMAL ATTIRE REQUESTED

LAISSEZ
LES BONS
TEMPS ROULER!

save the date for the wedding of

KOURTNEY & NATHANIEL

March 11, 2017
Paradise Valley Ranch
Hemet, CA

kourtneyandnate.com
"Laissez les bons
temps rouler!"

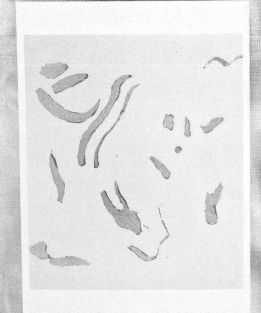

DETAILS

PREPARE FOR AN OUTDOOR CEREMONY
FOLLOWED BY RECEPTION,
DINNER, AND DANCING

WARM OUTERWEAR SUGGESTED FOR EVENING

PLEASE CONSIDER FOOTWEAR FOR
WALKING ON NATURAL TERRAIN
SUCH AS GRAVEL, GRASS, AND DIRT

FOR GIFT REGISTRY, RSVP, AND
ACCOMMODATION SUGGESTIONS, PLEASE VISIT
KOURTNEYANDNATE.COM

PLEASE RSVP BY
THE FIFTEENTH OF FEBRUARY

HIRING A STATIONER

Unless you are up for the task of designing and printing invitations yourself (basic templates can be found online at sites like Crane .com and Minted.com), a stationer is one of the first vendors you'll want to secure. Make an appointment with a few different people to view their wedding and nonwedding portfolios—some stationers will also have sample books from traditional companies like Crane & Co. and William Arthur. Learn about their process: Do they have on-site or off-site printing? (Having on-site capabilities, which is rare, means they can work with shorter turnaround times and make last-minute adjustments.) Do they offer professional calligraphy, foil-stamping, embossing, engraving, and die-cutting? Can they create custom wax seals? What about monogrammed cocktail napkins and matchboxes? And, of course, you'll want to talk about cost—couples are often surprised at the high cost of paper goods, so ask for an itemized proposal before you commit. Note that some stationers offer wedding packages for which all of the costs are listed up front, but these packages often leave very little room for alterations.

COST CONTROL While custom (or even semi-custom) stationery is the ideal, all of the details can quickly make a dent in your budget. Here are a few tips to help you keep costs in check.

- Allow enough time to avoid expedited freight and rush fees (see page 26).

- Get clear on your budget, and be direct with your stationer about it. If changes are made in design meetings, ask for an updated quote.

- Save costly printing techniques for the "big moments." For example, engrave/letterpress only the invitation, and flat print the rest of the pieces.

- Proof your invitations with the greatest care to avoid having to reprint.

- Do it yourself: make your own wax seals, hand-address your own envelopes, and handle your own mailing.

This artistic invitation was housed within a white folding card containing information about the rehearsal dinner and farewell brunch. A blush reply card was placed on the exterior.

SUITE DESIGN

A well-designed stationery suite is the sum of its many *many* parts. It's about layering dozens of elements, from the card stock to the stamps, in a cohesive way. Think about the invitation first. For your initial meeting with your stationer, you should have an idea of the time of year of the event, the venue, and the degree of formality. Any design inspiration you can bring (like your mood board—see page 17) will also help guide your stationer. Then look through their books of samples and evaluate each piece's individual elements. A sample may have a paper you love and a typeface you dislike, or vice versa. Combining all the elements that appeal to you will help to create your unique look. Once you have a general sense of the invite, you can work backward to create an "appetizer version" for the save-the-date (see page 46).

PAPER

Choosing your wedding stationery is such a tactile experience. Pick up and actually *feel* all the different options. Do you want a classic heavy card stock with a beveled edge? Or something light and layered? Textured or smooth? Remember that the heavier the card stock, the more costly it will be. If you are working with an online stationer or with someone out of town, ask them to send paper samples. Here is an overview of all the paper choices to consider.

Color: Ecru, white, or colored

Thickness: Paper weight is measured in grams per square meter (gsm) or in pounds (an ordinary piece of copy paper, for example, is about 75.2 gsm, or about a 20-pound bond)

Material: Cotton, wood fiber, linen, or vellum (a translucent type of parchment)

Format: Flat, fold-over, gatefold, or trifold (like a brochure)

Corners: Square or round

Edges: Straight, beveled, or deckle (torn)

TYPEFACE

Font choices for your invitation suite range widely, from simple block lettering to elaborate cursive script. When considering typefaces, pay special attention to the letters of your first and last names. Note that some typefaces offer alternate letterforms (called glyphs) for certain letters.

PRINTING TECHNIQUES

The printing process you choose is a key component of the overall design and cost of your suite. It's largely informed by your choices of font and paper, as they all need to be compatible. Engraving or letterpress, for example, cannot be done on an ultrathin paper such as vellum. Here are the different methods, ranging from the most straightforward to old-fashioned hand-lettered calligraphy.

Flat (or Digital): The most basic technique, flat printing takes a digital image and transfers it to paper—no special plates needed. Pros: You can use any color and font, it can be done quickly, and it's the least expensive option. Cons: The printing will be one-dimensional, and you can't use thick papers.

Offset: This is a similar process to digital printing, but here a metal plate is printed on a large rubber cylinder, which then offsets the image onto paper. Pros: Suitable for many weights and colors of paper, it costs less than most other methods and has a fast turnaround time. Con: It's one-dimensional.

Thermography: This technique, using ink and powder, gives the effect of engraving—at a much lower cost. Pro: It can be done on almost any kind of paper. Con: Paper snobs will know the difference.

Engraving and Blind Embossing: With engraving, text is raised on heavy card stock using etched copper plates. Blind embossing uses the same technique as engraving, but it's done without ink. Pro: Engraving offers beautiful old-world texture and detail. Cons: It is costly and has a slow turnaround time.

Letterpress: The opposite of engraving, letterpress debosses letters using metal or polymer plates coated with ink. It works best on smooth, heavy paper. This style has become very popular for weddings. Pros: It offers texture but is a little more subtle than engraving. Cons: Like engraving, it is costly and has a slow turnaround time.

Foil Stamping: This technique is similar to letterpress but uses metallic or pigmented foil (usually gold or silver) rather than ink. Pro: It provides a shiny, lustrous finish. Cons: Color choices are limited, and the process can be costly and slow.

Hand-Lettered Calligraphy: Decorative handwriting using a pen, brush, or quill can be done on any surface (although smooth paper is preferred). People usually think of hand-lettered calligraphy as stuffy and formal, but nowadays there are many artisans who offer more modern, playful interpretations. Pros: Every card feels like a piece of artwork, with lots of options for customization. Cons: It is the most expensive and slowest option (for these reasons, many couples opt to have their names on the invitation done in calligraphy and have the rest of the suite done in a less costly technique).

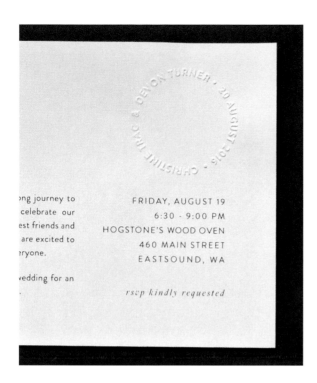

BLIND EMBOSSING AND FLAT PRINTING

LETTERPRESS

FOIL STAMPING

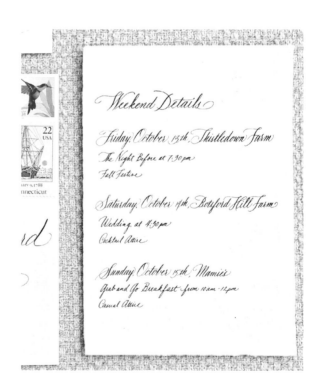

HAND-LETTERED CALLIGRAPHY

MR. AND MRS. RAYMOND REUDY
REQUEST THE PLEASURE OF YOUR COMPANY
AT THE MARRIAGE OF THEIR DAUGHTER

RAEANNA PATRICIA REUDY
TO
ROBERT LOPEZ
GRANDSON OF MARY ROSE MAGENO

SATURDAY, THE TWENTY-FOURTH OF JUNE
TWO THOUSAND SEVENTEEN
AT HALF PAST FOUR O'CLOCK
IN THE GARDEN
AT A PRIVATE ESTATE
ST. HELENA, CALIFORNIA

AND AFTERWARDS FOR DINNER & DANCING

Black tie optional

SAVE THE DATE
RAE & ROB
06.24.17

KINDLY REPLY
BY MAY TWENTY-FOURTH

NAME(S) _____
WILL ____ WILL NOT ____ ATTEND THE WELCOME PARTY
WILL ____ WILL NOT ____ ATTEND THE WEDDING

HOTEL: _____

MRS. RAYMOND REUDY
1520 HOOVER AVENUE
BURLINGAME, CALIFORNIA
94010

PLEASE JOIN US AT A
REHEARSAL DINNER
IN HONOR OF RAEANNA & ROBERT

THURSDAY, JUNE 22ND · 6PM — 9PM
INDIAN SPRINGS
1712 LINCOLN AVENUE · CALISTOGA

REPLY BY JUNE 1ST TO HAYLEY@LAURIEARONS.COM

Cocktail attire

RAE
AND
ROB

Mr. and Mrs. James Farrell Crowley
request the pleasure of your company

MRS. WINNIE AND MR. CHAVALIT FREDERICK TS
AND
MRS. IVY AND MR. JOW HSING PENG

EXTRA DESIGN DETAILS

First and foremost, your invitation suite needs to communicate information; but aside from the actual text, there are myriad ways to personalize your suite. A custom monogram, crest, or icon is a lovely way to visually connect different components of the suite—as well as napkins, matchbooks, and thank-you notes. There are several ways you can go about creating a custom image: you can design something yourself or commission an artist (there are a few great vendors on Etsy who specialize in monograms and icons), or your stationer can help you create something. And while crests and monograms are the most common choices, invitation suites can feature any kind of decorative artwork, including mural-like illustrations surrounding the text, watercolors, paintings, and/or drawings. Here are some other details to consider.

A decorative envelope liner can make for a strong first impression.

A layer of tissue over the invitation is an old-fashioned touch (once done as a way to protect the text from smearing).

Laser-cuts and die-cuts add extra dimension (this is frequently done for destination weddings in Mexico, to mimic the festive *papel picado* banners).

Inclusions such as dried or pressed flowers, leaves, and/or seeds will give each card a natural, handmade quality.

OPPOSITE:
MODERN MONOGRAM
This clean monogram, where the couple's initials are artfully intertwined, is reminiscent of a cool business logo and less traditional than a crest. Here, the first letter of the bride's and groom's names was the same—not all letters will work well together, so don't force it.

ABOVE, LEFT:
PLAYFUL CREST
A whimsical, hand-painted custom crest has become a beloved design statement for casual and formal weddings alike. A twist on traditional heraldry, it usually features a couple's initials (pictured) or a meaningful image. Couples can use it afterward for personal stationery and to monogram other home items.

ABOVE, RIGHT:
ELEGANT ICON
Symbols can be reflective of the wedding location, like a cactus for a desert wedding or a palm tree for a tropical fete. For this lunar-themed suite, the couple included a custom-designed navy crescent moon.

A RANGE OF SUITE STYLES

There are infinite ways to make your wedding suite unique. Start by thinking in general terms about style: do you want something colorful and exotic, or pared-down and minimal? To give you a better sense of how these ideas translate on paper, I turned to master stationer Jonathan Wright (who specializes in custom letterpress). Here is a sampling of his work, showcasing a wide range of styles.

CLEAN AND CLASSIC

This bright white, squared-edge card is accented with an ivory envelope liner and an image of a lily on the reverse side of the invitation. The emerald-green calligraphy on the envelope ties back to the lily.

BLACK AND WHITE

For an intimate wedding at the bride's parents' home, this modern invitation features white hand-lettered calligraphy on a black card. Black watercolor was used to stain the additional enclosure cards.

PALM READER

The classic hand-lettered calligraphy on this suite is modernized with a few distinguishing characteristics: a horizontal layout, a deep maroon ink, a tropical palm frond envelope liner, and a reverse-color enclosure card with information about additional events.

COLORFUL CRESTS

The monograms, color motifs, and special watercolor
calligraphy on this suite are light and reflective of
this wedding's tropical setting. For added texture and
formality, the small print is letterpress. The turquoise
envelopes add a pop of color.

OLD-WORLD CHARM

This delicate deckle-edged invitation "booklet"
features an illustration of the church where the
couple wed, drawn by the groom (a tattoo artist)
and finished in gold foil. The envelope is lined with
custom marbled paper.

ROYAL BLUE

An oversized, superthick card stock with an ornate gold
foil monogram, flourished hand-lettered calligraphy,
and old-fashioned rounded edges make this suite
supremely elegant. A velvet blue ribbon holds it
all together. It's finished with a collection of vintage
stamps.

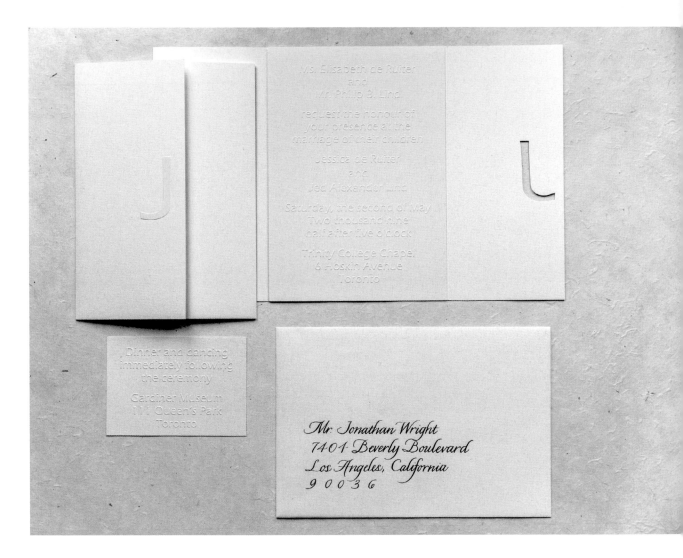

MODERN MINIMALIST

This suite is entirely blind embossed, save for the deep-oak-hued hand-lettered calligraphy on the envelope. The couple shared the same first initial ("J"), which was die-cut and embossed on the front of the gatefold cover.

BACKCOUNTRY VIBES

For an elegant Montana wedding, a wildflower frame surrounds the invitation like a fairy-tale mural, and elements of nature are seen throughout the suite (the envelope material is a rustic kraft paper). Each guest was greeted with a handwritten note from the bride on a bandana-inspired square.

REPLY CARDS

Before designing your reply cards, you need to decide who is invited to which events. For example, if you aren't inviting everyone to the rehearsal dinner, you'll need to design two different RSVP cards. (If you're inviting everyone to an ancillary event like drinks following the rehearsal dinner, that can be noted on a separate enclosure card.) Then you'll need to figure out with your caterer if your guests will need to pre-select their entrée choice so you can list the options on the reply card. Those pressed for time may forgo the card entirely and ask all their guests to RSVP to an email address or on their wedding website.

If you do send a physical reply card, make sure to include a self-addressed, stamped return envelope (do not provide stamps for international guests, as they will need to use their country's postage). If you don't get a reply by your due date, follow up with your guests via phone or email to find out their RSVP status (there always seem to be a few invitations that don't arrive for various reasons).

NUMBERING YOUR RSVP CARDS

Surprisingly, many guests will send back an RSVP card without filling out their name, so you may want to put a number on the back of the card that corresponds to the guest's name (include this in your spreadsheet—see page 24).

Asking guests to reply via email or through a wedding website cuts down on postage, paper goods, and time. Creating a separate email address to share with your partner is also a good way to keep track of all your wedding-related correspondence (it may also be used for your wedding hashtag).

RÉPONDEZ S'IL VOUS PLAÎT

Whether you are asking guests to respond to your invitation via email or phone, on a website, or using old-fashioned snail mail, design a card that is both practical and pretty. Here is a range of examples (you can see more RSVP card designs in the suites beginning on page 34).

THE MULTIPURPOSE CARD

Most people use one RSVP card for several different events. On this one, guests are invited to a welcome party, the wedding, and Sunday brunch. Their choice of entrée and where they will be staying (if applicable) are also requested.

BUSINESS-CARD INSPIRED

On this RSVP card, a Herend-esque panther gracefully stands above a phone number that had been set up for guests to call; similar to the email option, this is a faster (and more economical) method than asking everyone to mail back their card.

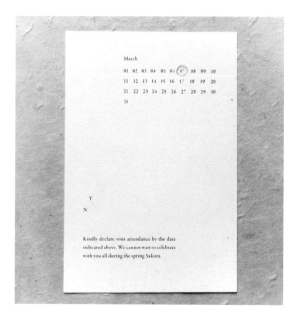

LEAVE A MESSAGE

This oversized reply card, with a beautiful hand-painted floral detail, encourages guests to write a note with well wishes to the couple along with their RSVP status. The notes make for a wonderful addition to your wedding album.

YES OR NO

This minimalist card has the reply-by date circled on a calendar. Below, guests are prompted to simply circle Y or N. The negative space on the card leaves room for the guests to leave a handwritten message, if they are so inclined.

OTHER ENCLOSURES

Some weddings are more straightforward than others. If you are having multiple events over the course of a few days, chances are you will need a few additional enclosure cards to communicate everything to your guests. You don't want to have so many enclosure cards that things get confusing, but you also don't want to cram too much information onto too few cards. As a general rule of thumb, let the invitation be its own moment, and then try to group similar items together on additional enclosures. Many couples now direct people to their wedding websites for information on mundane things like parking, accommodations, and directions. Here is a full list of what you might need to add to your wedding suite.

- Meal selection card (if not included on the reply card)

- Website information and social media hashtag (if using)

- Weekend itinerary

- Reception card (if the reception takes place at a different location than the ceremony)

- Invitations for rehearsal dinner and/or farewell brunch

- Maps and directions

- Accommodations

- Transportation and parking instructions

- Dress code (see page 50)

- Information about time and location for photos

MAPPING IT OUT

If your ceremony or reception site doesn't have an address or is difficult to find, include a map as an enclosure card with your stationery suite. A hand-drawn illustration is usually more compelling than a computer-generated map. A professional illustrator can create one that is in line with the style of your invitation, or if you are artistic, you can make one by tracing over a printout of the area. In addition to the map, you may want to list step-by-step directions.

HOLDING IT ALL TOGETHER

Since there are so many elements that make up an invitation suite, you'll want to think about how to hold everything together. Using an inner envelope (see page 53) is a formal, old-world idea, while wrapping the elements with ribbon, twine, fabric, or a leather string is an easily accomplished DIY project. If you want something more custom, you can work with your stationer on a matching paper band, or forgo the envelope in favor of a gift-like presentation box.

ENCLOSURE CARDS

Enclosure cards can be more creative than the formal invitation but should still be in the same general style.

A TROPICAL ITINERARY

A list of weekend activities for a wedding in Mexico includes welcome margaritas, yoga, and a pre-wedding fiesta (aka the rehearsal dinner).

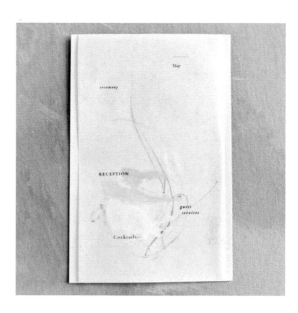

AN ARTIST'S MAP

This map was created in the form of an abstract painting and paired with an overlay with location names. After the wedding, guests could remove the overlay and have a one-of-a-kind piece of art to enjoy for years to come.

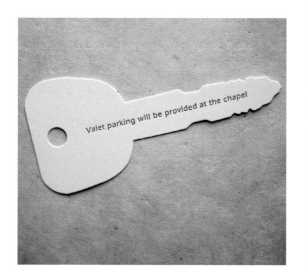

A VALET KEY

Presenting information about parking on a cutout key shape turns an otherwise mundane topic into a charming design moment.

AN ALL-IN-ONE BOOKLET

Instead of having a different enclosure card for everything you need to communicate, group information in a booklet that's easy for your guests to reference and bring along to the wedding.

SAVE-THE-DATES

Your save-the-date (or save-the-weekend) should echo the look and feel of your wedding invitation, so determine the general design of the invitation first (you don't need to decide on the exact wording). Unexpected paper shapes and artwork that might skew too informal for the invitation could be perfect here. In addition to the date and the location, inform guests of lodging options and other events, such as the rehearsal dinner and the farewell brunch, so they can plan their travel accordingly. If you've set up a social media hashtag and/or a website for your wedding, you might want to include it here rather than with the formal invitation suite.

If you don't have enough time to send a save-the-date via USPS (see the suggested timeline on page 26), send it by email. Your stationer or a graphic designer can design a PDF that matches your invitations, or use a service like Paperless Post.

OPPOSITE, CLOCKWISE FROM TOP LEFT:

A SCRIBBLED NOTE
Many save-the-dates are less formal than the invitation and include a picture of the couple. A postcard like this black-and-white one with gold writing is easy enough to create on your own.

A GARDEN PARTY
A modern script conveys a relaxed sensibility, but the fact that this one is done by hand—along with charming custom garden-themed illustrations and the monogram—signals that this will be a well-thought-out affair.

A PERSONAL VOICE
This save-the-date, written out in full sentences (rather than the more typical list format), makes an otherwise modern, minimalist card much more intimate.

A NOD TO TRADITION
The interlocking laurel crowns at the top of this card are a subtle reference to the Greek Orthodox wedding to come. The thick, smooth card stock with letterpress type feels formal and elevated.

SAVE the DATE
MIA + DAVID
JUNE 24, 2019
Los Angeles

Save the Date
for the wedding of

Kate Schlontein
and
Jacob Strumwasser

June 24, 2017
North Salem, NY

www.turkeyfarmwedding.com
Invitation to follow

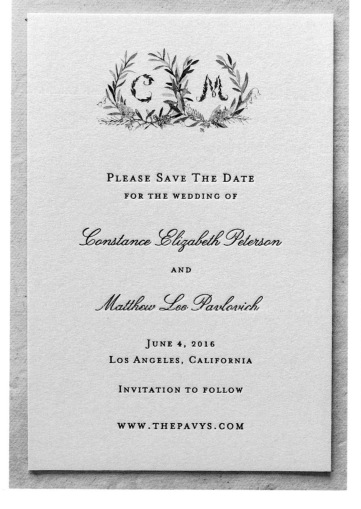

C M

PLEASE SAVE THE DATE
FOR THE WEDDING OF

Constance Elizabeth Peterson

AND

Matthew Leo Pavlovich

JUNE 4, 2016
LOS ANGELES, CALIFORNIA

INVITATION TO FOLLOW

WWW.THEPAVYS.COM

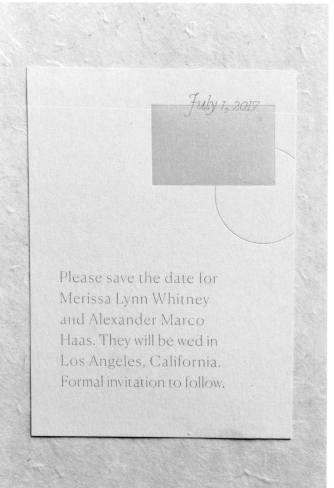

July 1, 2017

Please save the date for
Merissa Lynn Whitney
and Alexander Marco
Haas. They will be wed in
Los Angeles, California.
Formal invitation to follow.

INVITATION WORDING

It's important to remember that no matter how casual your event, a wedding of any budget or style assumes a basic level of formality. If you are taking many creative liberties in terms of the design of your invitation, use more formal wording to elevate the invitation so that it conveys "wedding." On the other hand, if your design is more formal, you may be able to use more casual language.

"HONOR" VS. "PLEASURE"
According to Crane's *Wedding Blue Book,* "request the honor of your presence" is to be used only for a wedding held in a place of worship. For other formal weddings, use "pleasure of your company."

This fruit-forward wedding featured a square invitation, on which both families were equally represented ("The Park Family & The Chae Family / Together, invite you to celebrate the marriage of . . ."). The choice of language, typeface, and lowercase script and the use of punctuation like the plus sign make this suite feel casual yet sophisticated.

WHO'S HOSTING?

Traditionally, the bride's parents are listed as the hosts, but in this day and age, some couples prefer to equally recognize the groom's parents or would not like parents included on the invitation at all. Tailor the wording to suit your specific needs—the language in the prompts below can all be mixed and matched. As a general rule, the woman's name goes first (and that's across the board, from escort cards to thank-you notes). For same-sex couples, use alphabetical order or your individual preference.

IF THE BRIDE'S PARENTS ARE HOSTING

Mr. and Mrs. William Davidoff
request the honor of your presence
at the marriage of their daughter
Constance Isabel
to
Mr. James Henry Stone

IF THE BRIDE'S PARENTS ARE HOSTING (TRADITIONAL JEWISH WEDDING)

Mr. and Mrs. William Davidoff
request the honor of your presence
at the marriage of their daughter
Constance Isabel
and
Mr. James Henry Stone
son of Dr. and Mrs. Jonathan Stone*

*An important distinction for a Jewish invitation is to list the groom's parents after the groom's name as "son of . . ." There is another belief that Jewish invitations should use the joining clause "and" instead of "to," which is traditionally used on invitations for Christian ceremonies, but this may not sound right, depending on the rest of your wording.

IF BOTH FAMILIES ARE HOSTING

With great love and excitement
the Davidoff family
and the Stone family
invite you to celebrate the marriage of
Constance Isabel
and
James Henry

IF THE COUPLE AND THEIR PARENTS ARE COHOSTING

Together with their families
Constance and James [or full names]
request the pleasure of your company at the
celebration of their marriage

IF THE COUPLE IS HOSTING

Constance Isabel Davidoff and James Henry Stone
invite you to share in the joy
of their wedding day

IF YOU DON'T WISH TO IDENTIFY HOSTS

With great joy
the pleasure of your company is requested at the
marriage of
Constance Davidoff and James Stone

DATE AND TIME

For a more formal event, one typically spells out the numerals on the invitation. For example, "at half after three o'clock in the afternoon" versus "3:30 p.m." And if you are spelling out the time, you may also choose the same treatment for the date, for example, "the twenty-first of June, two thousand and nineteen" versus "June 21, 2019." (The "and" is not required, so see what looks best with your design.)

ATTIRE

Crane's *Wedding Blue Book* stipulates that black tie is the only acceptable attire request to include on the invitation itself, and many old-school stationers agree that less formal guidelines belong on a separate enclosure card (see page 44). But if you are having a less formal wedding and don't mind the look of it, there are instances when putting a more casual dress code on the invitation works just fine. If you are including a separate reception card (for example, if you are getting married in a church, then hosting the reception at a different venue), the dress code should be listed on the reception card.

Beyond black tie, the wording you'll most often see is "black tie optional," "formal," and "cocktail attire," though people take many creative liberties when it comes to dress codes—"all white" is easy enough to understand, but others, like "California black tie" or "Aloha chic," may warrant further clarification on the wedding website or on an enclosure card. Also, make sure to note if any part of the event will take place on grass or sand or if there will be any walking required, so guests can dress accordingly.

For a wedding in Cuba, this minimalist pastel suite features the year, 2016, in Roman numerals: MMXVI.

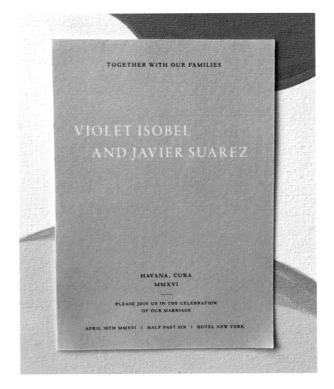

TOGETHER WITH OUR FAMILIES

VIOLET ISOBEL
AND JAVIER SUAREZ

HAVANA, CUBA
MMXVI

PLEASE JOIN US IN THE CELEBRATION
OF OUR MARRIAGE

APRIL 30TH MMXVI † HALF PAST SIX † HOTEL NEW YORK

ENVELOPES

MRS., MISS, OR MS.? "Mrs." can be used for a woman who is married, widowed, divorced, or separated, depending on her preference. "Ms." has the most universal application, but it is usually used for unmarried women and married women who kept their maiden name. "Miss" is used for girls under eighteen.

The envelope of your invitation is like the wrapping of a gift—so make it count. Envelopes are traditionally hand-addressed, which conveys a more personal, intimate quality than computer-generated addresses. You may choose to hire a calligrapher, ask a friend with good handwriting to help you, or do it yourself. If you have a very modern invitation suite, however, computer addressing might be appropriate—and it will certainly save time. Many couples will opt to computer-address the save-the-date and reserve hand-addressing for the actual invitation suite. Once you decide whether to address the invitations by hand or via the computer, think about how the other design choices on your envelope (font, color, inclusion of icons, stamps) will echo the contents inside.

ADDRESSING THE ENVELOPES

While it can be liberating to let go of some wedding traditions, how you address your guests isn't the place to get creative, as it's seen as a sign of respect. Only for a very casual event or for your close friends should you drop the titles and list both first names (for example, Constance and James Stone). If you have any doubt about how someone would like to be addressed, it is perfectly fine to just ask them (for more formal invitations, spell out the address instead of using abbreviations—for example, Street, Avenue, and Boulevard; Apartment or Number; and directions such as North or South). Here are a few tips for common addressing scenarios.

Opposite-Sex Couples: If the couple is married and the woman goes by her married name, use "Mr. and Mrs. James Henry Stone." If the woman goes by her maiden name or if the couple is unmarried, use: "Ms. Davidoff and Mr. Stone" or "Ms. Constance Davidoff and Mr. James Stone." The woman's name traditionally comes first. If the couple is not married, write the names on different lines and do not include "and" (married couples' names should appear on the same line and be joined with the word "and").

Same-Sex Couples: If the couple is unmarried, list each person with their appropriate title on separate lines, same as you would with an opposite-sex couple. Arrange the names in alphabetical order or begin with the person you know better first. If same-sex couples are married or consider themselves to be in a permanent union, put both names on the same line separated by an "and." For example, "Mrs. Constance Davidoff and Mrs. Katherine Smith" or "Ms. Constance Davidoff and Ms. Katherine Smith" are both correct; or use a plural title, for example "Messrs. James and Andrew Stone."

A Guest with a Plus One: If you know the name of the plus one, include that name on the outer envelope on a separate line. (Most etiquette junkies say to list the person you know first.) If you don't know the name of the guest, simply write "Constance Davidoff and Guest" on the same line.

Children Under Eighteen: Include their names only on the inner envelope, if you are including one. (If not, include them on the outer envelope under the parents' names.)

This whimsical matte-white script on a black envelope has a wonderful handmade quality. Note the use of French titles Mme. and M. (Madame and Monsieur), which is a nice touch if the recipients happen to be French or if you are a bit of a Francophile.

PROOFING Your stationer will create digital proofs for your approval. Print out the proofs and review each letter, one by one. Double-check all details such as day, date, addresses, and email addresses. The brain has an amazing ability to understand words that are misspelled, so you'll want a fresh pair of eyes to scan for things you may have missed. Ask an English major friend to look over the final version for grammar and spelling errors (ask this friend to take a look at your wedding website, too).

A Judge, a Doctor, or Military Personnel (Active or Retired): Include their appropriate title(s). If both people in an opposite-sex couple have a title, then list the woman's name first as you generally would. If the man has a professional title and the woman does not, then this is an exception where you would list his name first (for example, "The Honorable James Stone and Mrs. Stone").

INNER ENVELOPES

Traditionally, people send an invitation inside two envelopes—the outer envelope that gets dirty during transit can be discarded, and the recipient is presented with the clean inner envelope. In addition to being a great way to hold all the enclosure cards together, the inner envelope is also the place to clarify exactly who is invited to the wedding. Crane stipulates that the wording here should remain formal, but many take the opportunity to do something more relaxed, such as "Aunt Connie" or the use of nicknames. The inner envelope should include the names of all the people invited (it's generally understood that if someone's name isn't listed here, they aren't invited).

A FORMAL EXAMPLE

OUTER ENVELOPE:
Mr. and Mrs. James Stone

INNER ENVELOPE:
Mr. & Mrs. Stone

Audrey, Jon, and Grace
[children under eighteen living at home]

AN INFORMAL EXAMPLE

OUTER ENVELOPE:
The Stone Family

INNER ENVELOPE:
Constance, James, Audrey, Jon, and Grace

STAMPS & MAILING

For a fee, most stationers will assemble, post, and mail your save-the-dates and invitations. If it's within budget, it's nice not to have to worry about this, but it's easy enough to do yourself. Take a printed suite to the post office to get the exact weight for postage. Most invitations cost a minimum of 70 cents, which means you'll probably need more than one stamp (thick invitations, large envelopes, ribbons, and wax seals will all increase postage costs). And don't forget to get the exact postage for the reply cards, too. For an additional charge, you can ask the post office to "hand cancel" the stamps so there isn't a black mark over them.

The kind of postage you choose will make a strong first impression and should be carefully considered. Here are your options.

New: New stamps in many designs can be purchased from USPS.com and Stamps.com.

Custom: You can create a custom stamp through companies like Zazzle.com, Stamps.com, and Minted.com, but be warned that these companies will print their website address on the stamp in small print, and there is a black QLR code that isn't pretty. If you want to design a custom stamp using your own artwork (whether it's a crest, an icon, or another kind of graphic), it's best if it's not too detailed so that it is legible (the bar code and company name will take up a good portion of the stamp).

Vintage: Vintage stamps can be sourced from eBay or from a local dealer (just confirm that they are uncanceled). They will always take up more real estate on an envelope than new or custom postage since you will need to use more of them. Place them on the envelope before you stick or glue them on to find the best configuration.

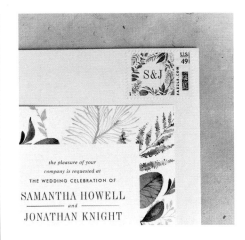

Echoing the green-and-white botanical print on the invitation, this custom Zazzle stamp feels deliberate and cohesive. Note that an odd-shaped envelope like this square one (what the post office deems "nonmachineable") will require higher postage.

WAX SEALS

A wax envelope seal is a wonderful old-world detail. It can be used to secure the envelope flap or to hold the different elements of the invitation suite together. If you are going to do this yourself, find sealing wax from a craft store or on Amazon, pop a cartridge into a glue gun (or melt the wax under a flame), and stamp the drippings with a signet ring or a stamp with your initials, a coat of arms, or an icon (those who want a cleaner look can do a wax seal but not stamp it with anything). A large, messy wax seal that isn't perfect has a charming, homespun quality. If you are asking your stationer to handle it, they may create the seals separately and then hand-glue them onto the envelope to ensure that no mistakes are made (some can work off a digital drawing, or you may have to leave a signet ring with them for a few days). Red wax against a white envelope with black text is the most classic option, but you could also go for something more modern, like white, black, silver, or gold wax, or anything that fits your color story (see page 17). An alternative to a wax seal is a monogrammed sticker. For the sake of consistency, you may want to use the same seal on your thank-you notes, too.

FOREIGN INVITEES

After you've checked the address format for the country where you are sending the invitation and addressed the envelopes accordingly, take the envelopes to the post office to determine exact postage. It's a good idea to also email your foreign guests a PDF of the invitation suite (which your stationer can provide) along with a note saying their invitation is on the way, since international mail can be very slow. Alternatively, you could expedite foreign invites using a service like FedEx or UPS. Instead of asking international guests to send back a physical reply card, provide an alternate way for them to RSVP, like on the wedding website or by email.

Stamping a wax seal with a couple's initials (or the initial of the groom's last name if the bride is taking his name) is the most common approach. A gold wax makes this detail feel instantly festive.

THE WEDDING WEBSITE

Creating a wedding website is standard practice these days, and it's easy enough for even the most low-tech couples (although some do hire web designers). The site can include the wedding itinerary, lodging options, and registry information. You might also want to clarify the dress code and include local activities, maps and directions, "your story," and photos and details about the wedding party. But a website should *not* be used in lieu of printed items—don't assume that everyone will visit your website, even if it's printed clearly on an enclosure card.

Giving your site a custom URL is a nice touch, especially if you are going to be including it on your printed invitation suite either as an enclosure card or on the invitation itself. Most build-your-own website companies offer custom URLs with their standard packages for an additional fee. If your first names are taken, do something more creative, like using nicknames, your wedding hashtag, or the name of your venue.

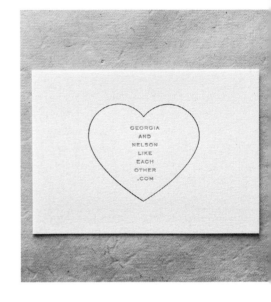

The address for your wedding website, even if it's a custom URL, may be too casual to include on a formal invitation. Here, it is provided on a separate enclosure, dressed up with a rose-gold foil heart.

WEBSITE PLATFORMS

When it comes to building your site, there are a number of different platforms to choose from, each with slightly different services, design templates, and cost structures. Here are a few to consider.

AppyCouple.com: If you want something bold, this is a good option. In addition to the website, they also create an app for your wedding where guests can upload photos.

Minted.com: This online design marketplace features not only hundreds of invitation styles (even custom stamps) but also the ability to create a matching wedding website.

RileyGrey.com: These modern, well-designed templates look like the work of a professional (fonts, backgrounds, and graphic elements on each template, though, cannot be altered).

SquareSpace.com: If you want to have more control over the design of your site, use one of this company's nonwedding templates and upload your own designs or create something totally unique. They also have designed wedding templates.

WEBSITE SPECIFICS

When thinking about how to build your wedding website, there are a few important considerations to keep in mind.

Will you be able to maintain visual consistency with your printed stationery? Some companies offer website templates with coordinating printed invitations; others will allow you to upload a custom crest you've already created.

Can you create a custom URL? It's much nicer to print something personalized than to have to list a company name as part of the website address.

Do you want password protection services for additional privacy? This is especially important if you need to provide home addresses or any other personal information on your site.

Do you want any additional planning services? Many companies provide helpful back-end services like guest list management, event RSVPs (so guests can RSVP on your wedding website instead of mailing back a card), photo-sharing, maps, planning timelines, and even event design.

What will it cost? The cost structure is either a onetime or a monthly fee. When thinking about cost, remember that you may want to leave the website up for a few months after the wedding if you are planning to post pictures on it and to keep the registry live—people will continue to give gifts long after the wedding is over.

A RIVER RUNS THROUGH IT

A bucolic second home near the Grand Tetons inspired a couple
to celebrate with thoughtful new family traditions.

Priscilla Fraser and Greg Chase fell in love with Jackson Hole shortly after they fell in love with each other. They eventually purchased a weekend home in the picturesque mountain town and now fly up from Los Angeles every chance they get—Greg, a scientist, is also an amateur pilot. After the pair became engaged, their issue wasn't so much *where* they would get married but *when*, as they soon learned they were also expecting their first child. They decided to delay the wedding until after their daughter, Lavinia, was born so they could focus on one thing at a time. While on maternity leave, Priscilla, an architect who is now the director of the MAK Center at the Schindler House in West Hollywood, began putting together ideas for the wedding between naps and feedings.

"Our perspective was that this was something we were doing for ourselves. We were getting married in a place we discovered together, and we had our daughter with us, so we thought, 'Let's just make it fun,'" she says. To that end, they brought on California-based planners Bash Please to help pull it all together.

The weekend kicked off with welcome drinks at the cowboy bar in town; on Saturday morning the couple hiked around Jenny Lake, followed by a BBQ at their house. The wedding on Sunday took place at Snake River Ranch, a cattle farm nearby. Against the backdrop of a grove of aspen trees and the Grand Tetons, Priscilla and Greg exchanged vows in front of 185 guests—Lavinia watched from her grandfather's lap. The bride's mother read a passage from Lavinia's favorite book, *Guess How Much I Love You* (the other readings, one from Plato's *Symposium* and another from astronomer Carl Sagan's *Cosmos*, were a bit more serious).

After the ceremony, guests were directed down a path along the river that led to a clearing where a gracious reception tent had been set up. Along the way, there was a bar, an appetizer buffet, a fire pit where guests could rest, and, finally, the escort card table. For the father-daughter dance to Bob Dylan's "Forever Young," Priscilla danced with her father and Greg danced with Lavinia. "In the end," says Priscilla, "our wedding was about traditions we were starting together as a new family."

AU NATUREL // The setting was "naturally
special," says Priscilla, so they didn't want to add too
much. In lieu of an altar structure, which would have
disrupted the view of the mountains, they opted
to line the aisle with white delphinium. At the end
of the aisle, the two rows formed a crescent where
Priscilla and Greg stood—the florist, Nicole Land of
Soil and Stem, called this part the "nest."

ABOVE, CLOCKWISE FROM TOP LEFT:

ROCK SOLID // Instead of traditional escort cards, small burlap bags were filled with skipping stones, tied with leather string, and attached with tags displaying the guests' names and table numbers. Guests were encouraged to skip the stones in the river as they walked along the path toward the reception tent. The florist decorated the trays with windswept sage branches, which are abundant on the property.

A BABE IN THE WOODS // The timing of their wedding was carefully considered. By the time they got married, Lavinia was seven months old and Priscilla was back to feeling like her old self. Lavinia's official title on the program was flower girl. Priscilla's dress was by Monique Lhuillier.

GOING STEADY // Priscilla's engagement ring (an oval solitaire in a low gold setting) is not conducive to stacking, so she decided to go with a different look for her wedding band. On her right hand she wears a thick gold ring engraved with Greg's EKG (hers is engraved on his)—it's a play on the idea of wrapping your heart around the other person's finger.

OPPOSITE, TOP:

SOMETHING BLUE // To complement the baby-blue table linens, larger arrangements featured cosmos, garden roses, oakleaf hydrangea (which is more elongated than typical hydrangea), and old-man's beard, which the florist gathered from the side of the highway. A snowberry sprig was included on the napkin treatment. Priscilla wanted the menu to reference an elevated steak house that was in step with the local cuisine. Their caterer sourced organic ingredients for the menu of Little Gem "wedge" salad and whole roasted Carter Country beef with wild mushrooms.

OPPOSITE, BOTTOM:

SCOUT'S HONOR // The bride called upon friend and designer Rachel Rogers to help create the paper goods. With the invitations, guests also received a custom patch that Priscilla designed (it was one of three the couple created—"The idea was that people would earn patches throughout the weekend, like at camp," says Priscilla). Among other things, it featured a palm tree and a pine tree, symbolizing Los Angeles and Jackson Hole. With the save-the-date, there was a Field Notes guide that detailed how the bride and groom met, tips on what to pack, and activities in Jackson Hole.

OPPOSITE:

INSIDE OUT // Under the gracious sailcloth structure, decor elements were kept natural: Smilax vines were wrapped around poles and strung with lanterns, and instead of wood flooring, the couple opted for grass underfoot. The sky-blue table linens helped pull everything together.

ABOVE, LEFT:

DRINK YOUR COLORS // One of the night's signature cocktails, a Huckleberry Fizz (huckleberries are native to the mountains of Wyoming), was pre-poured in elegant coupes and served up with patches (echoing the invitation suite) that were used as coasters. The purple, green, and white hues all reflected the wedding's color story.

ABOVE, RIGHT:

NOTES ON HIGH // A few high-tops were placed just outside the reception tent so guests could take in views of the Grand Tetons before dark. The soft blue linens and loose, colorful floral arrangements coordinated with the dining tables inside.

FOLLOWING PAGE:

BITE-SIZE // "The idea behind the cake was to do something that was easy for guests to grab and take back to the dance floor," says Priscilla. A small, two-tiered naked-style cake topped with wild berries was cut into bite-size pieces and offered on vintage dessert plates alongside homemade ice cream sandwiches and s'mores cookies.

THE REGISTRY

Here's a look at some of the items that topped Priscilla and Greg's wish list.

RACHEL ROGERS PAINTING

AVAILABLE FROM

RachelRogersDesign.com

HILL HOUSE HOME
WAVERLY SHEET SET

AVAILABLE FROM

HillHouseHome.com

COYUCHI KITCHEN
NAPKINS

AVAILABLE FROM

Coyuchi.com

YEAR & DAY
FLATWARE SET

AVAILABLE FROM

YearandDay.com

ROYAL COPENHAGEN
SERVING PLATE

AVAILABLE FROM

RoyalCopenhagen.com

WOODEN JAR SPOONS

AVAILABLE FROM

MarchSF.com

RICHARD BRENDON
CRYSTAL BARWARE

AVAILABLE FROM

MarchSF.com

ANTICA FARMACISTA
DIFFUSER

AVAILABLE FROM

AnticaFarmacista.com

JAPANESE
BASKET

AVAILABLE FROM

MarchSF.com

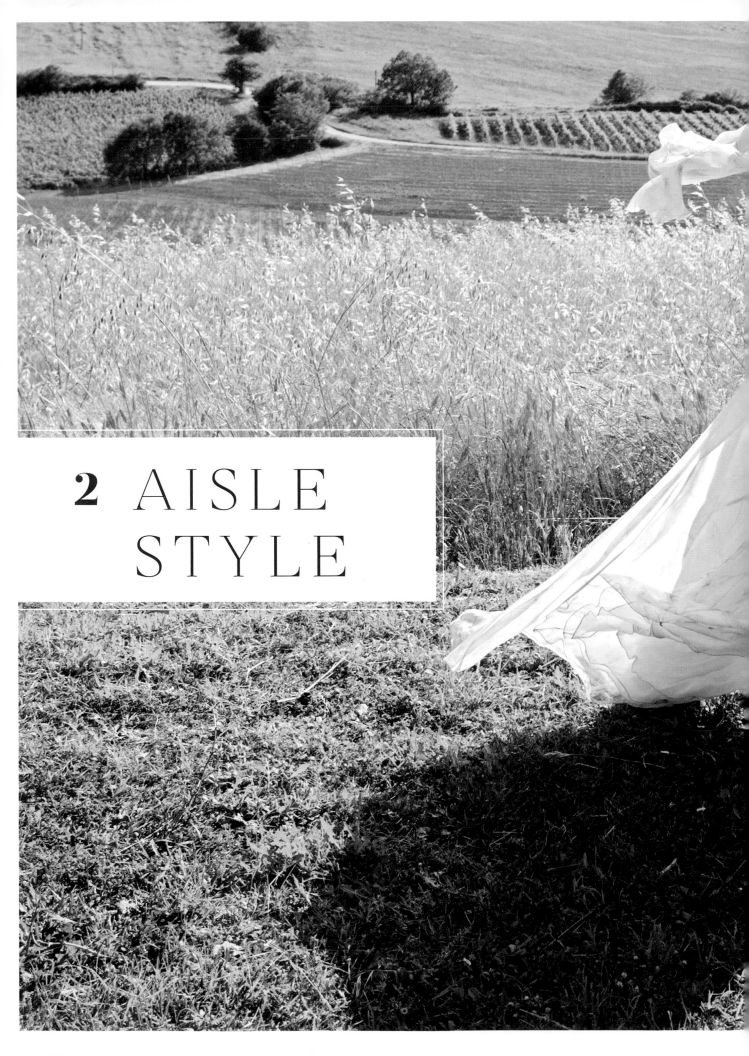

2 AISLE STYLE

Whether it's a simple sheath or an elaborate ball gown, the wedding dress is one of the most important components of your wedding story and something that needs to feel both of-the-moment and timeless. Finding the perfect dress—which requires strategy, research, and a bit of soul-searching—should come first, as it will inform almost everything else, from the bridesmaids' looks to the boutonnieres. This is also the time to break some of your bad habits and put in place new beauty and wellness routines that will continue long after the wedding. Finally, think of your wedding prep as a chance to invest in some of your relationships. Bring an old friend to a dress fitting, or take a cycling class with your future sister-in-law—sharing these preparatory moments with your loved ones will only bring you closer together.

THE DRESS

Finding a wedding dress is such a visceral experience. Sometimes you just know it when you see it. Or you might be completely overwhelmed by a sea of white fluff (which is the more common reaction!). A good place to start is a bridal boutique or a multi-brand store. Make appointments at all the boutiques you'd like to visit (they usually won't take walk-ins), and bring just one or two people you really trust. (If you bring your entire girl gang, you'll be bombarded with conflicting opinions. This should be a time when you are calm, focused, and listening—most important, to yourself. Going solo is also perfectly acceptable.)

Most bridal shops offer made-to-measure gowns, which means that the dresses are made from scratch using existing patterns. Start looking early, as it usually takes around six months to have a dress made by one of these designers, and once you receive your dress (ideally about two months before the wedding), it will need to be finished by a seamstress. The process of ordering a made-to-measure gown typically follows the sequence below.

SIZING Wedding dress sizing varies greatly among designers. If you are purchasing a dress from a European designer or company, you will probably need to order a dress that is two to three sizes larger than your "street size" (for example, a size 10 wedding dress might fit someone who usually wears a size 4). As for the American designers, some adhere to a European size chart, while others will fit true to your street size. Keep in mind that wedding dresses are always ordered based on a bride's largest measurement.

1 Selection: Make appointments at all the boutiques and department stores on your list. Tell each salesperson about the look you are going for, and don't be afraid to try on silhouettes that might be new to you. Once you settle on a gown, your measurements will be taken.

2 Ordering: The gown will be ordered according to your largest measurement, so when it arrives, it will typically require a fair amount of alteration. When you place your order, you will need to pay a deposit and sometimes sign a contract to protect the vendor from alteration costs in the event that your body changes dramatically. (Note: If you don't have six months to spare, rush orders can usually be accommodated, for a price.)

3 Alterations: Most brides need an average of three fittings: the first fitting takes place roughly six to eight weeks before the wedding, the second about four weeks out, and the last fitting, if necessary, one to two weeks before the date. The bridal salon will have an in-house seamstress or can recommend one in your area.

BEYOND THE BRIDAL BOUTIQUE

Bridal designers don't have a monopoly on white dresses. As you'll quickly discover, anything that falls under the category of "wedding" or "bridal" comes with a markup. Whether you are trying to avoid the hefty price tag or you simply want something less traditional, here are a few options to consider.

Ready-to-Wear: Resort, spring, and pre-fall collections usually boast an array of white looks that can be reinterpreted as a wedding gown or worn for other wedding-related events, such as the bridal shower or rehearsal dinner.

Vintage and Consignment Shops: There are many online and brick-and-mortar shops that have bridal departments or cater specifically to the bridal market.

Sample Sales: These are great opportunities to buy wedding dresses at less than market value—most designers host them after their spring and fall shows to clear inventory.

CUSTOM GOWNS

If you still can't find anything you love, or if you have something very specific in mind, it might be time to explore the idea of creating a custom gown. The easiest way to commission a bespoke dress is to ask a designer to re-create one of their existing patterns in white, which is much less time-consuming and expensive than creating a unique pattern. This is often done using a dress from a past collection. If budget truly isn't a factor, Paris's haute couture houses (e.g., Chanel, Christian Dior, Givenchy) set the standard for custom-made gowns; otherwise, find an experienced local dressmaker. Either way, leave plenty of time (at least three months) for them to create a sketch, build a muslin prototype, and produce the actual gown. And make sure you will be available for fittings, as you'll need at least three (at six to eight weeks out, then around four weeks, and a final fitting one to two weeks before the wedding for minor adjustments).

The A-line silhouette has become one of the most beloved shapes in bridalwear. For a beach wedding, this one by Cristiano Lucci is feminine and traditional with a sweetheart neckline, a dramatic beaded bodice, and a light tulle skirt.

SILHOUETTES

Before getting your heart set on a dress that you saw in a magazine (that looked perfect on a waifish 6-foot-tall model), think about what will actually be the most flattering for your shape. This means understanding how to accentuate the good and hide the bad. Here's a review.

A-Line: A universally flattering shape; it's fitted on top, then flares away from the body.

Ball Gown: Great for pear-shaped figures as the lower half of your body will be concealed underneath the skirt. It's best for taller brides—shorter frames will be overwhelmed by a voluminous skirt.

Empire: Ideal for shorter brides because the high waist of the empire cut creates the illusion of longer legs. It's also a nice option for plus-sized brides because the fabric falls away from the body.

Sheath, Slip Dress, and Column: Without a lot of built-in support, these styles are best for brides who are relatively slim. As their continuous lines have a lengthening effect, they are an especially nice choice for shorter brides.

Strapless: A good choice for women with a well-defined décolletage, minimal armpit bulge (the area just below the armpit that can appear smooshed in tight clothing), and a toned upper back, as well as small-busted brides who don't need a lot of support (bustier brides set on strapless should opt for a straight-across or off-the-shoulder neckline versus a sweetheart to minimize cleavage).

V-Neck: Shallow V-neck cuts are universally flattering; a deep V should be worn only if you have a smaller bustline.

Fit-and-Flare: Mermaid, trumpet, and drop-waist dresses, which cinch the waist and hug curves, are best for hourglass figures.

Both brides should wear
something that is the same
level of formality, meaning
one should not be wearing
a ball gown while the other
is in a casual jumpsuit.
Beyond that, each bride
should choose a look that
is reflective of her style,
be it minimalist, feminine,
or unconventional. If your
looks don't happen to be
in the same style category
(which is totally fine),
there are a host of ways
to visually connect them:
add an accent in the same
color or in complementary
colors; choose different
pieces in the same fabric
(such as a shared lace);
or choose coordinating
flowers and accessories
(veils, jewelry, clutches, etc.).

A SHOPPING STRATEGY

In order to avoid being overwhelmed by the aforementioned "sea
of white fluff," before you book your bridal salon appointments,
try to establish a general sense of which kinds of dresses you
definitely want to try on, a couple of new styles you might be open
to considering, and which styles are absolutely out of the question.
Doing this will streamline the process and make it more enjoyable.
Here are a few different ways to help you focus your approach.

Look in your closet. Which are your favorite dresses, and why? Are
you drawn to classic silhouettes or trend-based styles? Are they more
androgynous or feminine?

Consider your body type. You should wear whatever makes you
feel most comfortable, but a few tried-and-true combinations of
common silhouettes and body types are listed opposite.

Reference your mood board (see page 17). Look at your board
as a whole and try to identify commonalities and themes. When it's
time to go dress shopping, bring an image of your mood board to
show the sales associate and tell them some of the key words that
define the look you are going for.

Get practical. Think about factors like weather, location, and
budget. If you are getting married in a conservative church, find out
in advance if your dress needs to have a high neck and/or sleeves.
If you are working with a small budget, steer clear of Chantilly lace
ball gowns.

A DRESS FOR EVERY BRIDE

The bridalwear industry, once a bastion of tradition, has let go of many tired conventions and (finally!) reinvented itself with looks that are in keeping with today's styles. While classic strapless dresses are more fashion-forward than ever, brides are also experimenting with streamlined silhouettes, ready-to-wear options, and modern riffs on iconic French lace.

With the line between the bridal and ready-to-wear departments much less defined than it once was, the challenge now isn't finding something beautiful to wear—it's finding something that truly reflects your style. Before you begin shopping for a dress, it's important to try to pinpoint exactly what that is.

On the following pages, dresses are organized into categories that reflect the spirit of each bride, ranging from the unconventional to fairy-tale looks and everything in between. Go through each section and determine which category (or categories) feels most like you. Make notes along the way about which specific dresses you are drawn to and why—at the end of this exercise, you will have a much more clearly defined range of styles and "key words" to use while you are shopping.

This bride paired a silky, deep V-neck gown from Monique Lhuillier with an airy bouquet of white scabiosa and dried elements and a classic side-part bun to which a chapel-length veil was secured for portraits and the ceremony.

A STYLIST'S TIPS Wedding stylist Cynthia Cook Smith has many years of experience when it comes to wedding dress shopping. Here are her suggestions for brides-to-be.

Let the dress come to you. Search the market, and find the best thing that exists rather than looking for something superspecific.

Don't choose a dress that's too revealing or sexy. Your wedding look should be timeless and classic. (If you want something a little more risqué, save it for the reception.)

Keep an open mind. Many times brides will say they absolutely don't want strapless or they want only a certain designer, but when they try things on, it's a different story.

Don't just view the collections online. Wedding dresses look so different in person, so go with a friend you really trust to a store where you can see everything on the rack.

Sleep on it. When you think you've found the one, take pictures, think on it for a bit, and go back for another appointment to try it on again.

SLEEK AND MINIMAL

Whether it's a slinky slip dress or a body-skimming sheath, these styles are for the lover of simple, streamlined silhouettes free of embellishment, tulle, or decorative lace. Recalling an elegant Carolyn Bessette Kennedy and generally less bridal in feeling, they offer a refreshing antidote to the big, puffy gowns of the past. These styles are often unforgiving and tend to work best for small-chested, slim, and athletic body types. Stylist Cynthia Cook Smith warns that these dresses sometimes wander into lingerie or nightgown territory, which you should be careful to avoid. She also recommends that if you are struggling between choices, these styles often work well as a second look to wear for the reception.

A FINE BALANCE

DESIGNER: Custom Saint Laurent

WHY IT WORKS: The deep V and a high leg slit are offset with full-length sleeves to give this look a sense of modesty. This bride's wedding was held in a colder climate, so the sleeves were also a practical choice.

THE SIMPLEST SHEATH

DESIGNER: Charlie Brear

WHY IT WORKS: With a classic boatneck and a subtle puddle train (and a low V in the back), this bias-cut dress is timeless and can easily be layered with jewelry and outerwear.

BACK-AND-FORTH

DESIGNER: Marchesa

WHY IT WORKS: From the front, this look feels very streamlined and minimalist due to its straight-across neckline, but a dramatic chapel-length train begins mid-back and has a modern squared edge.

UNEXPECTED ACCENTS

DESIGNER: Custom Carolina Herrera

WHY IT WORKS: A classic column dress with a romantic off-the-shoulder neckline is given an edgy twist with contrasting black straps.

'90S INSPIRED

DESIGNER: A.L.C.

WHY IT WORKS: A simple silhouette in double-faced silk with a very low back and barely-there spaghetti straps is perfect for a more casual party.

SWEET AND SIMPLE

These styles are for the laid-back, go-with-the-flow bride who wants something easy to wear. Think relaxed, bohemian silhouettes (off-the-shoulder necklines, ruffles, and breathable maxi skirts) and hemlines that just graze the floor to reveal a pair of flat shoes. They are perfect for backyard or beach weddings. Veils are either kept short or skipped entirely. Make sure the rest of the look is natural: loose hair, light makeup, and a garden-inspired bouquet. The best part? There's usually no need to change into a reception dress.

FULL OF MOVEMENT

DESIGNER: Zimmermann

WHY IT WORKS: Whimsical silk tiers make this dress fun to dance in, while the high neckline offers the right amount of modesty to balance the hint of midriff.

NEW AGAIN

DESIGNER: Laura Ashley, circa 1982

WHY IT WORKS: A pink, puffy '80s gown that belonged to the bride's mother was transformed into this clean, minimalist column with a few soft details like the sweetheart neckline and off-the-shoulder sleeves.

HAUTE HIPPIE

DESIGNER: Co

WHY IT WORKS: This modern riff on a retro silhouette features a few details that make it special: a sash to cinch the waist, breezy three-quarter-length sleeves, a keyhole neckline, and dotted textured lace.

TO THE MAX

DESIGNER: Valentino Resort

WHY IT WORKS: Inspired by the 1970s and artist Frida Kahlo, this delicate cotton broderie anglaise maxi dress is a festive choice for a casual beach wedding, without coming off as theme-y.

EASY STRAPLESS

DESIGNER: Leila Hafzi

WHY IT WORKS: Instead of a more formal and conservative strapless style, this column gown with Grecian style ruffles feels relaxed, especially when paired with natural hair and makeup.

LADYLIKE LACE

Lace has been synonymous with bridalwear for centuries, and it is still the choice for brides who want something that exudes old-fashioned romance and femininity. Handmade lace is expensive, so you can expect to see higher price tags here. The main thing to consider when thinking about a lace wedding gown is whether you want something delicate and lightweight, like an embroidered French Chantilly, or a heavier fabric with more of a cutout feel, such as eyelet, Venise, or guipure lace. Many lace dresses will include beads, crystals, and pearl accents, whether they're outlining a lace pattern on the length of the dress or hand-sewn in just a few specific spots.

STRAIGHT-LINE STRAPLESS

DESIGNER: Custom Brock Collection

WHY IT WORKS: Chantilly lace and silk organza add texture and softness to a voluminous silhouette, while the straight-across neckline gives the dress a cool, modern touch.

BUTTONED-UP

DESIGNER: Samuelle Couture

WHY IT WORKS: With a high neck and three-quarter-length sleeves, this dress is at once conservative and flattering thanks to its body-conscious silhouette.

SHEER ROMANCE

DESIGNER: Inbal Dror

WHY IT WORKS: This off-the-shoulder illusion dress—with long sleeves and a corseted bodice in delicate bishop lace—has an old-world Victorian air.

3-D TEXTURE

DESIGNER: Marchesa

WHY IT WORKS: This re-embroidered fit-and-flare gown with a plunging V-neck and flutter sleeves is lightened by whimsical organza flowers.

A CLASSY COLUMN

DESIGNER: Amir Taghi

WHY IT WORKS: A floor-length strapless lace column dress gives the illusion of off-the-shoulder sleeves thanks to a cape secured with bows, which the bride removed for dinner.

STATEMENT MAKERS

Now is the time to indulge your fairy-tale fantasy. Surprisingly, many of these looks are actually quite easy to wear (a full skirt and a corseted bodice mean you don't have to worry about "sucking in" for photos), but a big skirt isn't really conducive to sitting down for a lengthy meal, so you may want to choose a second look for the reception. Offset a dramatic dress with natural hair and makeup and a low-key bouquet so your look doesn't feel too fussy.

A NEW CONTEXT

DESIGNER: Thakoon

WHY IT WORKS: A long train doesn't necessarily require a formal setting. This diaphanous cathedral-length train feels surprisingly at home in the woods of New Hampshire.

EPIC PROPORTIONS

DESIGNER: Ines di Santo

WHY IT WORKS: A sleeveless asymmetrical floral-print ball gown is perfect for a wedding in a villa or fancy old hotel.

SUPERFEMININE

DESIGNER: Vera Wang

WHY IT WORKS: A boned, strapless lace bodice adds structure above a puff of tulle. While the skirt is voluminous, the absence of a train makes it quite wearable.

CHANGE UP

DESIGNER: Oscar de la Renta

WHY IT WORKS: This traditional strapless gown features a removable lace overcoat, eliminating the need for a reception dress. This bride paired the look with an unembellished tulle veil.

CLOUD-LIKE

DESIGNER: Marchesa

WHY IT WORKS: For an elegant oceanfront wedding, a plunging lace neckline above a cascading tulle skirt was full of movement as it fluttered in the breeze.

THE UNCONVENTIONALISTS

With a high wearability factor after the big day, separates, suits, and jumpsuits are wonderful options for elopements and encore weddings, and for brides working with a short engagement period (since most of these options can be purchased off the rack). If you want to completely buck convention, you may even opt for a bold color or a print.

HOLDING COURT

DESIGNER: Zimmermann

WHY IT WORKS: This ivory jumpsuit was perfect for a quick daytime trip to city hall and a post-ceremony lunch at a nearby hotel.

NEW-FASHIONED SHIRTDRESS

DESIGNER: Style Paris by Susan Sutherland

WHY IT WORKS: With a deep V—neck, long sleeves, and a full flowing skirt with a slit, this bridal shirtdress is comfortable, breathable, and easy to dance and run around in.

SUIT UP

DESIGNER: Chanel

WHY IT WORKS: A vintage three-piece Chanel skirt suit is a versatile, casual look that you can wear again and again.

SHORT AND SWEET

DESIGNER: Kaviar Gauche

WHY IT WORKS: A casual, warm-weather wedding may call for a raised hemline. If you want it to still look bridal, opt for a traditional fabric such as lace.

FINE PRINT

DESIGNER: Valentino

WHY IT WORKS: An easy way to set yourself apart is by wearing a color or a print. A bird print on this breezy, slightly bohemian silhouette feels effortless yet still worthy of a special occasion.

TRAINS

Train lengths—in order from shortest to longest—are fishtail, puddle, court, chapel, Watteau (a cape-like fabric panel that begins just below the shoulder blades), cathedral, and royal. The three most popular lengths are a low-maintenance puddle, which is less than a foot long; a midlength chapel train, which is generally 3 to 4 feet long; and cathedral length, 6 to 7 feet long, for those who want to make an ultra-dramatic statement.

Designers don't always adhere to these specific lengths, so just use these names as a general guide and think more loosely about trains as short, medium, and long. The general rule is, the more formal the event, the longer the train. (But, of course, that isn't always the case.) Then there is the matter of shape—most trains are rounded, but some modern styles have a straight edge.

If you have a long train, practice walking in the dress beforehand (only on a clean floor!); and on your wedding day, ask your attendants and your groom to help lift it off the ground when you are moving between locations. You might also want to roll out an aisle runner if you are having an outdoor wedding so the train doesn't drag directly on the ground, but be prepared for it to get dirty regardless.

Chapel and cathedral trains usually require an outfit change or a bustle for the reception. Until then, enjoy it and don't stress about it getting dirty as it trails behind you. This Toni Maticevski dress features a squared Watteau train that begins just below the shoulders.

BUSTLES

If you aren't changing into a different dress for the reception, think seriously about your range of motion and if you want to bustle your dress for the reception. The two most common techniques are the standard style (where the train is pinned on the outside of the skirt—see below) and the French style (where the train is tied underneath the skirt using a series of ribbons). If you don't want to alter your dress's silhouette, you could also attach the train to a finger- or wrist-loop to hold it off the ground or simply sling it over your arm. Bustling should be done with the help of a bridesmaid or family member who has practiced beforehand (invite them to one of the fittings so the seamstress can show them how it works).

BEFORE
This Grecian goddess–like hammered silk dress from Elizabeth Fillmore Bridal has a generous chapel-length train.

AFTER
For the reception, the train was secured with a standard bustle. This style shows the mechanics of the bustle and may be preferable if you want people to understand that this is not the dress's original silhouette.

UNDERGARMENTS   Don't forget about your foundation garments. Lacy lingerie might be a romantic idea, but most gowns will require something more practical. Bring options (Spanx, nipple petals, bras, thongs, etc.) with you to one of your dress fittings to ensure that you have what you need. Then take a picture with your dress on to see if any undergarments are visible in a photograph (you might not be able to tell in person).

VEILS

The different veil styles—in order from shortest to longest—are birdcage, flyaway, blusher (or shoulder-length), fountain, elbow, waterfall, fingertip, waltz, floor-length, mantilla, chapel (or sweep), and cathedral. Veils are not mandatory, but they are traditional (particularly in Jewish weddings, where they are used in an unveiling ceremony called the *bedecken*), and they lend an ethereal quality to your look. Many modern brides employ a long veil as a more practical alternative to a train. This is not a hard-and-fast rule, but the veil is generally not cut to the same exact length as the dress—it's either longer or shorter. The designer who sold you the dress will most likely be able to help you with the veil (many veils are edged with the same fabric as the dress to visually connect the two).

The placement of the veil will make it feel more or less formal. A spunky, tufted veil placed at the top of the head is fun and casual while a veil secured to a low bun runs more formal. Heavy, intricate mantilla veils are an exception; they are pinned to the top of the head and are very formal and traditional. Think about whether you want to secure your veil with something more visible than a comb, like a small tiara or a diamond barrette.

Traditional brides will keep their face veiled until the first kiss, but others might just wear a veil for a few portrait photos or keep their face unveiled and let the fabric float behind them. If you are planning to cover your face for any part of the ceremony, though, order a double-layer veil (one layer is pulled in front of your face and the other covers your back). Once it's time to sit down for dinner, most brides will have removed the veil.

BIRDCAGE

Most birdcage-style veils are a bit retro, but this *Black Swan*–inspired example is decidedly more fashion-forward thanks to the use of a wing-like remnant piece of lace sewn on one side.

MANTILLA

A mantilla veil is usually distinguished by an intricate lace pattern and its placement on top of the head (typically about 2 inches from the hairline so that the lace gently drapes over the sides of the face and shoulders).

FLYAWAY

For a bride who wants to soften her look with a veil that won't get in the way, a playful two-tiered puff of tulle that gently graces the shoulders is perfect for a casual daytime wedding.

ELBOW-LENGTH

Echoing the shape of the bride's dress, this embroidered elbow-length veil is somewhat formal but still allows for mobility.

CHAPEL

Without any embellishments or lace edging, a graceful chapel-length veil feels light and airy—perfect for an intricate gown or one with a busy train.

CATHEDRAL

A voluminous hand-embroidered veil adds structure and drama to a simple bias-cut silk slip dress.

SHOES

Ideally, you would choose your bridal shoes after you select your dress but before your first fitting, so that you can alter the dress according to the heel height. If you are slightly taller than your groom, you may want to wear a pair of stilettos for your bridal portrait, then walk down the aisle and take group portraits in flats. In that case, be sure to consider how your dress will look with different shoes. And if you are going with one pair, make sure they are comfortable enough to spend the entire evening in (removing your shoes during the reception because your feet hurt is a no-no for traditionalists).

A great bridal shoe is surprisingly difficult to find, partly because so few designers have bridal collections (and those who do, such as Manolo Blahnik and Jimmy Choo, have a limited selection). So be resourceful and seek out classic shapes (slingbacks, stilettos, ankle-strap sandals, etc.). The truth is, if your skirt will cover your shoes, you can probably get away with buying white shoes off the rack that are a close if not perfect match. But if you want your shoes to exactly match your dress, there are two ways to achieve this, with the help of an experienced cobbler.

❶ **Re-cover your shoes.** Ask your dress designer for extra fabric from your gown to use to re-cover your shoes. If that isn't possible, visit a fabric store to source a couple of yards of fabric that you think will be a good match.

❷ **Dye your shoes.** A pair of neutral silk or satin shoes can be dyed to the exact hue of your dress (a quick online search for "dyeable shoes" will yield a handful of options—Stuart Weitzman, for example, makes its iconic Nudist sandal in dyeable white satin in a couple of heel heights). Most people will dye shoes based on indoor lighting, so if you are getting married outside, be sure to ask the cobbler to adjust the dye accordingly.

A bridal wardrobe stocked with choices (from left to right): strappy metallic sandals, blush-colored satin block sandals, white satin block sandals, classic low-heeled white satin slingbacks, and silver metallic flats. The Manolo Blahnik sandals (middle) that the bride wore for portraits were black suede before she had them re-covered in white satin to match her gown.

Beyond white footwear, metallic silver shoes generally pair well with beaded dresses, and nude-colored shoes (embellished or plain) are always a good choice if you can't find the right white for your dress—or if you don't want the matchy-matchy look. Of course, you can always go for a bold color if you want to make a statement.

As for the shoes' silhouette, traditionalists will say that a closed-toed shoe is necessary for formal events, but an elegant sandal is perfectly acceptable as long as it's silk or satin (consider a closed-toe shoe if you are getting married in a church or a city, however).

When you do settle on the perfect pair, break in your shoes at home, add pads as needed, and scuff the bottoms to prevent slipping.

LIGHT LAYERS

If you are getting married in a Conservative or Orthodox synagogue or in a Catholic church, be sure to find out if there are restrictions on having bare shoulders. If so, or if you simply want to be a little more modest for the ceremony—or because it might actually be chilly—a veil, bolero, blazer, fur (or faux fur) shrug, capelet, wrap, or even a cape should do the trick. Of course, you could also get a dress with sleeves.

CAPE
Mimicking the lines of the dress, this custom cape was worn over a V-neck dress during the ceremony. Secured at the collarbone, it created a keyhole shape, revealing hints of the dress underneath. The cutout armholes made it even more practical.

CAPELET
As the temperatures started to drop during a late-autumn wedding, this bride put on a feathery pink capelet to join her guests for the outdoor cocktail reception.

VEIL
Wrapping a veil around your arms and shoulders (as you might a pashmina) offers a subtle amount of coverage. The advantages are that it feels bridal and, since you can still see the gown, it won't alter your silhouette. The downside is that it won't do much to keep you warm.

The bride's vintage diamond engagement and wedding rings (left and center) are set on yellow gold bands that subtly match the groom's ring (right).

WEDDING RINGS

Traditionally, the bride and groom exchange matching yellow gold bands. But in this day and age, a couple's wedding rings don't have to match, nor do they have to necessarily be made of gold. The design of the bride's ring is usually informed by her engagement ring; she should decide if she wants the wedding ring to match or if she wants to mix metals (for example, a classic yellow gold band paired with a diamond infinity band). Here are the different options (for men and women).

Gold: Yellow gold is the most traditional (24 karat is the purest form, but it's usually considered too soft for an everyday ring, so people opt for 14 or 18 karat). In addition to yellow gold, there's rose gold and white gold. Trinity bands (three interconnected gold bands of either matching or varying colors) have also come into fashion.

Platinum: Stronger and more expensive than gold, platinum is considered a "cool" metal that works well against skin with pink undertones, and it is hypoallergenic (gold can contain irritants such as nickel).

Eternity: This style of band, with diamonds all the way around, is often chosen to match a bride's engagement ring. Beyond white diamonds, different gemstones or colors can be used. The setting options include claw prong (the most traditional option and most suitable for large, round brilliant stones), channel (stones are placed flush between two metal edges; it's the most secure and almost snag-proof), and bar (diamonds of equal size are held together by a bar separating them, which lets in a lot of light).

BRIDAL BLING

Beyond the wedding and engagement rings, the other jewelry you select for the occasion is a wonderful way to showcase your personal style. If you've chosen a rather traditional dress, think about offsetting it with more modern accessories, like an arm cuff, a double-pierce earring, or a dramatic drop earring. Alternatively, if your dress is more fashion-forward, consider wearing traditional pieces like pearl or diamond studs and a tennis bracelet or two. If you are gifted family heirlooms (or they are loaned to you for the special occasion) and you aren't able to modernize the setting, you can always incorporate the pieces into your look in different ways— for example, by securing a brooch to your bouquet or attaching it to your clutch.

PRECIOUS CARGO
An assortment of new and vintage jewelry for this wedding weekend included everything from classic diamond-and-pearl drop earrings to the dramatic dangling diamond fan earrings (her something borrowed) the bride wore for the reception.

ABOVE:

HOLLYWOOD GLAM

Dangly diamond-encrusted chandelier earrings and a matching diamond barrette add a glitzy touch, perfect for an evening reception.

RIGHT:

DOUBLE UP

A diamond drop earring is a classic style; when accompanied by a second, small diamond stud, the look is youthful and fashion-forward.

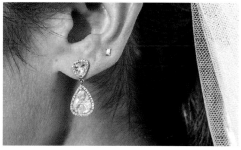

BELOW:

STATEMENT NECKLACE

A bold diamond necklace like this one works best with simple strapless dresses. Keep the earrings and the rest of your jewelry minimal so that it doesn't appear heavy.

RIGHT:

THE GO-TO STACK

Most brides tend to keep their bracelet game simple and just stick to one or two bands, but if your everyday stack is formal enough (like this gold assortment), there's no need to part with it for your wedding.

BRIDESMAIDS

The concept of a bridal party is something that's broadly interpreted these days. If you and your fiancé each have ten best friends, then maybe a big wedding party is in order, but the tendency toward smaller wedding parties, which are easier to manage and more intimate, is growing. A bridal party might consist of one or two people and may even include men (on the groom's side, there may be groomsmaids, too). The idea that you need to have the same number of bridesmaids as there are groomsmen is also not always realistic.

Every bride's relationship to her bridesmaids is unique, so you may have a different dress-selection process with each maid. Most bridesmaids want to be involved in the selection of their dress in some way, so the bride usually dictates the larger vision for the dresses (whether it's a general color palette or specific styles to choose from), then lets the bridesmaid make choices within a given set of parameters. However, some bridesmaids would rather have the bride select their dress and not have to deal with it at all—especially if the bride has incredible taste. If you are flexible, you may want to have a conversation with your maids before starting the process to solicit their input.

When it comes to dressing your bridesmaids, there are two schools of thought.

❶ Identical Dresses: Same silhouette and color/pattern. It's the easiest route and looks clean and usually more formal. Let each maid personalize the look by choosing her own shoes or jewelry to add subtle dimension.

❷ Different Dresses: Varied silhouettes and colors/patterns. It's more visually interesting and better accommodates different body types, skin coloring, and possibly budgets.

For this Nantucket wedding, the bridal party wore romantic, custom silk taffeta off-the-shoulder dresses by Brock Collection in a muted gray-and-pink floral pattern. The maid of honor's look (center) was distinguished with a slightly different patterned dress (same florals, but on a white background), a small train, and a white bouquet.

The color palette for your bridesmaids' dresses, whether the bridal party is wearing the same dress or different dresses, will depend on the setting and the time of year; for example, dark jewel tones for a fall/winter wedding or pastels for a springtime wedding—soft, neutral colors (grays, beige, etc.) will work year-round. Traditionalists may not like it, but black or white dresses for bridesmaids are perfectly acceptable options, too!

A big factor in dress selection, of course, is who will be paying for it. If it's within budget, it's a lovely gesture for the bride (or the groom, in the case of a groomsmaid) to pay for the gowns. If you want to ensure that your maids wear something exactly to your taste, it's nice to offer to foot the bill. But this isn't always possible, especially if you have half a dozen bridesmaids. If you are asking them to pay for their own dresses, be very mindful of the cost, and give them some flexibility (for example, ask them to buy a dress within a certain color palette or choose a dress at a price point you know is reasonable for everyone). If you have your heart set on a style that is not within everyone's budget, then you should very discreetly offer to help pay for the dresses of those who can't afford it; if this can't be done discreetly, it's best to find another dress.

The same concept applies for footwear: Most brides will ask their maids to wear something neutral that they already own, but if you want them to wear something new, ideally you would pay for it or at least make sure to be very cost conscious and give them some choice in the matter.

It's generally best to avoid bridesmaids' fashion lines altogether, due to poor quality and lack of originality—instead, stick with the designers you love. Just make sure to select the bridesmaids' gowns with enough time for alterations, which each maid should do on her own (leaving about a month for alterations is usually safe).

The most relaxed couples won't put any stipulations on what the wedding party wears. In this case, the maids should just adhere to the general dress code.

JUNIOR BRIDESMAIDS

Junior bridesmaids (between nine and fourteen years old) should wear dresses that echo those of the rest of the bridesmaids in color and style. Modesty is crucially important here (girls this age are often between children's and adult sizing, so you may want to consult with their parents). If possible, the bride should cover the cost of their ensemble.

BEYOND MATCHING BRIDESMAIDS' DRESSES

This method requires a bit of strategizing to look cohesive. The feeling of a dress is the most important thing—you don't want a stiff modern dress next to a ruffled romantic gown, even if they are the same color.

SEA GLASS COLORS

For a tropical wedding, light blues and greens are more natural colors and less expected than the usual pink or champagne. The maids' varying looks were unified by laurel crowns and little white posies.

MIX IT UP

Each bridesmaid in this wedding party wore something different yet relaxed in spirit. For cohesiveness, each wore a laurel crown and carried a bouquet of peonies.

INVESTMENT PIECES

This bride opted for timeless dresses and separates in gray and white, made from sustainable fabrics, from designer Elizabeth Suzann.

A PLAY ON PRINTS

Sticking with a black-and-white color scheme, the bride asked each maid at this wedding to select a dress from designer Juan Carlos Obando.

THE LITTLEST ATTENDANTS

The general rule of thumb when it comes to dressing your flower children and ring bearers is that they should look their age. Whatever the style of your event, young members of the wedding party should be in cotton or linen—all white always works here. For the flower girls, white Battenberg lace aprons or traditional smock dresses with a bow or a flower crown and a pair of Mary Janes (with white stockings for a more formal event or ruffled socks for a more casual daytime party) are classic—a floral print or pastel hue can also be sweet. Many times a sash is added to tie in with the color scheme. And for the ring bearer, a linen or cotton suit with a white tie and buck shoes is adorable.

While it's customary for the bride to select the ensembles of the attendants (and also pay for them), it's probably a good idea to go over your selection with their parents when you inquire about sizing information. And don't forget about grooming. If possible, ask your hairdresser to spend a few minutes with your young helpers.

ABOVE:
TWO OF A KIND
Adding colorful sashes (such as these burgundy ribbons) to all-white dresses is an easy way to connect the flower girls' looks with the rest of the wedding's color story. While the dresses here are identical, the looks are differentiated by the girls' hairstyles and shoes.

OPPOSITE:
THE NEW FORMAL
For a woodsy wedding in Northern California, the "flower children" were each given a nest of flower buds to toss as they walked down the aisle. The girls wore baby's-breath crowns and white linen lawn dresses with blue velvet sashes; the boys wore classic white linen suits and boutonnieres.

BOUQUETS

The bridal bouquet is one of the most iconic elements of a wedding. Treat it like you would a piece of jewelry or any other accessory. It will be with you during portraits and as you walk down the aisle (unless you are holding both parents' hands); afterward, it's usually placed on the cake table until the end of the evening, when you may decide to toss it.

Unless having a romantic and billowing presentation-style bouquet is an integral part of your vision, smaller arrangements tend to feel more elegant than big, bulky ones, which can be distracting and not proportional to your frame, not to mention heavy (you don't want to walk down the aisle with flexed arms). Find ways to balance your look: if you have a big dress, then consider scaling back on the bouquet, for example, to a posy of just three peonies instead of ten to fifteen. Think about the shape of the bouquet, too, and how to secure it—do you want something compact or more airy and loose? Most bridal bouquets these days are hand-tied (meaning the different stems are placed in a florist's hand and then tied together, leaving the stems exposed for a natural look), but you may also have the stems wrapped with a satin ribbon for a more formal look.

When it comes to the color of your bouquet, decide between a traditional all-white arrangement and something that might tie in with your color story (see page 17) and the rest of the ceremony flowers and centerpieces. This can be achieved by using a single flower variety or a few different kinds of flowers, which will give it a little more dimension. The pages that follow offer a look at a range of different combinations to help inform your choice.

WORKING WITH DRIED FLOWERS

Aside from their longevity *after* the ceremony (imagine displaying your wedding bouquet in a favorite vase), one of the benefits of working with dried flowers is that this kind of arrangement can be made well in advance (hello, DIY project). It's an especially good option for winter weddings when there's not much in season. Some of the best varieties to use are lunaria pods, bunny tail or pampas grass, eucalyptus, lavender, wheatgrass, sola flowers, and berry branches. Keep in mind that dried arrangements tend to be stiffer than fresh, so consider mixing in a few fresh stems to soften the look.

An exotic bridal bouquet for a wedding in Big Sur featured an unexpected combination of lady's slipper and Sharry Baby orchids, chocolate cosmos, Queen Anne's lace, and blue acacia.

HOW TO CARRY YOUR BOUQUET

Some bouquets are meant to be held down at your side, across your arms, or so that they trail behind you, but to hold a traditional hand bouquet, create a diamond shape with your arms, carrying the bouquet slightly lower than your belly button, relax your arm muscles, keep your elbows at your waist (so they don't stick out), and slightly tilt the flowers forward to show the top of the arrangement. For presentation-style bouquets, the flowers should rest across the forearm at belly-button height, with the opposite hand gently holding the stems (if necessary). When in doubt, ask your florist for their recommendation.

WHITE BOUQUETS

LIGHTEN UP

KEY INGREDIENT: Baby's breath

WHY IT WORKS: A round baby's-breath bouquet is feminine, traditional, and perfect for a formal occasion, yet it's very low cost.

A DELICATE DRIFT

KEY INGREDIENTS: Jasmine, grapevine, gardenias, Purity garden roses

WHY IT WORKS: For a cascading look without the weight, opt for light, vinelike stems with undulating leaves and blooms.

TWO-TONE

KEY INGREDIENTS: Panda anemones, Queen Anne's lace, flannel flowers

WHY IT WORKS: A loose arrangement of flowers with dark inky centers subtly injects contrast into an all-white arrangement.

ALMOST UNTOUCHED

KEY INGREDIENT: Dogwood

WHY IT WORKS: A lush drift of blooming dogwood is deliberately wild yet incredibly simple. To make it a more manageable handheld bouquet, the stems were cut short.

ELEGANT SIMPLICITY

KEY INGREDIENTS: Garden roses, olive leaves

WHY IT WORKS: A round, midsized bouquet can be created with many different kinds of flowers (roses, peonies, ranunculus, hydrangea, etc.). Hints of greenery make it feel slightly less formal and traditional.

LONG AND LEAN

KEY INGREDIENT: White peonies

WHY IT WORKS: Grouping large blooms in differing heights is a wonderful way to showcase the beauty of each individual blossom.

A BREATH OF FRESH AIR

KEY INGREDIENT: Phalaenopsis orchids

WHY IT WORKS: Orchids are frequently added to bouquets as accent flowers, but this avant-garde arrangement is composed of them exclusively. They are extremely delicate, so handle with care (no tossing!).

THE NEW POSY

KEY INGREDIENTS: Clematis flowers, lunaria pods

WHY IT WORKS: This modern alternative to a lily-of-the valley bouquet (see page 107) is tied with an ivory upholstery tassel.

COLORFUL BOUQUETS

A TROPICAL MEDLEY

KEY INGREDIENTS: Pink Ice protea, anthurium, peonies, caladium leaf, philodendron leaf

WHY IT WORKS: In a vibrant palette of orange, pink, and red, this lush arrangement is hardy enough to last without water for many hours and can also withstand hot temperatures.

A SINGLE VARIETY

KEY INGREDIENT: Matilija poppies

WHY IT WORKS: Wrapping the stems in white ribbon makes this collection of soft, crepe-like wildflowers feel more formal.

MOODY ROMANCE

KEY INGREDIENTS: Anemone, lisianthus, fritillaria, hellebore, chocolate cosmos, fern, ninebark, chocolate lace

WHY IT WORKS: Perfect for an autumnal wedding, inky eggplant hues and shades of emerald green evoke a sophisticated yet unexpected sensibility.

DARK TO LIGHT

KEY INGREDIENTS: Garden roses, delphinium, snowberry, smokebush foliage, scabiosa, Japanese anemone, *pieris Japonica*

WHY IT WORKS: This bouquet embraces every hue in the wedding's color story, with pastels reflected in the baby-blue ribbon and blush-colored roses. Local foliage provides a touch of darkness.

A HINT OF PINK

KEY INGREDIENTS: Hyacinth, delphinium, lily of the valley, pepper grass, lisianthus, ranunculus, hellebores, carnation

WHY IT WORKS: A few blush stems were tucked into a white foundation (along with the rosy silk ribbon) to subtly add color and connect this loose and leggy arrangement back to the wedding's feminine palette.

FORMAL TONES

KEY INGREDIENTS: Lily of the valley, forget-me-nots

WHY IT WORKS: Inject some color into a traditional lily-of-the-valley bouquet by interspersing something colorful and equally delicate among the stems.

PINT-SIZED

KEY INGREDIENTS: Chocolate cosmos, hellebores

WHY IT WORKS: Fashion-forward brides often opt for a small posy that won't distract from the dress or come off as too "bridal." The best part? It's easy on the budget.

WILD ONE

KEY INGREDIENTS: Pink peonies, Queen Anne's lace, chrysanthemum, seeded eucalyptus

WHY IT WORKS: Without a defined structure, this just-picked-from-the-garden-style bouquet feels even more unexpected with a few moody dahlias juxtaposed against the ultrafeminine peonies.

THE ORIGINALS

Some unconventional brides have turned the idea of a wedding bouquet completely on its head, holding just a single stem, something nonfloral, or a very abstract concept of a bouquet. Let your imagination run wild and find a true floral artist to help manifest your vision—or turn this into a DIY project.

LEAVING A TRAIL

KEY INGREDIENT: Passion vine

WHY IT WORKS: A foraged passion vine reinforced with orchid blooms and additional passion flowers has no real front or back. It gently glided on the ground behind the bride.

THE MOST MINIMAL

KEY INGREDIENT: Magnolia branch

WHY IT WORKS: For a purposefully understyled look, consider a single perfect stem. It's a wonderful way to offset a busy dress or complement a simple sheath, and it's often easy enough to do on your own.

GOING GREEN

KEY INGREDIENTS: Seeded and baby-blue eucalyptus, wax flowers, lavender

WHY IT WORKS: Having a beautiful bouquet doesn't necessarily mean using only expensive, rare blooms. Easy-to-find varieties such as eucalyptus, wax flowers, and olive branches feel more discreet, androgynous, and natural.

NONFLORAL

KEY INGREDIENTS: Silver brunia, Billy balls, scabiosa pods, pine cones and sprigs

WHY IT WORKS: Incorporate a few dried stems into a fresh-cut arrangement or create a petite bouquet made exclusively of dried flowers, such as this one. (For more on working with dried flowers, see page 102.)

THE BRIDESMAIDS' BOUQUETS

Bridesmaids' bouquets usually differ in composition from and are slightly smaller than the bridal bouquet, but they can also be slightly larger. Remember that not all of the bridesmaids' bouquets need to be identical. The important thing is that all the hand arrangements complement one another, which can be done by carrying a few similar stems through the arrangements or by strategically incorporating different hues within your color story. The same idea applies if you are offering corsages to other family members.

Echoing the texture and style of the white bridal bouquet (see page 104), these arrangements of yarrow, cattail grass, scabiosa, and dried grasses were each slightly different while remaining within a muted palette that coordinated with the dresses.

A PERFECT MATCH

Whether you are using similar elements or completely different varieties, here are a few examples of how to translate the bridal bouquet (left) into the bridesmaids' bouquets (right).

BLUSH TONES

KEY INGREDIENTS: Garden tea roses, peonies, Veronica, astilbe, oregano, scabiosa, sweet peas

WHY IT WORKS: While the bridal bouquet is a mix of garden flowers, the bridesmaids' bouquets are almost exclusively composed of pink peonies. Though different in composition, they both have a soft palette and speak to the same relaxed aesthetic.

A TIGHT EDIT

KEY INGREDIENTS: New Zealand ferns, white ranunculus, rosy hellebores

WHY IT WORKS: The foundational elements of both the arrangements are the same, but the bridesmaids' bouquets are considerably smaller, and instead of being predominately white, they feature pink accents thanks to a few fresh-cut hellebores.

CLASSIC CUTS

KEY INGREDIENTS: Lily of the valley, sweet pea, maidenhair fern

WHY IT WORKS: A small and compact bridal bouquet is perfectly offset by a loose, whimsical, larger bridesmaid's arrangement. The green-and-white palette is a timeless choice.

FLOWER CROWNS

Once relegated to the flower girl, a floral crown is a modern, ethereal accessory for brides and bridesmaids alike. A delicate green-and-white circlet tends to be more formal than a crown with larger, more colorful types of flowers. You can offer crowns to all the women in attendance by placing them at the dinner tables or by setting up a station where guests can make their own during the reception (see page 295). For adults, place the crown at a slight angle (lower in the back, higher in the front) rather than directly on top of the head (which might be suitable for small children), and make sure all the flowers are facing outward so that people can see them.

ABOVE:
EARTH ANGELS

A baby's-breath crown for the littlest attendants is a formal and traditional choice. Add volume if you want to create more of a halo effect (for adults, a slim, more discreet baby's-breath crown is more elegant).

OPPOSITE:
LA BOHÈME

An understated crown made of twigs and a few dainty rosebuds won't overpower your look and is easy to wear.

ABOVE:
GREEN GODDESS

If you want a crown that blends in with your look instead of taking center stage, a small green circlet with white accents is a nice solution. For the base, consider rosemary, ferns, mint, eucalyptus, or olive branches; for accents, use small spray roses, baby's breath, feverfew, snowberries, or wax flowers.

BEAUTY

Most brides seek out the services of a professional to do their hair and makeup for the wedding. Assistants to big-name makeup artists are often perfect for weddings as they are accustomed to helping out on busy editorial shoots and are trying to make a name for themselves. You'll want to schedule trials in advance, even if you are asking a friend to do it or if you are doing it yourself, so you can test out products and techniques (see page 120). Note that getting your makeup and hair done at the same time will usually take about two hours (uninterrupted).

If budget allows, offer hair and makeup services to those getting ready for the wedding with you. If possible, ask your hair and makeup team to refresh your look just before the reception. It's also worth finding out if it's within budget to have your hair and makeup done for other events during your wedding weekend, like the rehearsal dinner.

HAIR

Intricate, complicated updos have largely fallen out of favor, replaced by styles that are more natural and relaxed and don't require constant maintenance as the night progresses: low ponytails, loose waves, simple buns, or even a great blow-out. Your wedding hairstyle should be based on three factors.

1 Your Typical Hairstyle: If you always part your hair on the same side, or always wear it a certain way for formal events, sticking with what you know and love will help you feel like a glamorous version of yourself.

2 Your Dress: Different dress silhouettes call for different hairstyles. A high neckline with intricate beading might seem busy if your hair is down; you may want to show off a dramatic open-back gown by putting your hair up.

3 The Weather: If you are getting married in the summer or outside in humid weather (or if you plan on dancing and socializing for hours on end), consider wearing your hair down for a few pictures and even the ceremony, but then putting it up.

If you are even *considering* an updo, let your hair grow out the year before the wedding, or you may need to get a few extensions put in. Then bring inspiration pictures (including a photo of your dress) and anything you might want to put in your hair (flowers and/or a flower crown, a tiara, barrettes, ribbons, etc.) to the trial with your hairstylist. Note, most stylists will advise you not to wash your hair the morning of the wedding in order to maintain its natural texture.

NATURAL UPDOS

Unlike the updos of the past (where your hair would be filled with pins that would inevitably fall out during the course of the evening), today's updos are simpler and more discreet.

RELAXED BUN

This casual version of a classic, sleek bun might be more in line with how you style your hair on a daily basis. It's also a great way to soften a minimalist dress.

LADYLIKE BUN

A round or knotted low chignon with a side or center part, or no part at all, works for almost everyone—it can offset a busy dress or complement a simple sheath.

MILKMAID BRAIDS

This European style can be worn either low or as a crown on top of the head and will stand up to a night of dancing. Pull out a few strands of hair around your face and add a couple of tiny flowers to soften the look.

LOW KNOTTED PONY

A hybrid between a low ponytail and a bun pairs particularly well with a classic silhouette like this one, which has a high neckline and a low back.

SHOULDER-GRAZING LOOKS

Whether your down look is relaxed or controlled, it will require more maintenance throughout the night than an updo—and if it's a windy day, you may want to have a plan B location for pictures.

EFFORTLESS BLOW-OUT

A professional blow-out works for casual weddings or to offset a formal dress. It's also ideal for strapless styles, where it helps soften the neckline.

TOPKNOT

This playful style, with a small high bun and loose, tousled locks underneath, feels young and fresh. It's a great way to keep your hair out of your face on a windy day.

OLD HOLLYWOOD WAVES

A smooth 1950s S-wave with a deep side part is an incredibly polished style. While it's glamorous, it's also high-maintenance and not suitable for hot weather or lots of dancing.

FISHTAIL BRAID

This loose, cascading, goddess-like braid recalls the Irish tradition of brides braiding their hair to symbolize feminine power and luck. It's best for brides with very long hair.

HAIR ACCESSORIES

Whether it's a few delicate flowers or a glitzy, diamond-encrusted barrette, adding accessories to your coif is a wonderful way to dress down or dress up your overall look.

FLOWERS

In lieu of a flower crown, a few strategically placed flowers will soften any look. Try baby's breath, feverfew, hypericum berries, hellebores, or daisies.

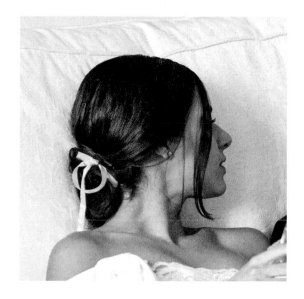

RIBBON

A black, white, or blush ribbon secured to a half-up/half-down look or a pony or bun exudes cool French-girl style. A bow is more feminine than a double knot.

BARRETTE

Your hair can be a great place to incorporate a piece of jewelry if you aren't wearing a necklace or bracelet(s).

HEADBAND

A flat double-banded headband tucked behind a few curls is reminiscent of a tiara but feels much more discreet.

MAKEUP: GETTING THE NATURAL LOOK

One of the most common regrets brides have is that they felt like they were wearing too much makeup on their wedding day. There are usually several reasons for this, one being that most people don't have a lot of experience having their makeup professionally applied and either don't know how to direct their makeup artist or unwittingly leave their fate in the hands of someone who may not share their vision. That's why being able to clearly articulate to your makeup artist the look you are trying to achieve is crucially important. And if you are doing your own makeup, you need to familiarize yourself with certain practices and techniques in the months leading up to the wedding as a way of training. So, for those who need a course in Makeup 101, here's a breakdown of all the elements, in order of application.

1. PRIMER

Before applying any makeup, use an illuminating primer as a base. It's what will make your skin glow. A good primer also means your foundation won't have to work as hard and you won't inadvertently overapply it. (Note: The same applies to eye primers and lip primers.) This step may not be necessary if you have clear skin.

2. FOUNDATION

If you are someone who doesn't typically wear foundation, you may choose to skip this step entirely or apply a very light tinted moisturizer, but foundation is the answer if you want to cover up dark circles, pimples, uneven skin tones, and imperfections. It is usually applied with a sponge but can also be applied with a brush or your fingers depending on the consistency.

The color of your foundation should exactly match your skin tone—otherwise your face will be a different color than the rest of your body and there will be a line on your neck or jaw where the foundation ends. When searching for the right shade, test it on your face in natural lighting—go outside and make sure the foundation disappears into your skin.

Some things you may want from your foundation: shimmer (to impart extra dewiness), waterproofness (if you tend to get emotional), that it be oil-free (use a water-based formula if you have particularly oily skin—see box, opposite), a built-in primer (to make it longer lasting), and an SPF (for daytime weddings). Here are the different options depending on the amount of coverage you need (obviously, the more of the product you apply, the more coverage you get).

Tinted Moisturizer: Does double duty by moisturizing the skin while imparting a hint of color (or triple duty if it contains an SPF). Best for people who already have clear, even skin.

Sheer Foundation: Won't mask your skin but will even out texture. It's made with liquid silicone, so it glides on smoothly and you can layer it. Works best for brides with normal to dry skin and older brides who may have wrinkles and fine lines because this light formula won't settle into depressions in the skin.

BB Cream: Lighter than a standard foundation but thicker than a tinted moisturizer. Many BB creams are made with silicone and are packed with antioxidants, making them light and moisturizing.

Mousse (or Whipped Foundation): Has a powdery, matte finish that is suitable for all skin types and offers medium to full coverage.

Liquid (or Cream) Foundation: Offers medium to full coverage depending on application, and comes in many specialized versions (twenty-four-hour, oil-based, oil-free, waterproof, etc.). Works best on well-moisturized skin because it can emphasize fine lines and wrinkles. It will cover blemishes and pigmentation issues.

OIL-BASED VS. OIL-FREE FOUNDATION Oil-based foundations are great for anyone with dry skin and for older brides who want to minimize the appearance of fine lines. Oil in the product instantly plumps up the skin.

Oil-free (or matte) foundations are water-based and ideal for women with naturally oily skin. Use a good moisturizer or a foundation primer for an extra layer of moisture.

3. CONCEALER

Concealer is similar to foundation but has a thicker consistency used to mask blemishes, pimples, dark under-eye circles, and other imperfections. For under-eye concealer, choose one that is a shade or two lighter than your skin color (yellow-toned concealers will better hide bluish undertones, and peach-toned concealers will better hide brown and yellow spots); for your face, pick a color that exactly matches your skin tone.

4. BRONZER AND BLUSH

You can do neither, one, or both. If you do decide to use both bronzer and blush, the trick is to avoid applying too much product. Start with the bronzer (your bronzer shade should be one shade darker than your natural skin tone; avoid bronzers with orange undertones—they don't look good on anyone). Bronzer should be gently applied with an angled contour brush to areas of the skin that would naturally be tanned by the sun: the tops of the cheeks, the bridge of the nose, and your forehead along the hairline.

Blush should be applied using a round or flat-head brush. To determine the right color, pinch your cheeks and find the color that most closely resembles your natural flush. Smile when you apply blush so that it is transferred only to the apples of your cheeks.

5. EYEBROW PENCIL

Shape and fill in your brows with a pencil that's one to two shades lighter than your brow. The goal is a full, natural brow—not something too plucked or thin, or too dark. Comb and then set with a gel or some Vaseline.

6. EYE SHADOW, LINER, AND MASCARA

The general strategy when applying eye makeup is to add intensity as you go, starting with shadow to contour the area. A black smoky eye is typically too dramatic for the ceremony, so stick with a lighter, translucent shadow with a little shimmer for the ceremony and add heavier shadow for the reception if you want. Classic, slightly winged-out eyeliner is always chic.

Next, place a few strategic individual false lashes, if needed, then curl your eyelashes and apply a thin coat or two of mascara, making sure there are no particles or clumping.

7. LIPSTICK

Generally, if you've gone heavier with your eye makeup, you'll want to stick with a nude lip; conversely, if your eye makeup is light, you can get away with something bolder. Of course, if you want to keep everything natural, lightly done eyes and a nude lip work beautifully. If you are worried that a bold lip will get smudged during the first kiss, wear a nude color for the ceremony and something more colorful for the reception. The trick to longevity here is to fill in your lips with a pencil before applying lipstick (lip stains are also longer lasting than traditional lipsticks). If you want a shiny finish, add a clear or tinted gloss.

8. SETTING POWDER

Makeup artists will often use a translucent powder to set makeup, followed by a setting spray. This combo will keep your makeup in place for hours. Some even swear by a quick mist of hair spray over the face to set makeup (just remember to close your eyes!).

THE MAKEUP TRIAL
It's important to bring reference photos and any personal products that you'd like to use to the makeup trial. Remember to take photos in different kinds of light (indoor and outdoor, night and day) after the trial and make edits to your look as needed. If many changes are needed, you may want to schedule another trial, find a different makeup artist, or consider doing your makeup yourself.

FOUR CLASSIC LOOKS

Whichever look you decide on for the day, remember that the guiding philosophy behind natural makeup is that less is *always* more (and that imperfections can always be resolved in Photoshop!).

A HINT OF COLOR

A soft, rosy blush will add warmth and brightness and still feel appropriate for a daytime wedding, when evening makeup may appear too heavy. Finish with a glossy, natural lip to match.

DEFINED EYES

For a look that can transition from day to night, a thin black line placed just on the upper lids doesn't feel too heavy. If you want more drama, continue the line to make a very subtle winged-out cat eye.

SHINE BRIGHT

Shimmer placed on the eyelids, cheeks, and lips instantly adds to the celebratory mood. (Keep the lips nude so the look doesn't become overdone.)

THE BOLD LIP

A wine-stained or bright red lip is an elegant touch for an evening wedding, and it can also work for daytime if the rest of your makeup is kept very light. This choice largely depends on your personal style—if you like a bold lip, don't miss the opportunity.

THE NATURAL NAIL

A nude manicure and pedicure will elongate the limbs and work with any ensemble (and will also do double duty on your honeymoon). Choose a shade that complements the undertones of your complexion the same way you would shop for foundation. Some tried-and-true shades include "Samoan Sands" and "Bubble Bath" by OPI, "Mademoiselle" by Essie, and "Ballerina" by Chanel. Buy the color you want and bring it to the salon (oftentimes, nail salons will dilute their bottles with nail polish remover, which stretches the bottle but compromises the quality of the polish). Gel manicures and pedicures are not the most healthy, but they will be more resistant to chipping. If you want something even more natural looking than nude nail polish, ask your technician for a "buff," where a buffing block is used to build shine on the nail to look like you're wearing a clear gloss polish.

DAY-OF BAG

In addition to an evening clutch (which might hold basics like lip gloss, face powder, a room key, mints, and maybe a few tissues), ask a bridesmaid or a friend to have a bag of beauty essentials on hand, including the following.

- Bobby pins and hair elastics

- Travel-size hair spray

- Pain reliever

- Tampons

- Fashion tape

- Dental floss

- Safety pins

- Stain remover wipes

- Blotting papers

- Makeup remover and makeup (for smears and touch-ups)

- Band-Aids

Ask your nail technician to file your nails into a slightly rounded shape that follows the natural lines of your fingertips before applying a sheer gloss (this might mean applying only one coat instead of two).

PRE-WEDDING BEAUTY CHECKLIST

6 MONTHS BEFORE

○ TREATMENTS: Start seeing an aesthetician for facials and to troubleshoot any other topical issues.

○ PROCEDURES: If you've been meaning to get a mole removed or do any small procedures, such as lightening acne or sun-damaged skin with a laser treatment, microdermabrasion, or a peel, scheduling it now will give you plenty of time to recover before the wedding.

○ EXERCISE: If you don't already have a workout routine, start one that you can continue up to and after the big day.

○ CLEANSE: If you are interested in doing an elimination diet to identify chronic skin issues or to reduce inflammation, now is the time. Similarly, a cleanse to boost energy and skin quality is best done early.

○ BIRTH CONTROL: If you take birth control pills and don't want to have your time of the month coincide with your wedding date, talk to your doctor about altering your schedule.

3 MONTHS BEFORE

○ MAKEUP/HAIR TRIAL: Many brides-to-be schedule these to coincide with their shower or a big night out.

THE MONTH OF

○ TEETH WHITENING: Make an appointment with your dentist or start a box of at-home strips.

○ BOTOX: This isn't on everyone's to-do list, but if it is on yours, don't do it too close to the wedding on the off chance that the injection causes bruising. It also takes a week or so to kick in.

○ HAIR: If your wedding hairstyle calls for it, make an appointment with your hairstylist for a cut, color, and/or extensions two to three weeks before the wedding.

THE WEEK OF

○ TAN: If you want that sun-kissed look, find a spray-tan professional whom you really, *really* trust (you may even want to do a trial in the months prior to the wedding).

○ WAXING/THREADING: Attend to those unruly eyebrows, upper lip, legs, bikini line, and any other areas that need a little taming. Be sure to schedule this a few days in advance in case any redness results.

○ CORTISONE SHOTS: If you feel a pimple coming on, your dermatologist can give you a cortisone shot to prevent a breakout. You can usually make a same-day appointment.

○ MANICURE/PEDICURE: Do this as close to the wedding as possible.

○ EXTRA SLEEP AND WATER: A few additional hours of beauty sleep and staying hydrated will help prevent dark circles and make you feel energized.

THE DAY OF

○ MASK: Your makeup artist might suggest a hydrating sheet mask in the morning (try this a month or so in advance to make sure you don't have a reaction to anything in it). It's also a fun thing to do with your bridesmaids while you're getting ready.

○ COOL OFF: If you are a little puffy from the night before, putting a cold compress on your face will help bring down the swelling.

GETTING READY

The idea of waking up on your wedding day and having a leisurely breakfast followed by a walk or a yoga session is wonderful—in theory. The truth is that most brides opt to spend the day in the hair-and-makeup chair and request that their bridesmaids get ready with them. It's important to be considerate of your bridesmaids' time—anything beyond two to three hours can start to become wearisome. If you are getting ready with your maids, consider providing a breakfast or lunch spread, or snacks, and have a few bottles of water (and Champagne!) on hand. You may also want to ask someone to make a playlist and bring speakers. When it comes time to put on the dress, it's customary for the mother of the bride to help her daughter.

If you are less traditional about things, you may choose to get ready with your soon-to-be husband, which can be an incredibly intimate and sweet time to spend together. What you wear while getting ready should be something that won't disrupt your hair and makeup, like a pajama set, silk robe, or basic white button-down.

INNER STRENGTH

For all the attention placed on beautification, it's just as important to take care of your inner wellness. Whether through meditation, massage, gardening, sound therapy, acupuncture, reading, cooking, or taking a bath, it's imperative to do things to center your thoughts as often as possible before the wedding.

THE GROOM'S GUIDE

Men's dressing essentially boils down to three basic options: a tuxedo, a suit, or slacks and a button-down. Your first step should be to go to a store (whether it's a department store or a designer boutique) where you can try on five to ten tuxedos or suits, and figure out what you like: Do you prefer wearing a double-breasted jacket? Do you like a shawl lapel or a peaked lapel? A satin or a grosgrain tie? Edit down the options until you find a style that works for you.

The general rule of thumb is that the groom should dress in accordance with the dress code listed on the invitation. If you want to be a tad more formal, that's fine, but you shouldn't overdo it at the risk of making the guests feel underdressed.

TUXEDO 101

Making your wedding black tie (i.e., choosing to wear a tuxedo for your wedding) is a decision that should be made with other guests in mind—find out if your friends have tuxedos or if they will need to rent or buy one for your wedding. If the majority don't own a tux, you may want to opt for a suit, or at least consider making the dress code black-tie optional. Tux rentals are better now than they used to be, but it is still far more preferable to wear something that you've purchased, because the quality and fit will be much better. If you do decide to rent a tux, find and reserve your tuxedo at least a month in advance. If possible, go for a higher-quality rental, which usually runs somewhere between $100 and $150 just for the suit— some rental companies will allow small alterations to be made. All the accessories (bow ties, studs, cummerbunds, shirts, shoes, etc.) are additional costs, so you may want to consider purchasing some or all of these items to elevate and personalize your rental tux.

Thinking about buying a new tuxedo? Familiarize yourself with all the options so you can make the most informed choice.

Grooms should wear something equal in formality to what their spouse is wearing, but within these parameters there are myriad options for personalization. Here, two grooms wore contrasting tuxedos, one with a classic black peaked-lapel jacket and one with a white shawl-collar jacket, united by matching boutonnieres.

JACKET STYLES

Single-Breasted: Features one to four buttons and can be worn with a cummerbund or a vest.

Double-Breasted: Features two to six buttons, where the front flaps overlap. This style is always worn closed without a vest or a cummerbund.

LAPELS

There are three different lapel styles to choose from for your tuxedo jacket:

Notched lapels are the most common and are similar to the collar of a business suit.

Peaked lapels are the most dramatic with sharp edges that point upward.

Shawl lapels are rounded and have an old-fashioned sensibility.

COLOR

The classic look is a black jacket with black trousers, but there are a couple of interesting alternatives. Black trousers with a white bow tie and a white jacket feels a little more swanky, while a navy tuxedo (or a navy jacket with black pants) is more subtle.

SHIRTING

The groom should decide if he wants to wear a bow tie, a tie, or no neckpiece at all (see page 135) before deciding on the collar. Shirting options include the following.

The band collar (also known as a standing or Mandarin-style collar) doesn't have any collar leaves and can be worn with a bolo tie or without a neckpiece.

The classic collar (or a turndown collar) is the most versatile and works well with a tie or bow tie. A more modern groom is likely to wear this

style, as opposed to a wingtip collar, with a tuxedo. A variation of this includes a spread collar, with wider collar points.

The wingtip collar (or winged collar) is the most formal collar and is almost always worn with a tuxedo.

PLAIN, PLEATED, OR PIQUÉD

When it comes to the front of the shirt, a plain front is the most relaxed, pleated is more conservative, and a piquéd bib style is the most formal and old-fashioned option.

CUFFS AND BUTTONS

A shirt with French cuffs is the only style that requires cuff links. All other cuffs (square, round, and angle cut) have a button closure. Most pleated or smooth-front tuxedo shirts are worn with studs (decorative fasteners that usually match the cuff links) or button covers. If you want a cleaner look, use a fly-front detail to conceal the fastenings (a plain strip of fabric that is placed over the buttons).

TUXEDO ACCESSORIES

- Cuff links (if the shirt has French cuffs)
- Suspenders (see page 135)
- Cummerbund
- Tie or bow tie (see page 135)
- Scarf
- Waistcoat or vest
- Amulet
- Pocket watch or wristwatch
- Pocket square (see page 135)
- Boutonniere (see page 136)

PERSONALIZING YOUR TUXEDO

Traditionalists like Kirk Miller, owner of bespoke and ready-to-wear men's shop Miller's Oath, insist that menswear is always best when it's classic. That said, personalizing your look is encouraged, if done in a tasteful and discreet way. To dress down a formal tuxedo, for example, he suggests trying a pair of black leather tennis shoes. Here are a few more personalization ideas to consider.

- Make one buttonhole on your sleeve the same color as the bridesmaids' dresses.

- Have your wedding date embroidered on the inside of your jacket.

- Add a beautiful watch chain.

- Opt for a white or velvet dinner jacket.

- Get a cool pair of trousers—for example, a morning stripe trouser or even a muted plaid with a tuxedo stripe.

- Design the back panel of your tux shirt in a different color.

- Make the lining of your tux something unexpected.

CUSTOM SUITING

There are only a handful of tailors in the country who offer true bespoke craftsmanship—where a suit is designed based on an original pattern requiring multiple fittings, and the options for customization are endless. Made to measure, which is often confused with bespoke, is essentially a hybrid of ready-to-wear and bespoke that relies on modifying an existing pattern. The process of creating a bespoke suit takes ten to twelve weeks (it could possibly be done in eight weeks if you're in a rush) and will run well over $1,000, but the result is truly special. Besides getting a suit that fits perfectly, at the end you will also have a pattern and a detailed set of measurements that you can use to make additional garments in the future. Here's what you can expect if you go the custom route.

1 Creating a Pattern: You and your tailor will discuss style and fabrics. The tailor will then take around fifty measurements of your body, which they will use to draft a paper pattern. In addition to measurements, the tailor will make note of details such as the slope of your shoulder and the arch of your back.

2 Fittings: Fabric is cut by hand according to the specific pattern and loosely sewn together. You return for a basted fitting (which usually takes around thirty minutes). At this stage, the entire suit can be taken apart again so any necessary changes can be made to the suit/tuxedo; and also, importantly, the pattern itself can be changed at this time. Adjustments are made and a second fitting (and, if necessary, a third fitting) takes place.

3 Hand-Finishing: Once the fit is perfect and all stylistic adjustments have been made, the white basting thread is removed and the garment is hand-finished.

THE ULTRA-FORMAL GROOM If black tie isn't refined enough for your taste, there are a few options reserved for the most formal occasions.

White Tie (or Full Evening Dress): The rarest and most formal dress code of all, this designation calls for a black tailcoat paired with a white starched shirt, a white vest, a white bow tie worn around a detachable collar, high-waisted black trousers, and patent-leather shoes.

Morning Dress: This daytime formal dress code consists of a morning coat (a cutaway coat), a waistcoat, and striped trousers (which are usually gray). The semiformal counterpart to this look is a stroller jacket (similar to a tuxedo jacket, without the satin detail).

A TUX FOR EVERY TASTE

A tuxedo is an investment that you will have for life, so try to pick something that you will feel comfortable in now *and* thirty years down the road.

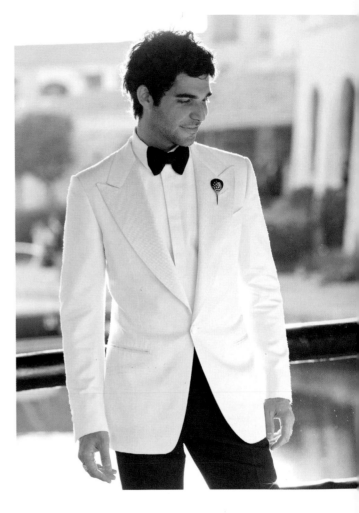

WHITE TIE

This look exudes old-school elegance with a shawl lapel, a crisp piquéd bib-style shirt with a clean fly-front finish, a classic white rose boutonniere, and (not pictured) a pair of velvet evening slippers.

WHITE JACKET

The white dinner jacket is a throwback style that's making a resurgence among sartorially minded grooms. It can be worn with a white bow tie or a black one, for contrast. Here, it is paired with a dramatic peaked lapel, a feathered boutonniere, and a shirt with a clean fly-front finish.

BLACK AND BLUE

This navy tuxedo with black buttons and a black notched lapel is slightly more casual than an all-black or all-white version. Free of adornment (like a boutonniere or a pocket square), it feels clean and modern.

DOUBLE-BREASTED

This double-breasted jacket, with a peaked lapel and wide, overlapping front flaps, is an old-school choice that exudes confident conservatism. As it is heavier than a traditional single-breasted tux (and should always remain buttoned), it's best for colder climes.

SUITING

A classic, well-tailored suit is an extremely versatile option for a groom and his groomsmen. Most men own a suit, and if not, your wedding is the perfect excuse to buy one. Lighter shades (like gray and beige) are usually worn for daytime parties while evening weddings typically call for darker shades (black, navy, charcoal). If you are having a less formal event, ditch the tie and undo a couple of buttons. Only the most casual groom will completely eschew a jacket and tie.

DRESSING UP A SUIT If you want to make a classic suit more formal without having to venture into tuxedo territory, Kirk Miller advises choosing one in a very dark color (navy and charcoal can both be used) and pairing it with a *very* crisp white shirt and a dark, solid-colored tie or bow tie. One main point of differentiation between a tuxedo and a suit is the addition of a belt. If you want a more formal-looking suit, wear a belt that blends in instead of one that contrasts.

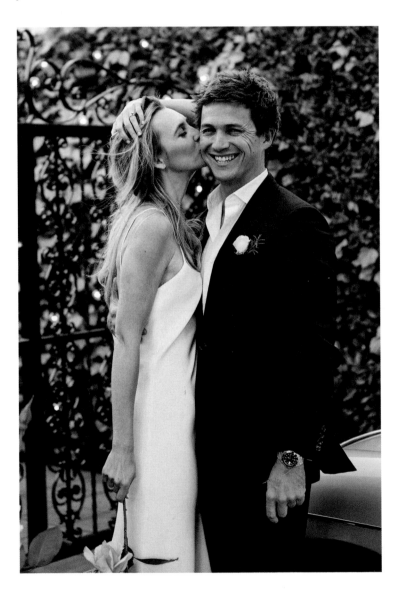

A classic black suit with a crisp white shirt and a traditional white rose boutonniere was perfectly appropriate for a low-key backyard ceremony.

SUIT SELECTION

Just because a suit is less formal than a tuxedo, it doesn't necessarily mean it requires less consideration. If you are wearing something you already own, make sure it fits like a glove (you may need to take it to the tailor), and think about ways to customize it and make it feel elevated for your wedding.

THE FORMAL OPTION

A dark suit with a dark tie is suitable for an evening party—black on black is classic, though navy is also handsome.

LIGHT GRAY

A crisp light gray suit is a sharp choice for daytime or early afternoon festivities. Adding a darker tie makes the look more elegant.

LINEN

A beige linen suit is ideal for a tropical beach wedding and can be worn with brown loafers without socks (or sandals). Since linen has a tendency to droop, make sure your suit is well-fitted.

NO TIE REQUIRED

For a more casual wedding, a dark suit sans tie is cool and relaxed. Just undo one shirt button (two maximum).

FOOTWEAR

With a tuxedo, it's customary to wear black patent oxfords or velvet evening slippers (without socks), although some modern grooms might opt for fashion sneakers. (The most formal groom in white tie may wear black patent court pumps with grosgrain ribbon.) A classic suit is typically paired with leather oxfords or loafers. For casual affairs, you'll see everything from drivers and boat shoes to sandals. Ditch the socks with drivers and evening slippers for a more European look. And as a general rule of thumb, most styles look best if the toe is elongated, not squared. Only for the most laid-back beach ceremony should a groom consider being barefoot (and even then it may seem odd if the rest of the guests are wearing shoes).

CLASSIC PATENT LEATHER
Elegant lace-up patent leather shoes can scuff easily, so make sure they are shined to a mirror finish before the wedding.

BROWN LEATHER
When choosing brown leather shoes, be sure they are consistent in color, meaning no intentional (or unintentional) distressing. The darker the brown, the more formal the shoe.

VELVET EVENING SLIPPERS
Round-toed black velvet evening slippers are distinctly debonair—nowadays many feature embroidered icons and heraldry for added effect.

SNEAKERS
Lace-up Vans skate sneakers are an irreverent yet fashion-forward choice for a casual groom.

A mix of old and new accessories
for the groom: a vintage gold pocket
watch, a silk handkerchief with
discreet skull icons to match the
cuff links, and a classic black bow tie.

TIES AND BOW TIES

One of the easiest ways to personalize a tuxedo or suit is with
a neckpiece. Traditionally, grooms wear a bow tie with a tuxedo
and a standard tie with a suit, but nowadays many grooms wear a
standard tie with a tuxedo.

When it comes to bow ties, classic black and white bows in
silk, satin, and velvet are the most common. Grooms can also find
printed options to match the bridesmaids' gowns or altar flowers.
Aside from color and fabric, there are many different styles of bows
to choose from, including a lavaliere bow, a layered or flat bow, a
double bow, and a bow with elongated points. Grooms who wear
a bow tie will want a set of tuxedo studs, typically in black onyx or
mother-of-pearl, to cover up the exposed buttons on the front of
their shirt.

Ties also come in a wide spectrum of options. Beyond the
classic black silk tie that most men pair with a black tuxedo or suit,
there are different textures (satin, grosgrain, crochet, velvet) and an
array of prints and colors. Then there's shape: traditional, square,
or skinny (the latter tends to feel more modern). An Ascot tie is
usually reserved for the most formal daytime events and paired
with a cutaway coat. And consider adding a tie pin, which can be a
silver bar or something more embellished, like a fabric flower. An
alternative to a traditional fabric tie is a Western-style bolo made
of leather.

SUSPENDERS AND BELTS

Suspenders are worn with tuxedos; belts should be worn with a
suit or for a more casual event. If you want the groomsmen to have
a uniform look, instruct them to wear a certain color or style, or
purchase a pair of suspenders or a belt for each of them.

POCKET SQUARES

Pocket squares can be included in any look, whether the groom
is wearing a formal tuxedo or a casual linen blazer, and with or
without a boutonniere. The type of fold (classic, Pesko, flower,
crown, or puff) depends on the material (usually white linen,
cotton, or silk). A monogram of his initials and the date hidden in
the fold is also a nice touch.

BOUTONNIERES

Boutonnieres should echo the style of the bridal bouquet and are usually worn by the groom, groomsmen, ushers, ring bearers, and fathers of the bride and groom. If you've chosen a particularly delicate boutonniere, it's not a bad idea to have a few extra on hand in case you need a fresh one later in the evening.

When fastening the boutonniere, secure it through a buttonhole (*boutonnière* is the French word for "buttonhole") on the left lapel. Avoid piercing a satin lapel, as it will damage the cloth. If there is no buttonhole, just stick with a pocket square or use magnets to secure the flowers.

This textured boutonniere was made of heuchera leaf and blushing bride.

COLLAR CUES

Whether your taste is more traditional or you want something bold and colorful, the boutonniere is a wonderful place to express your personality. Here, a range of styles by Los Angeles–based florist Hollyflora.

WHITE DONE RIGHT

In the classic green-and-white color palette, fanlike bay leaves are paired with a couple of delicate *Pieris japonica* tendrils.

EARTH TONES

Perfect for a rustic outdoor wedding, this sweet combination of peach strawflower and berries is wrapped with a leather string.

REAL MEN WEAR PINK

This bold boutonniere features an unexpected pairing of a soft, blooming ranunculus and fiery maple leaves.

TROPICAL

Speckled leaves with oversized pink blooms are perfect for a summer beach wedding.

A NEUTRAL GREEN

Going green doesn't mean you have to forgo flowers, as proven by this look with a few dainty hellebore buds.

DRIED

Strawflowers, pampas grass, and a lunaria pod all mingle together in this arrangement, which is delicate yet durable.

GROOMSMEN

Groomsmen are typically instructed to wear the same thing as the groom or a slight variation (usually a different neckpiece and/or boutonniere), though the most laid-back groom will allow them to select their own look (within the dress code). If you are concerned about how your groomsmen's choices will look together, ask them to send pictures so you can make any adjustments beforehand. Whatever direction you give your groomsmen should echo the direction given to the bridesmaids. For example, if each bridesmaid is wearing the same dress, it might look odd if the groomsmen are wearing a range of looks. Another good rule of thumb: the groom should not be dressed in a more or less formal style than his groomsmen (meaning if the groom is wearing a tuxedo, then his wedding party should also wear tuxedos, not suits).

If the groomsmen are instructed to wear tuxedos, the groom would ideally offer to pay for all of the rentals, or at least discreetly offer to pay for those groomsmen who need assistance. If this cannot be done discreetly, then the groom should consider asking the groomsmen to wear a dark suit instead (most men own a dark suit or can more easily borrow one). If the groomsmen own their own tuxedos but they don't perfectly match (for example, some are shawl collar and some are notched), don't worry about the slight differences in style.

The groom should gift his groomsmen any accessories he wishes them to wear on the wedding day or ask that they purchase their own accessories within a certain set of parameters (for example, a navy tie and a white pocket square). The groom doesn't need to specify basic leather oxfords or loafers for the wedding, but if he wants the groomsmen in a more niche style, like a Sperry boat shoe or an espadrille, he should either provide this as a gift or select an option at a reasonable price point. He should also inform the groomsmen of what he will be providing in advance so that they know exactly what they are responsible for.

OPPOSITE, TOP:
BLACK TIE
To take the guesswork out of dressing a large wedding party, stick with the same look for each groomsman. Here, the groom (second from left) and his father (third from left) wore peaked lapel tuxedos while the groomsmen wore tuxedos with shawl lapels.

OPPOSITE, BOTTOM:
UNIFIED BUT NOT UNIFORM
In matching blue suits and Vans sneakers, the groomsmen wore different shirts, ties, and pocket squares (the groom is pictured in the center).

GROOMING Men should partake in some pre-wedding beautification, too. A trip to the barbershop the week of the wedding is almost always in order. A fun activity is to organize an old-fashioned hot-lather-and-straight-razor shave with the groomsmen. And the day of the wedding, you might want to employ a groomer (or ask your hairdresser) to style your coif and touch up any facial hair.

SUPER TUSCAN

A couple's weeklong celebration in the Italian countryside
took inspiration from the region's sun-drenched terra firma.

Nicole Cari would often come home for lunch when she worked as the marketing director for the fashion label Band of Outsiders. Her office was just a few minutes from the bungalow she shared with her boyfriend, Jacob Soboroff, a correspondent for MSNBC. One day, as she arrived for one of their weekly lunch dates, Jacob surprised her with a spread of Italian cheeses, bread, prosecco, flowers, and, best of all, a diamond engagement ring that had belonged to her late stepmother. The couple immediately started making plans for a wedding at Nicole's father's vacation home—an eighteenth-century farmhouse in the Chianti region of Tuscany.

Part of Nicole's job at Band of Outsiders (and now with brands including jewelry designer Sophie Buhai) was to produce all the company's events, dinner parties, and fashion shows, so organizing a weeklong celebration for one hundred out-of-town guests was something that came quite naturally. "I felt like I had so much to show and so much to share that one or two days just wouldn't have been enough," she explains. Leading up to the Thursday wedding

(house rentals in Europe are usually Saturday to Saturday, hence the midweek wedding), there was a welcome BBQ at the house, a beach day for Nicole and Jacob and their friends, and a rehearsal dinner at a nearby inn.

On the day of the wedding, Nicole's friends organized a sage circle to offer advice and loving words. The couple married overlooking a dramatic vista before cocktails and dinner were served around the pool. Nicole's instinct was to let the venue speak for itself and to bring in elements that were authentic to the area: hay bales served as ceremony seating, wine barrels were used as high-tops, and an existing stone patio was home to a raucous dance party before the *polizia* arrived. The festivities concluded with a late-night skinny-dip in the pool, and everyone reconvened (fully clothed, although some in pajamas) the next day for brunch. Looking back on it all, Nicole says, "It went by so fast, but I really felt that we had not only gotten to see everyone who came to the wedding but that we actually spent time with everyone—including each other."

VIEWFINDER // The couple worked with planner Annie Adair at Tuscan Tour to make the most of the setting. Wine barrels doubled as tables at the sunset cocktail hour overlooking the countryside; a string quartet played classical music. There was a setup of cheese, prosciutto, and breadsticks, with some passed appetizers including stuffed local zucchini flowers. "The cocktail hour was probably my favorite part of the whole wedding," says Nicole.

THE CLOTHESLINE-INSPIRED ESCORT DISPLAY // Table assignment cards by Rifle Paper Co. were secured to tree branches with simple wooden clothespins.

SWEET BEGINNINGS // The traditional Italian wedding cake was made by local bakers as guests looked on. The menu for the evening featured classic Italian staples and wine from nearby vineyards.

SITTING PRETTY // The Tuscan countryside is dotted with hay bales—usually in barrel form, though they come in rectangular shapes, too. For the ceremony, bales were draped with burlap and used as benches. Nicole's friend Keith Malloy played the processional music—"Sea of Love"—on his guitar. For the readings, Jacob's best man, Nicole's man of honor, and Jacob's siblings lifted passages from love letters the couple had exchanged over the years to tell the story of their relationship.

BENVENUTI! // Of the hundred guests, half rented homes while the other half stayed at a nearby hotel, which is where the rehearsal dinner took place. The welcome crates, which were shared among guests, featured a bevy of local products (pasta, wine, cookies, and sprigs of rosemary and lavender) in addition to mosquito repellent, sunscreen, water, Advil, and a local guidebook that Nicole and Jacob wrote and printed themselves.

LOCAL FLAVOR // A colorful tomato can doubled as a casual container for a drift of wildflowers, lavender, and rosemary at the rehearsal dinner.

OPPOSITE:

DINING POOLSIDE // There were two long tables arranged in an "L" shape around the pool. Nicole worked with a local wedding planner to help organize the elements, which were classic and casual: silver candelabras, rustic wooden tables, simple white china, and bistro-style folding chairs. The centerpieces were exclusively green hydrangeas, which are abundant in the gardens around Tuscany.

ABOVE:

AN ALFRESCO AFFAIR // The after-dinner reception was held in a garden strung with bistro-style lights and blooming potted flowers. Dancing took place on the existing brick hardscape surrounded by casual rattan seating arrangements.

FOLLOWING PAGE:

FLOWER GIRL // Nicole's silk Valentino resort dress featured a faint calla lily print on the bottom. She paired it with nude Valentino sandals and an arm cuff, which was a gift from Jacob. Nicole wasn't the only one in flats—the dress code on the invitations simply read "no ties, no heels."

THE REGISTRY

Here's a look at some of the items that topped Nicole and Jacob's wish list.

VITAMIX 780

AVAILABLE FROM

Vitamix.com

HEATH CERAMICS SALT AND PEPPER SHAKERS

AVAILABLE FROM

HeathCeramics.com

HEATHER TAYLOR HOME NAPKINS

AVAILABLE FROM

HeatherTaylorHome.com

EDWARD WOHL CUTTING BOARD

AVAILABLE FROM

HeathCeramics.com

DAVID MELLOR KNIFE SET

AVAILABLE FROM

HeathCeramics.com

LE CREUSET DUTCH OVEN

AVAILABLE FROM

Williams-Sonoma.com

ASTIER DE VILLATTE VASE

AVAILABLE FROM

NickeyKehoe.com

DOLCE VITA ITALIAN FLATWARE

AVAILABLE FROM

NickeyKehoe.com

ICHENDORF MILANO ITALIAN GLASSWARE

AVAILABLE FROM

NickeyKehoe.com

3 THE CEREMONY

Distracted by the complexity of an expensive reception, couples often lose sight of the importance of the ceremony. Whether it's in front of three friends at a courthouse or one hundred guests in your parents' backyard, the ceremony is the heart and soul of every wedding—and it's what everyone remembers most. Church and hotel weddings are still popular, but more and more couples are heading outdoors and taking their design cues from the natural surroundings.

The pages that follow will show you how to create an ethereal ceremony from scratch, whether you want an upgraded twist on the traditional white arbor or a more design-forward alternative. Beyond what your ceremony looks like, there are myriad ways to modernize the content of the service so that it reflects the uniqueness of your relationship.

SCHEDULE OF EVENTS

Before you start planning the details of your ceremony, you need to decide what time of day you are going to get married—and for that matter, when everything else is going to happen. There are lots of things that will influence your schedule. First, decide what kind of wedding you want to have—most people have an afternoon ceremony followed by cocktails, dinner, and a few hours of dancing, but you should think about what's most important to you. If you want to spend the day doing other activities (hiking, playing tennis, doing yoga, having lunch with family, meditating, going on a swim in the ocean . . .), you might want to delay your ceremony start time. If you want to get married exactly as the sun sets, you may decide to deviate from the traditional order of the day and put the cocktail hour before the ceremony. Of course, you need to find out what your venue allows: do they have an early curfew, or restrictions on noise? And, like any good host, you should be mindful of your guests. If you are having a wedding with mostly young guests, you might be able to get away with a later start time, but older guests may want to be home earlier—especially if they will be driving. If you are working with a planner, they will be able to help you create a timeline. Once it's set, share your timeline with all of your vendors and your wedding party, and make sure an abbreviated version is on your wedding website for guests to refer to.

A basket of booklet-style programs set out for guests at the ceremony. In addition to the order of the ceremony, you'll need to create a detailed schedule for the entire day.

SAMPLE WEDDING DAY SCHEDULE

Here's an example of how an evening wedding might flow. Adjust the hours as needed based on your ceremony start time, and add time between the ceremony and the cocktail hour if you are moving to a second location and/or taking group pictures. Note that religious ceremonies tend to run longer than the twenty minutes allotted here for a secular ceremony.

12:00 P.M.	Bride and bridal party begin hair and makeup; wedding parties have lunch
1:00 P.M.	Vendors arrive at ceremony site to set up
4:00 P.M.	Pictures are taken with wedding party and family
5:30 P.M.	Doors open and early guests arrive to ceremony
6:00 P.M.	Time listed on invitation and when most guests arrive
6:15 P.M.	Ceremony begins
6:35 P.M.	Ceremony ends
6:45 P.M.	Cocktail hour begins; couple takes additional pictures
7:30 P.M.	Couple joins end of cocktail hour
7:45 P.M.	Dinner begins
9:00 P.M.	Toasts
9:45 P.M.	First dance and other protocol dances (see page 290); general dancing
10:30 P.M.	Cake cutting
11:45 P.M.	End time (guests depart)
12:45 A.M.	Breakdown complete and vendors depart

LOCATION

These days, you can get married just about anywhere. If you aren't having a religious ceremony in a place of worship, there are so many possibilities to consider: Is there an art gallery in your neighborhood that you have always loved? A favorite restaurant or antiques store? How about a garden or historic house?

It's very important to find a venue that you won't have to completely transform, which can put a serious dent in your budget and never feels truly authentic. Instead, try to find a place where many of the decor elements are built in (for example, a garden path as an aisle, a mountain or ocean backdrop, or a beautiful picture window to frame the setting) and where, ideally, you would just need to bring in a few florals to enhance the setting. Factors like guest count, budget, and time of year will all weigh heavily in your choice of venue (or venues), so make sure to look at the big picture.

You may be confronted with the decision of holding the ceremony and the reception in two different locations. While this might be less convenient, if it means your ceremony will be more beautiful and in a more meaningful space, then it might be worth it. (For more on reception locations, see page 270.)

MEADOW

While there are many pros to tying the knot in a verdant meadow or field (low venue and floral costs, beautiful vistas, a unique setting, and an abundance of space), there are also a few big cons (unpredictable weather; the need for bathroom facilities, lighting, and transportation; accessibility; insects). If you are using a public space, the first order of business is handling permitting issues (take this up with the local parks and recreation bureau). Find out the restrictions on filming, photography, noise, bathroom trailers, and curfew. Then embrace your setting with design elements that blend in with the surrounding landscape (think wood accents, foliage, berry branches, and native flowers).

A weathered wooden aisle flanked by acrylic ghost chairs strikes the perfect balance of rustic and modern, old and new. Low hedge-like rows of wildflowers in matte black containers feel natural to the bucolic setting and don't block the view.

OCEANFRONT

There are two types of beach weddings: those held in the tropical settings that everyone instinctively thinks of and ceremonies without a palm tree or coconut in sight—the ones that take place along the craggy New England shore, on the dunes of Amagansett, or atop the cliffs of Big Sur. Wherever you stage your beach wedding, there are a few things to look out for when you do a site visit: tide times, wind, sound (crashing waves can drown out voices), and other beachgoers—if you are getting married on a private beach, you'll have more control over who is around; otherwise, you may want to have planners and assistants on the perimeter asking people to keep away (unwilling strangers can usually be bribed with a few bucks). If you are setting up right on the sand, make sure to alert your guests so they can dress appropriately (see page 50).

Set back far from the waterline, where the sand is firmer, bamboo folding chairs were arranged in a slight curve around the chuppah to face the sunset. The fabric on the chuppah is tightly secured, as is the tablecloth underneath it. An aisle was created by simply "combing" the sand with a rake to make it smooth (using large palm leaves would also work).

For this intimate backyard ceremony, the chuppah was placed at the edge of the pool so that it was far enough from the back door to create a short aisle. If you live in a residential area, it's a good idea to speak with your neighbors beforehand and ask them to be mindful of creating noise during your ceremony (with lawn mowers, music, etc.) and, conversely, to warn them of the noise your reception could cause (bringing a small gift is usually helpful when asking for cooperation).

BACKYARD

If you are lucky enough to live in a place that can accommodate your guest count, start by getting estimates from rental companies, caterers, and valet companies. Consider if you'll need or want to move out your furniture and put down additional protective flooring, because this will add to the cost. You may also need to pull permits from the town if it's a large party. And keep in mind that being "on-site" (i.e., being home while everything is happening) can add to your wedding-day anxiety.

Now the positives: There is so much of your personality already built in, and you can relive the wedding every day. Plus, having an at-home wedding is a great excuse to fix up your house, whether you are repainting a few rooms or improving the landscaping.

Some couples, if they are short on space, opt to have just the ceremony at home, then host the reception at a nearby restaurant or event space. There are a few alternatives if your own home won't work: the home of a close friend or family member or a rental (many historical properties are often available for events).

HOTEL BALLROOM

Getting hitched at a hotel is often a very practical choice from a financial and logistical perspective, since so much is already on-site (furniture, catering, security, parking—some venues even come with an in-house coordinator or manager who will oversee everything). A small, boutique hotel will make your wedding feel more intimate than a larger venue, especially if your wedding guests happen to rent out the whole place. Try to find a hotel with plenty of architectural charm so you don't have to spend a small fortune transforming a sterile ballroom—or ask if you can get married on the grounds of the property.

Sometimes, a total transformation is required. Here, a generic ballroom was enhanced with aromatic mature pine trees along the walls of the room, tree clippings down the aisle, wooden flooring, drapes to soften the walls, and hundreds of ivory pillar candles that created a natural glow. An elevated platform was built so everyone could see the altar.

COURTHOUSE

Having a civil union doesn't mean sacrificing on style. At the Santa Barbara courthouse, the Mural Room features artist John B. Smeraldi's Mudejar-style paintings. Ceremonies here can also be held outside in the sunken gardens.

Once consigned to quickie or second marriages (or what people nowadays call "encore weddings"), courthouse ceremonies are becoming more and more mainstream. It's easy to see why, when you look at some of the beautiful city halls in this country. Take St. Louis's Parisian-style rotunda or the beautiful Beaux Arts landmark in San Francisco, for example. Both can accommodate a few hundred guests. Since these services take place during regular business hours, you might consider having a lunch reception at a nearby restaurant or a catered picnic.

HOUSE OF WORSHIP

In terms of logistics, a wedding in a church, synagogue, or mosque is usually the easiest (and least expensive) route, after a courthouse wedding. In most cases, there's not much you can or need to bring in aside from flower arrangements and possibly a musician. Ideally, this would be a place where you are an active member. If not, it's a nice idea to attend services before the big day to get to know the community.

A few things to keep in mind: First, some churches and synagogues require that couples take marriage classes before the wedding. Second, larger sanctuaries tend to feel empty if your guests take up only the first few rows; sometimes couples will cover the empty rows with fabric, or ask to hold the ceremony in a side sanctuary or usable outdoor space on the grounds. And last, these venues tend to book up quickly, especially in the summer months, so plan ahead.

St. John's Anglican Church, a local landmark in the Bahamas, is often simply referred to as the "pink church." Pink and green were used throughout this wedding: tropical palms reflective of the island's natural landscape marked the entrance of the cozy chapel, and the reception was later held on a pink sand beach.

INDUSTRIAL LOFT

At an event space in Brooklyn, a wall of opaque windows backlit the ceremony space. The industrial feel of the concrete floors was softened with a delicate hanging installation of dried lunaria seeds.

For some nonconventional urban couples, getting married in a converted warehouse or factory, or even in an art gallery, makes a lot of sense: the gritty style is more aligned with their aesthetic, there is no need for a weather-contingent plan B, and the spaces are usually wide-open rooms (and therefore easy to put your mark on). Because many were not intended as event spaces, you will need to bring in everything from sound equipment to the furniture and find creative ways to delineate different areas within a large open space.

CEREMONY STRUCTURE

Beyond religious ceremonies held in a place of worship, couples are free to design any kind of ceremony structure they wish. The most popular type of structure is an arch adorned with white flowers such as garden roses, baby's breath, or something more extravagant like dendrobium orchids. Variations on the classic arch include a structure that is square at the top instead of round and the use of less traditional types of flowers, more greenery, or an arrangement that's asymmetrical or less densely populated with blooms. Good rental companies will have options for arches, arbors, and chuppahs in their inventory. Florists who do a lot of weddings will also likely have some in stock. Or you may want to create a custom structure with a carpenter.

LEFT:
THE NATURAL CHUPPAH
A chuppah is used in Jewish ceremonies, although couples of other denominations may choose to incorporate one if they like the look of a square structure to stand under. It features a canopy made out of a prayer shawl or a piece of lace that's supported by four poles. This one is covered in greenery and white blooms, making it seem like it is growing from the ground.

OPPOSITE:
THE NEW-FASHIONED ARCH
Atop an aisle of wood chips, this white arch constructed of branches of tiny white blooms (instead of a dense collage of heavy cut flowers) is perfectly balanced with its setting.

RETHINKING THE CEREMONY STRUCTURE

While it's hard not to love an oversized arch or a classic chuppah, there are a host of other options for your ceremony structure. The most minimal couples may choose not to have anything to delineate the ceremony space at all.

LAYING LOW

Many people dislike the feeling of being on a stage, so they'll choose a design that is more modest—like this circle of mixed flower buds that the couple and the officiant stood inside. A minimal structure like this keeps the focus on you, reduces floral costs, and takes advantage of whatever beautiful setting might be in the backdrop.

BRANCHING OUT

While delineating the space and marking a clear stopping point at the end of the aisle, this frame of greenery also feels like an extension of the tree itself. A hanging option is great for a curved seating arrangement, as there are no poles or columns to obstruct the view—for the guests or the photographers.

FRAMEWORK

Whether it's a pair of oversized French doors or the entrance to a rustic old barn, doorways (with a little adornment) make excellent ceremony focal points.

WALL FLOWERS

It requires a bit of imagination (and a skilled florist) to fashion a beautiful ceremony space from a blank wall. Here, an abstract arch of greenery creates a natural frame and looks like a vine growing along the wall.

CEREMONY SEATING

There are a couple of things to consider when it comes to seating: the configuration and the type of chair. A circular or semicircular arrangement with the couple in the middle is cozy and familial. (If you wish to have 360-degree seating, make sure you feel comfortable at every angle and that your ceremony structure is unobtrusive.) Alternatively, straight rows of benches, pews, couches, and chairs are traditional and work best if you want to have a more prominent altar structure. If you are arranging chairs on land, ensure that the ground is firm enough that they won't start sinking.

There are unexpected ways to mix it up, such as alternating couches or benches with individual chairs or clustering seats together in a nonlinear way, say, around natural dividers like trees or bushes. You can also use seating to change the curvature of the aisle: a winding path to the altar is less predictable and has softer lines. Before you select your ceremony seating, decide if you'll be repurposing the chairs for dinner, as you may need them to work for both settings.

ABOVE:
GATHER TOGETHER
Natural wooden benches like these keep a low profile and are perfect for big groups because they don't take up as much room as individual chairs. They are casual and encourage people to sit closer to one another.

LEFT:
VARIETY SHOW
In order to keep this small outdoor ceremony from looking too much like a church wedding, wooden pews adorned with flowers were mixed with cross-back chairs to make the seating less formal and more appropriate for the environs.

OPPOSITE:
SURROUND YOURSELF
Despite the large guest count at this Santa Barbara wedding, arranging the bentwood chairs in a circular style created an incredibly intimate ceremony. A simple chuppah was elevated on a platform, ensuring that each guest could clearly see the proceedings. In addition to the main aisle, secondary aisles (to be used by guests) segmented the seating area into quadrants for symmetry and flow.

THE AISLE

Your aisle decor should be informed by your choice of ceremony structure. If you plan to have a dense, oversized arbor as your focal point, you should scale back on the aisle decor and perhaps even leave the aisle bare. On the other hand, if you have a minimal ceremony structure, incorporating flowers and plants along the aisle may be a more understated and certainly more unexpected way of incorporating flowers in your ceremony. Whatever you do, make sure your aisle decor will not obstruct your guests' view and that the elements echo the palette on the altar and in the personal arrangements. How you style this passageway (with flowers, rugs, candles, plants, etc.) should be purposeful and also practical.

AISLE LENGTH
Consider the distance you'll need to walk before reaching the altar. If it's too far (and will take you more than around ten seconds to walk), you might start to feel a little awkward, as people will be watching your every step. If the aisle is too short, your guests won't have the opportunity to stand up to honor your arrival, and your walk could come off as rushed.

OPPOSITE, CLOCKWISE FROM TOP LEFT:

BOTANICAL BOOKENDS
Placing an arrangement at the end of each row (or every other row) works well on solid surfaces. They can even be repurposed as centerpieces on the dining tables or transported to the cake table or to the bar after the ceremony.

A CLIMBING ROSE
Twisting vines and blush-colored garden roses were gently secured around the backs of just a few chairs at this outdoor ceremony, to help tie in with the lush garden setting.

OFF THE GROUND
Tying arrangements or pieces of fabric to the last chair in each row (or every few rows) to adorn your aisle is ideal for small areas since it frees up space on the ground below. These bundles were made up of pampas grass and lunaria; this look can also be achieved with garlands.

MARK THE ENTRANCE
Two large arrangements of cut flowers are a beautiful and dramatic way to adorn the beginning of the aisle. If you don't want to use cut flowers here (which can be costly if the displays are big), this is also a good opportunity to use potted plants and/or flowers or even trees that can be replanted at home.

THE GARDEN PATH

For an outdoor wedding, consider "planted" arrangements (i.e., concealed containers that appear to be growing from the ground). It's an organic idea that works best when a small hedge is created using tall bushy plant varieties such as delphinium, ferns, pampas grasses, or lavender (pictured). Here, vines were also used to conceal the base of the arrangement.

BY CANDLELIGHT

For an indoor evening ceremony, white pillar candles
of different heights (in protective glass hurricanes)
illuminate the aisle and offer a more intimate and
flattering glow than standard indoor downlights. Make
sure your venue will allow open flames.

AISLE COVERS

Creating a beautiful pathway will instantly make the ceremony seem more pulled-together. To protect the aisle from foot traffic, consider roping it off. Here are a range of options beyond the standard white runner (which can be easily sourced on Amazon or Etsy for less than $100).

THE CUSTOM RUNNER

A sturdy carpet-like runner can be designed to cover the aisle and the ceremony area—a natural fabric like sisal will skew more casual while something with a velvet finish will seem more formal. (Make sure runners are secured to the floor using a mat or an adhesive because thin material will bunch and cause a tripping hazard.)

WOOD FLOORING

Laying down wood flooring for the aisle is a great way to level an uneven walking surface. Here, it was slightly curved to accommodate an irregular space. This is a pricey custom job and will probably take a carpenter a day or two to complete.

FLOWER PETALS

Simply cover the path with flower petals for an easy, natural look. Under this canopy of trees in Ojai, California, white rose petals were scattered along the aisle before the processional.

VINTAGE RUGS

Rugs are a wonderful bohemian touch for those who want something colorful and relaxed. You can rent vintage rugs from design-forward rental companies—or, better yet, borrow them or bring them from home.

PRE-CEREMONY TOUCHES

Even though you likely won't be there to greet your guests when they arrive for the ceremony, you want to make them feel welcome. Beyond tissues and hankies for the tender moments, there are a host of other items you may want to consider providing to ensure that your guests will be comfortable. Many of these small comforts can double as favors.

OPPOSITE, CLOCKWISE FROM TOP LEFT:

FANS

For outdoor summer weddings, your guests will appreciate a fan to help beat the heat. Sun umbrellas are another popular idea, but these oftentimes block people's views and are more expensive.

CRACKED COCONUTS

Offering refreshments before the ceremony is a hospitable touch on a hot summer day (it will also buy you some time to wait for any stragglers to arrive). For this wedding in Mexico, coconut water was served directly from cracked coconuts that were set up on a festive buffet.

YARMULKES

For a Jewish ceremony, navy blue yarmulkes (in keeping with the wedding's navy and orange color story) and a dish of bobby pins were arranged on a table with programs and a small flower arrangement. Be sure to order enough for everyone who may wish to wear one during the ceremony (including guests of different faiths, and women).

PASHMINAS

Even if you've warned guests about dressing appropriately for the weather, you may want to have some pashminas on hand for female guests if you are getting married in a colder climate.

PROGRAMS

Programs aren't a wedding requirement, but if you choose to have one, it should list all the elements of the ceremony. It's also a great place to make requests—like asking guests to refrain from using their cell phones during the ceremony, which can be so distracting. Depending on the design and the amount of information you want to include, programs can be printed in a booklet (held with a ribbon or a piece of twine), on a brochure-like trifold, or on flat cards, which is usually the least expensive option. You may choose to place each program atop individual seats (if wind isn't an issue), ask an usher to hand them out, or place them on a table where guests can help themselves.

Here is an example of the kind of information you might want to include in a program with multiple pages.

Page 1: Your names, the location of the wedding, and the date (include your wedding logo here if you have one)

Page 2: A list of the people in the wedding party and anyone participating in the ceremony

Page 3: Elements of the ceremony (ask your officiant to provide this information)

Page 4: An explanation of traditions (this is especially nice for an interfaith ceremony—have your officiant look this over beforehand)

Page 5: A remembrance page (the names of loved ones who have passed away whom the bride and groom or their families wish to acknowledge)

Page 6: Notes from the couple. If you'd like to talk to guests about cell phone use, photography, or wedding hashtags, this is the ideal place. You can also take the opportunity to thank your guests for coming. A quote or passage from a book here is nice, too, especially if you aren't doing a reading.

PROGRAM FORMATS

The format of your wedding program will depend on your personal style, how much information you need or want to convey, and what's left in your stationery budget.

BROCHURE

A brochure format typically offers six pages on which to place information. In the center of this design, the couple explained the different traditions of a Jewish ceremony, as only half of their guests were Jewish.

DOUBLE-SIDED

On the front of this card, the couple included a series of custom totemic symbols by artist Kris Chau. The quote at the bottom is by one of the couple's favorite poets, Gary Snyder. The reverse side identified the officiants, the musician, the readers, and the members of the wedding party and offered a word of thanks from the couple.

BOOKLET

Adorned with a gilded, old-world crest and matching gold bow, this formal program booklet provided plenty of room for information about the ceremony.

SHORT AND SWEET

For a casual ceremony, this hand-painted flat card included all the relevant information. Since creating something like this can be very time-consuming, instead of making one per person, you may want to make just enough for couples to share.

THE PROCESSIONAL

Each culture has its own traditions when it comes to the processional (see opposite). Nowadays, though, there are many variations on the traditional processional—and for good reason. A bride should be able to select the person who gives her away, whether it's her father, her mother, or a close friend. Some brides want to walk down the aisle with both of their parents, while others wish to walk alone as a sign of independence. Some even do half and half, where they walk half the aisle unescorted before being joined by their escort. Then there are the couples who walk down the aisle together holding hands—a particularly lovely idea for a same-sex wedding.

If you have a small wedding party or the number of bridesmaids to groomsmen is unequal, you may want everyone to walk down the aisle individually. If you have a very large wedding party, you may want people to walk in multiples (for example, one groomsman to escort two bridesmaids). Whatever the arrangement, make sure your aisle is wide enough to accommodate your processional—you don't want to feel squeezed.

ESCORTING 101

If the bride is escorted by her father (or another man), she should place her right hand around his left arm just above the elbow (this goes for the rest of the bridal party, too), or she may hold hands with him. Men should have a lightly closed fist—no limp wrists.

If the bride is walking down the aisle escorted by both parents, one on each side, they should very lightly hold their daughter's biceps just above her elbows (not putting any weight on her) while the bride holds her bouquet in front (see page 103). If the bride wants to hold hands with her parents, her mother can hold the bouquet in her free hand. And everyone should stand up straight!

For a traditional Jewish processional, it's customary for both the bride and groom to be escorted down the aisle by both of their respective parents. Here, the bride's parents lightly place their hands on the back of her arms. Since the groom doesn't have a bouquet to hold, he may hold hands with his parents.

PROCESSIONAL ORDER

	TRADITIONAL CHRISTIAN ORDER	TRADITIONAL JEWISH ORDER*
1	Officiant	Rabbi and cantor (if you have one)
2	Groom's grandparents	Groom's grandparents
3	Bride's grandparents	Bride's grandparents
4	Groom's parents	Best man
5	Bride's mother (who is usually escorted by a son, another male relative, or the father of the bride—who would then return to escort the bride)	Groom escorted by both of his parents
6	Best man	Groomsmen and bridesmaids
7	Groom (typically enters from the side)	Maid of honor
8	Groomsmen and bridesmaids	Ring bearer
9	Maid of honor	Flower girl(s)
10	Ring bearer	Bride escorted by both of her parents
11	Flower girl(s)	
12	Bride escorted by her father	

*While there's no strict rule about order, this is the most common sequence.

JOBS FOR THE LITTLE ONES

Traditionally, a flower girl scatters rose petals along the aisle, but if she is too young, that can be an overwhelming task. Instead, you might ask her to simply carry a small floral pomander. Similarly, if your ring bearer is not responsible enough to carry the real ring box, you can give him a symbolic one and the job of escorting the flower girl. For that matter, not every attendant needs an actual job—they can simply walk down the aisle and then take their seats, and they will feel honored just to be included.

INCLUDING YOUR PETS If you want your dog to participate in the ceremony, make sure your venue is pet-friendly (if not, ask if they will make an exception). Once you get the green light, get your pooch groomed and find a floral leash or collar. Unless the dog is highly trained, don't give your pet any responsibility other than walking down the aisle and posing for a few pictures. Ask a friend or family member to pet-sit during the ceremony (don't forget to have some cleanup bags and treats on hand).

RING CONTAINERS

Ring boxes are a small detail, but they always seem to end up on a photographer's shot list. It's a great place to incorporate an heirloom, if you have one. If not, you can purchase a traditional velvet box or pillow, or think outside the box (literally!).

BIRCH BOXES

Here, wooden display boxes (which can be sourced from a craft store) hold wedding bands stuffed with cotton. If you have matching bands, make a mark on the bottom of one of the boxes to delineate his and hers.

THE RING BASKET

For a wedding in Mexico, the couple purchased a small basket made by a local craftsman and used a folded palm leaf as a cushion. The rings were then tied together with a piece of ribbon that connected to their color story. Any shallow bowl will offer a similar look.

A MOSSY PILLOW

A variation on the traditional ring pillow, this moss-covered version is natural yet polished thanks to a neutral ribbon—tie a knot, then secure the rings with a tight bow.

VELVET BOX

Traditional square boxes in cushy velvet are also beautiful places to store your ring after the big day. For the ceremony, you may use two boxes or share one.

THE OFFICIANT

The most important thing you need to know about your officiant is if they can legally marry you; if not, you may be required to have a civil ceremony as well. If you get married outside the United States, for example, you may need to have a civil ceremony back home for it to be legally binding (most people who have a destination wedding schedule the courthouse ceremony beforehand to avoid going through complex foreign legalities and simply have a symbolic ceremony abroad).

Ideally, you should have a personal relationship with the person who marries you, so they can add stories and anecdotes to the service—it's also a way of honoring your relationship with that person. If you aren't having a religious ceremony, you may want to ask a friend or family member to conduct the ceremony. State laws regarding who can perform a marriage ceremony vary, so make sure to check all the regulations listed on your state's Department of Public Health website. In some states, it's sufficient to be ordained through organizations like the Universal Life Church Monastery and American Marriage Ministries, which can easily be done online. Others require that an ordained minister actually have a ministry or congregation. Still others simply require officiants to get a one-day marriage designation or become a temporary officiant. Couples married by Buddhist, Islamic, Hindu, and Sikh clergy members in the United States will also be required to have a civil ceremony for the marriage to be legally recognized.

When you find your officiant, work closely with them on the exact wording and flow of the ceremony. If you are at all concerned or curious about the actual language that will be used in your ceremony, politely ask your officiant to go through it with you beforehand so you can point out things that you like and dislike.

ADDING A SOUND TRACK Whether you've hired an acoustic guitarist or are using a prerecorded track, you'll need to pick songs for the prelude (to be played as the guests arrive and find their seats), processional (to be played as the wedding party and bride walk down the aisle; many couples opt to use a special song to announce the bride), and recessional (to be played as the newlyweds, wedding party, and guests walk up the aisle). Unless Pachelbel's "Canon in D" or Wagner's "Bridal Chorus" has special meaning to you, why not try something a little more original for the processional? (Wagner is widely known for his anti-Semitic beliefs, so this traditional piece is a particularly divisive choice.)

The recessional is typically louder and more joyful than the processional. If you aren't doing a first dance to "your song," you may want to feature it here.

THE KISS Here are some tips to keep in mind: the bride's face should turn in toward the officiant (so her face doesn't appear smooshed in photos), don't go in for a dip (unless you are very confident about it), keep it under five seconds, and it's probably best to err on the conservative side (your guests may not want to see you French kiss, and doing so can also mess up your makeup). But the only thing that's *really* important here is to ask the officiant to step out of the frame (make the request at the rehearsal) so they don't inadvertently photobomb this moment.

READINGS & VOWS

The truth about readings is that they tend to be long and overly serious instead of a creative way to engage your audience. For some, the choices are limited—traditional Catholic ceremonies specifically require readings from the Old and New Testaments and passages from Psalms and the Gospels. If you don't have such restrictions, think carefully about what would truly enhance your ceremony, and remember that readings don't have to exclusively be about love and marriage—they can be musings about life from the Dalai Lama or ideas about happiness from a loved one (like a wise grandparent). Consider including lyrics from "your song," snippets from love letters you've exchanged over the years, or excerpts from nontraditional sources, like your favorite children's story or a movie. Context is important, so, if possible, ask your reader to explain why the specific passages were chosen and the meaning behind them. If you can't find something that feels exactly right, don't settle—it might be better not to have a reading at all.

Depending on the order of your ceremony, the vow exchange usually happens after the readings. In addition to any traditional religious vows that you might ask your officiant to lead, you may choose to write your own vows and exchange them in private or read them during the ceremony. Instead of making promises to each other, many couples approach their vows as a verbal love letter—a chance to shower each other with praise and show how excited they are for their future together. It might be a good idea to keep a journal of ideas for your vows as you go through the planning process—you never know when you'll feel inspired. If someone else will be holding your vows before handing them to you during the ceremony, enclose them in a booklet for privacy. Or you may want to write them on monogrammed note cards so you can preserve them in your wedding album.

CUSTOMS

If you are having a conservative religious ceremony, you may not have too much wiggle room in what traditions you can include. If not, familiarize yourself with all the options and pick what's right for you. Interfaith couples may choose to incorporate ideas from both sides. Here's an overview of customs, organized by religion.

	CHRISTIAN	HINDU	ISLAMIC	JEWISH
WHERE AND WHEN?	Catholic weddings take place in a chapel or a church unless you receive permission from the vicar-general. Protestant, Episcopalian, and Unitarian weddings can take place outside of a church. Most parishes avoid scheduling weddings on Sundays or during Lent and the Holy Triduum to avoid interrupting services or church activities.	Hindu weddings can generally take place outside the temple. Some couples will let a priest or family member choose an auspicious date.	A Muslim wedding usually takes place outside of a mosque, although they can be held there, too.	Orthodox weddings take place in a synagogue. Conservative and Reform services can take place outside of the synagogue. Jewish ceremonies often take place on Saturday evenings or on Sundays, since most rabbis will not conduct weddings on Shabbat.
OFFICIANT	Priest, minister, or ordained clergy member	Priest	A male family member who is familiar with Islamic law, an imam, or the mosque's marriage officer	Rabbi
BEFORE THE WEDDING	Premarital classes are often required for Catholics.	The first night of the three-day celebration is the Ganesh Puja ("Prayer to Lord Ganesh") ceremony, held at home with close family. Typically, the second night includes the mehndi (henna) and sangeet (which involves singing, dancing, and music) ceremonies.	There are many rituals, but the dholki, a night of singing and dancing at the house of the bride, takes place a few weeks before the wedding, and the henna ceremony happens a few days prior.	Premarital classes are often required for Conservative ceremonies. Orthodox brides will visit the mikvah (ritual bathing place) within four days of the wedding. During the bedeken, which is conducted just prior to Reform, Conservative, and Orthodox ceremonies, the groom unveils the bride to symbolically confirm her identity.
CEREMONY STRUCTURE		Mandap		Chuppah

	CHRISTIAN	HINDU	ISLAMIC	JEWISH
WHAT TO WEAR	In conservative churches, the bride may be asked to cover her shoulders.	Brides traditionally wear a gold-and-red sari (or a two-piece ensemble called a bridal lehenga) with a dupatta (a long scarf), gold jewelry, and a bindi. Grooms typically wear a white sherwani (with or without a turban), a dhoti, or a Western-style suit.	Depending on their backgrounds, conservative brides may wear an elaborate dress with long sleeves and a shawl or a hijab. Grooms may wear a sherwani (a long, button-front coat). Less conservative couples may both wear Western dress.	In Conservative synagogues, the bride may be asked to cover her shoulders. In Orthodox ceremonies, she will adhere to the Orthodox dress code (wearing a wig or kerchief on her head and wearing a dress that covers from the neckline to the knee).
RELIGIOUS DOCUMENTS		Before the ceremony some couples will sign a lagna patrika, a written promise to each other.	The meher, the Muslim marriage contract, is signed during the nikah, the wedding ceremony.	The ketubah, the Jewish marriage contract, is signed before the ceremony and often displayed on an easel during the wedding ceremony.
ELEMENTS OF THE CEREMONY	Opening prayers, scripture readings, a sermon, exchange of vows, special songs or readings, Communion, ring exchange, the kiss, a blessing, and a closing prayer. Catholic ceremonies will feature a nuptial mass after the ceremony.	Customs vary greatly by location and/or family, but most start with the kanyadaan (where the father gives away his daughter), then the priest ties the couple's hands together and conducts the mangal fera, where the couple circles a sacred fire seven times. Then the groom puts sindhoor (a red powder) in the bride's hair, signifying that she is married.	While festivities can last for days, the nikah, the wedding ceremony itself, is relatively short. During the nikah, the wedding contract is signed and the officiant may read from the Quran. The couple may exchange vows. After the ceremony, though not necessarily on the same day, the groom's family will host a wedding feast called the walima.	After signing the ketubah and doing the bedeken, the ceremony opens with prayers and a kiddush, then a reading of the ketubah and the Sheva Brachot ("seven blessings") before the ring exchange and the kiss. Couples may also include vows and readings. The groom breaks a glass at the end of the ceremony.
OTHER CUSTOMS	Lighting a unity candle	The priest chants Sanskrit mantras. The bride and groom also exchange floral garlands.	After the signing of the marriage contract, the couple may share a sweet fruit, such as a date.	In Ashkenazi ceremonies, the bride may encircle the groom during the hakafot.
DO YOU NEED AN ADDITIONAL CIVIL CEREMONY FOR IT TO BE LEGAL?	No	Usually yes	Usually yes	No

BOHEMIAN, MYSTICAL, AND OTHER SECULAR IDEAS

Whether in lieu of or in addition to a traditional religious ceremony, how you conduct a nondenominational service is entirely up to you. Many couples dream up creative new ways to inject spiritual energy into their ceremony, or adapt new age ideas from other cultures and traditions. Here are just a few examples.

- Ask an astrologist to help you find an auspicious wedding date.

- Host a tea ceremony just before the wedding ceremony (similar to the Chinese tradition or a Japanese sake ceremony), to promote closeness between the couple, the wedding party, and their families. (Oftentimes this will be done just with the bridal party, with friends taking turns offering loving words to the bride.)

- Write joint vows, alternate reading each line, then read the last line together.

- Add mystical touches to the ceremony, such as a sage blessing or strategically placed crystals, to promote positive energy.

- Engage your audience by asking your officiant to lead a communal reading, meditation, or song.

ABOVE:
TIED TOGETHER
The ancient Celtic and Wiccan practice of tying the couple's hands together symbolizes their connection. It's often done during the exchange of vows, and it is where the expression "tying the knot" comes from.

OPPOSITE:
NEW AGE RITUALS
An assortment of alternative items to add to a ceremony could include palo santo wood, herbal tea, and a bundle of sage to cleanse the air.

THE
SEND-OFF

If you are torn between doing a send-off here or at the end of the evening, don't feel like you need to choose one over the other. Mark the end of the ceremony with a celebratory recessional that includes something for your guests to toss into the air, then do something different after the reception (see page 296 for ideas).

In movies, couples are showered with rice as they make their way out of the church after they have been pronounced husband and wife. This sweet tradition stems from the ancient Romans, who threw seeds to symbolize growth and fruitfulness. Unfortunately, rice is harmful to birds and other animals, so unless you can clean it up immediately afterward, you should find a safer alternative. For a daytime ceremony, this could be fresh or dried flowers (something fragrant, like lavender, rose hip, or chamomile is a lovely idea), fallen leaves (if it's an autumnal wedding), seeds, dried herbs, or even shredded coconut.

TRANSPORTATION

If your ceremony will take place in a different location than your reception, you'll need to think about how to transport your nondriving guests. Depending on your guest count, this could be with a few town cars, an open-air trolley, a shuttle bus, or even an old-fashioned yellow school bus. If your group is particularly tech-savvy, you could also provide guests with a single-use Uber passcode. And if people will be driving themselves, explain parking instructions in advance (see page 44) or offer valet service.

As for *your* mode of transportation, it really does elevate the experience if you have a fun ride. Renting a town car with a driver for the day is luxurious. Maybe you have a friend or relative with a classic convertible you can borrow, or you may want to rent one (you should hire a driver or ask a sober friend to do the honors so you can enjoy the moment together in the backseat). Decorate the rear of the car with flowers and signs (or string cans from the bumper if you are in a rural place) to make it festive.

ABOVE:
SOFT PETALS
Instead of individual containers filled with flowers to toss, these large baskets were placed at the end of each row and filled with a "potpourri" of flowers (million-star baby's breath, café au lait carnations, and garden roses) for guests to share.

OPPOSITE:
A NAUTICAL EXIT
If you happen to be getting married near a lake or a still body of water, a mahogany Chris-Craft or vintage boat would make for a charming getaway vehicle.

CONSCIOUS COUPLING

For this creative pair, an intimate backyard ceremony in Hawaii honored
the traditions of the land while reflecting their laid-back spirit.

A few years ago, Jess Bianchi, a filmmaker, bought
a small piece of land in Kauai from a friend. He
built a small, wabi-sabi-style surf shack and never
imagined it would be anything but a tropical
bachelor pad. Then he started dating jewelry
designer Malia Grace Mau, who is part Hawaiian,
and everything changed. They began splitting their
time between California and Kauai and got engaged
after just nine months. ("I wanted to propose
sooner," says Jess. "When you know, you know.")
The plan was to get married at a botanic garden
near their island home and host a small reception
in their backyard, but when they visited the garden
a few weeks before the wedding, the property was
besieged by mosquitoes and in complete disarray.
"We realized we needed to change the location of
the ceremony and at the last minute decided to
have it at our house. That was the best decision we
could have made," says Malia.

As a tropical storm rolled across the island the
morning of the wedding, the couple woke up and
had a leisurely breakfast at home. Afterward, Malia
hosted a tea ceremony with her friends while Jess
practiced yoga before they got ready together.
Then at 4:00 p.m., as if on cue, the clouds cleared.

Hand in hand, Jess and Malia walked out the front
door and down the long driveway to the back of
the property, where the ceremony took place.
Underneath a double rainbow (the result of the
day's storm), they were married in a traditional
Hawaiian service, which included several powerful
oli chants and a water ceremony. At one point the
couple also exchanged leis with their mothers,
siblings, and Jess's father. "We made promises to
everyone, not just to each other," says Jess. "We
really wanted to touch on the heart of what was
happening, because we're only doing it once."

The reception following the ceremony was
very fluid in structure: There was a bar in the
driveway, where guests could order a fresh juice
or a cocktail—some even took their drinks to the
property's tree house. A buffet set up in a side
garden offered fresh, organic fare from local farms
in Kilauea, and there were two decorated picnic
tables for those who wanted to sit down. There
was dancing, a tarot card reader, a photo booth,
and a palm weaver who kept the kids entertained
for hours making hats and opening up coconuts.
"It was very personal," says Jess. "So much of our
relationship grew on that property."

BACKYARD GOALS // At the back of the
property filled with overgrown palms, the couple
married in a private ceremony in front of one
hundred guests. Florists Emma Chidgey and Julie
Lock adorned the ceremony structure with king
protea, dendrobium and cymbidium orchids, majolica
and South American roses, and anthurium. "It was so
nice to have everything in one place," says Jess. "We
wanted to reduce any stress and just keep things as
simple as possible."

ABOVE, LEFT:

BOHEMIAN RHAPSODY // Malia found her silk crepe Cortana dress at LOHO Bride in San Francisco. "I loved how low-maintenance it was. I didn't have to iron it; I didn't have to steam it. I just put it in my suitcase and brought it to Kauai." In keeping with Hawaiian tradition, all of the flowers from the wedding were later placed in the ocean as an offering—except for Malia's tropical flower crown, which she hung to dry in the cottage. She is also wearing a gold and rough-cut turquoise necklace from her own collection.

ABOVE, RIGHT:

PSYCHEDELIC PIES // The couple's close friend Stephen McCarty, chef/owner of Sukhavati Raw Desserts in Los Angeles, made five 12-inch raw vegan cheesecakes with local ingredients. The flavors: coconut caramel cacao, coconut lime, lemon rainbow, chocolate banana peanut butter, and pineapple mango coconut lime. To decorate the cakes, he meditated and channeled the couple's spirit to inform the different designs.

OPPOSITE, CLOCKWISE FROM TOP:

VINTAGE CHARM // The couple owns a '70s Volkswagen van almost identical to this one (it's Malia's island car), but this is actually a photo booth they hired for the day and had set up in the driveway.

CUSTOM CRAFTS // Malia made the gold wedding rings at her home studio in Topanga Canyon, California, using an ancient lost wax technique.

RECLAIMED SIGNS // Malia and Jess don't drink alcohol, so the bar featured a variety of fresh juices and kombucha in addition to cocktails, beer, and wine. The bar menu was painted on an old wooden board.

FOLLOWING PAGE:

SEAT YOURSELF // Since they were limited on space, Malia and Jess decided to do a cocktail-style reception instead of a traditional seated dinner. For those who wanted to sit down, there were two rectangular tables topped with *Ruscus aculeatus* (butcher's broom) garlands adorned with orchids and roses.

BAR menu

cocktails

- kauai mai tai -
- mint colada -
  vodka or rum
- lilikoi lemonaderita -
- pink drink -
  watermelon w/ vodka

beer	wine
lihūē lager	riesling
tropical armadillo	chardonnay
	pinot grigio

juice
- mint colada
  coco H₂O · pineapple · mint
- watermelon
- lilikoi lemonade
- passion orange guava
- soda H₂O
- dragonfruit pineapple
- lilikoi lychee

bush
kombucha on tap

THE REGISTRY

Here's a look at some of the items that topped Malia and Jess's wish list.

HASAMI PORCELAIN MUGS

AVAILABLE FROM
TortoiseGeneralStore.com

HASAMI PORCELAIN BOWLS

AVAILABLE FROM
TortoiseGeneralStore.com

AĒSOP HAND WASH

AVAILABLE FROM
Aesop.com

**AMY DOV WALL HANGING
CERAMICS**

AVAILABLE FROM
AmyDovStudio.com

ALEPH GEDDIS SCULPTURE

AVAILABLE FROM
GlasswingShop.com

KAT & ROGER CERAMICS

AVAILABLE FROM
AlphaShadows.com

ROPE INCENSE

AVAILABLE FROM
SivanaSpirit.com

**POPPY AND SOMEDAY
MARFA MOON MIST**

AVAILABLE FROM
PoppyandSomeday.com

**MYSTIC MAMMA
DESK CALENDAR**

AVAILABLE FROM
MysticMammaShop.com

4 TABLESCAPES

Curating all the details of a tablescape is truly an art form—the chairs, flowers, plates, linens, silverware, and candles should be unified, but in a way that doesn't feel fussy or overly complicated. To achieve this balance, experiment with scale, juxtapose heights and textures, and feature a few unexpected elements that will hold your guests' attention. If you love the look of an unwieldy foraged centerpiece, for example, make sure to offset it with a more minimalist place setting. Or if you have a busy heirloom lace tablecloth, think about doing a single-variety floral arrangement. Pulling it off is easier than you think: if you adhere to your color story (see page 17) and let the design elements reflect your surroundings, you'll be well on your way.

THE TABLE

Before you meet with a rental company, you'll need to figure out the table shapes that will work with your venue. The basic options are round and rectangular—or a mix of the two (oval and square shapes are less common). In general, uniform shapes lend a more formal feel, while a mix of shapes skews a little more casual. Many people instinctively select the same table shape as the dining table they have at home because they are familiar with how to decorate it. Whatever shape you choose, tables should be 60 inches from the wall (and from one another), and you should allot about 24 inches for each person at the table.

Incorporating different table shapes within the same setting creates a more casual and variegated look. Here, under a sailcloth tent, round tables with full-length white tablecloths are positioned alongside a wooden banquet table topped with a white runner.

RECTANGULAR VS. ROUND TABLES

	RECTANGULAR	ROUND
WHERE IT WORKS BEST	Smaller, narrower spaces	Large, open spaces
SERVING STYLE	Best for plated courses or family-style (with so many people at one table, a trip to the buffet will create long lines)	Anything goes: plated, buffet, or family-style
STANDARD SIZING	A 48-inch-long table seats four.* A 72-inch-long table seats six.* A 96-inch-long table seats eight.*	A 54-inch-diameter table seats six. A 60-inch-diameter table seats eight. A 72-inch-diameter table seats ten.
CENTERPIECES	The standard table width is just 30 inches across, so centerpieces should be low and tight or tall and skinny (alternatively, try hanging arrangements).	Opt for wide and sprawling arrangements here.
NOTES	When aligning rectangular tables together, be careful when seating guests in the joints—there will be a dip in the surface and bothersome table legs underneath.	Last-minute cancellations (or wedding crashers) are more easily accommodated with this shape, by tightening or opening the circle.

Add two if seating on the ends.

THE HEAD TABLE

In most cases, the head table (where the bride and groom are seated) should be in the center of the room so those on the perimeter don't feel like they are in the cheap seats. Couples with divorced parents often view the sweetheart table (a separate table with only two seats for the new couple) as a safe middle ground since it prevents them from having to pick a side to sit with. But there are other options that are more inclusive: placing the couple at a siblings-only table or at a table with only the wedding party can eliminate awkward situations. Some couples employ a long banquet table and seat family on either end, typically with the bride and groom seated in the middle.

THE KIDS' TABLE

Children often play an integral part in the ceremony as ring bearers and flower girls, but what happens when it comes time to sit down to dinner? While some couples will seat older children with their parents, younger kids often prefer to have their own table where they can carry on as loudly as they'd like. Make sure their table is far enough from the main seating area that the noise won't be a distraction but not so far that their parents can't keep an eye on what's going on. The tablescape should be in harmony with the adults' tables—minus the steak knives and candles—and be sure to provide plenty of coloring books, crayons, card games, and arts-and-crafts projects to keep them occupied.

If your guest count is small enough, having one extra-long banquet table like this one will ensure that everyone feels like they are at the head table.

SETTING YOUR SEATS APART

Whether you choose to do an old-school sweetheart table or sit among your family and friends, find a way to distinguish your chairs from the others, whether it's by using a different style of chair (a couple of dramatic peacock chairs, for example) or decorating your chair backs.

BOW-TIED

A cloth panel (made of extra table linens) was woven into the backs of these two French cross-back chairs, then tied with a bow.

PAPER FLOWERS

A garland of panda anemones constructed out of paper accented the backs of this bride's and groom's black cross-back chairs.

A POP OF COLOR

Echoing the bright bougainvillea in the centerpieces, a loose arrangement angled across the backs of two white cross-back chairs makes a sweet, low-key statement.

CURVE APPEAL

Following the lines of the round cane-back upholstered chairs, two lush olive leaf wreaths were accented with flowers to connect with the pastel and white centerpieces.

SEATING

Chairs are, of course, an essential element of any tablescape. Think of them as you would a frame for a piece of artwork: a border that should blend with the environment and not be a focal point. If your chairs are doing double duty for the ceremony and the reception, make sure they work for both settings. And since you might end up spending three or four hours at the table, be sure they are comfortable. Here is an overview of the standard options.

Chiavari chairs are universally popular and feature vertical back slats that have the appearance of notched bamboo. Rental outfits carry almost every finish (white, gold, and silver skew more formal; light or dark-stained wood are perfect for the outdoors). They are also very easy to transport.

Classic bentwood chairs have a cane or solid seat and a rustic, midcentury vibe that's perfect for more casual events. They come in a variety of dark and light stains.

Eames Eiffel chairs are a hallmark of midcentury design (their single-shell form was created in the 1950s). Today they are a great choice for modern indoor events.

Folding chairs, whether bamboo, natural wood, cloth covered, or Fermob-style bistro chairs (the classic all-metal French-style chair with curved slats), are usually the least expensive option.

Wooden cross-back chairs (also referred to as X-back or farm chairs) are hugely popular for polished outdoor weddings. They are a little more formal than a traditional wooden folding chair and are easy to stack. You may choose to add a pad for comfort and to tie in with your color story (see page 17).

Metal tabouret chairs have a distinct vintage industrial look. They usually come in classic silver but can also be found in bronze and a range of colors.

CHIAVARI

BENTWOOD

FOLDING

**CROSS-BACK AND
UPHOLSTERED**

Upholstered chairs are usually the most expensive seating option, but they tend to be the most comfortable. They range from a simple slipper chair (tufted or smooth) to the more elaborate wingback chair or round cane-back chair with a linen seat. Be aware that many upholstered chairs run wide, so they won't follow the standard chair-to-table ratio (as described on page 200).

Translucent acrylic ghost chairs lend an ultramodern touch. They come both with and without arms.

Benches are a great option for a very casual meal taking place at a rectangular table. If you are tight on space, they are ideal for seating guests close together.

SEATING CHARTS

Create a seating chart as soon as all the RSVPs are in. There's the old-fashioned way: write each guest's name on a sticky note and arrange the notes on sheets of paper, then take a picture or transcribe the information into a spreadsheet. For those who are a little more high-tech, there are a number of digital platforms to help: AllSeated.com, WeddingWire.com, and WeddingMapper .com allow users to import master guest lists from a spreadsheet, design floor plans, and send their final plans via email to vendors and planners.

Couples should be seated together, but the tradition of alternating boy-girl-boy-girl just doesn't seem relevant anymore. Also, don't be surprised when your naughty guests move the place cards around—despite all your planning, it might happen. If you are working with smaller tables, you can make things simple by assigning people to tables instead of to individual seats.

TEXTILES

Formal tablescapes usually have a tablecloth, while more casual ones will either have a runner or no linens at all. If you are covering your table with a cloth, you can use generic folding tables since no one will see them; if not, you will need to rent a beautiful table since it will be visible.

TABLECLOTHS

Just as putting a fresh coat of paint on the walls can set the tone for a room, a tablecloth can do a lot of the legwork in establishing the color story of your tablescape (see page 17). It's easiest to choose something neutral—off-white, beige, or gray, or a muted color—upon which to layer bolder hues. The choices for tablecloth length (which is referred to as the drop length) are described below—typically, the longer the drop, the more formal the table.

Short: Hanging less than a foot below the table (usually 6 to 10 inches), this length is used for informal or casual events.

Half: A half drop, as you might have guessed, hangs exactly half the length to the floor. A typical dining table is 30 inches high, so this would be a roughly 15-inch drop.

Full: Usually considered the most formal option, a full drop means the tablecloth is exactly the length of the table and just skims the ground.

Puddle Drop: Here, the cloth extends the full length of the table and gently puddles on the ground. Even though it's longer than a full drop, this style can feel more relaxed.

When choosing the fabric of your tablecloth, consider the formality of your event. If your look is more polished, you may want a pressed cotton, linen, or even simple burlap cloth. For something less formal, embrace the wrinkles of unpressed linens, loosely bunched and draped on the table. A heavy lace overlay is a beautiful way to add texture, as is macramé.

In most major cities, there are rental companies that specialize in textiles, and they will ship almost anywhere. If you are planning a destination event, consider bringing linens with you. You can also create custom cloths by sourcing material at a fabric store and then taking it to a tailor to finish.

RUNNERS

If you want to show off a beautiful wooden table but also want to inject a pop of color into your tablescape—or if you are trying to add dimension to an existing tablecloth—a runner can make a world of difference. The standard runner is 15 inches wide, extends between 36 and 108 inches in length, and is meant to hang about 6 inches off either end of a rectangular table (it could also stop at the end of the table or go all the way to the floor). People often choose a bolder color for a runner than they would for a larger tablecloth—for example, a deep blue velvet to play off of blue-and-white china, or a burnt orange to complement Umbrian-style earthenware.

On large round tables, a mix of blue-and-white patterned tablecloths was a perfect juxtaposition to the garnet-colored flowers. If you worry that an oversized tablecloth will get in the way, tuck it under (as pictured opposite).

TABLETOP TEXTILES

If you choose to incorporate a runner or a tablecloth, think carefully about its length, color, and texture, which will influence the formality of your tablescape.

A SHORT RUNNER

A hemstitched linen runner that stops before the end of the table is perfect for a more casual setting. Here, it offered protection from wax spills and water rings from the vases without concealing the beautiful wooden farm table beneath.

HALF DROP

A lightweight natural cloth in a fabric such as burlap is just enough to make a tablescape feel polished but not too fussy. The half-drop length is easy to work with since guests' legs and shoes will not disrupt or sully the fabric.

FULL LENGTH

For a formal dinner setting, the corners of this cream-colored tablecloth are gently folded under, resulting in a crisp, polished look.

PUDDLE DROP

A tablecloth is a perfect opportunity to emphasize your color story (see page 17). Here, a navy cloth with a slight puddle drop has a relaxed, European sensibility—just make sure it's not so long that people might trip over it.

NAPKINS

Napkins should always be made from a natural fabric like cotton, hemp, or linen. If you want to incorporate a print on the table, napkins are a good place to throw in a soft stripe, floral, or mud cloth pattern. As with the tablecloth, think about if you want the napkins to be pressed and folded for a more polished look or if you prefer a softer texture—a fringed edge is especially nice when juxtaposed against a flat tablecloth. And, in the same way one might mix and match china, feel free to do the same with a slightly different napkin at each setting.

Once you decide on the napkin itself, you'll need to choose how you want to style it on the table. This is referred to as the napkin treatment, and it is a key element to a well-designed tablescape—one that is almost always on a photographer's shot list. To begin, you'll need to decide where the napkin will live: folded on top of the plate, on the side, or underneath. Then consider ways to dress it up.

INTO THE FOLD

In this simple, restaurant-quality presentation, each napkin was folded to create a pocket for the menu, with the name card placed on top.

FRUIT-FORWARD

For a wedding in Ojai, California, kumquats were a natural choice to tie in the yellow and orange hues on the table. Lemons, pomegranates, figs, and grapes are all wonderful alternatives.

BEST BUDS

Blooms that don't make it into the centerpieces or that are rescued from the floor of your florist's workroom (like this sprig of dried wheatgrass) can be trimmed, cleaned, and used as perfect napkin treatments.

PUT A RING ON IT

A napkin ring evokes a familial, intimate vibe—like something you might use at home. Here, a natural wooden ring complements the warm wood and blush tones of this modern tablescape.

TIED UP WITH STRING

For this Wyoming wedding, a raw leather string (which can be sourced at a craft or bead store) held the napkin, a name card, and a sprig of wild berries.

LOVE KNOTS

This napkin was meant to resemble a Boy Scout neckerchief with an elegant twist. The place cards were tied to a little bundle of palo santo wood with a copper wire on top of speckleware china from Crate & Barrel.

CENTERPIECES

The centerpiece is a great opportunity to show off your creativity during a wedding. The old-school philosophy when it came to centerpieces was "the bigger, the better"—the more flowers you had on the table, the more special your event was or the more memorable it would be. But that way of thinking has gone out the window in favor of arrangements that are more thoughtful—where different shapes and sizes might coexist on one table so that each guest has a unique perspective. The only rule of centerpiece design that truly matters is that the arrangements shouldn't hinder how your guests interact (meaning they should be kept low enough or high enough so that everyone can make eye contact and converse easily).

The first consideration in determining the best design should be how you plan to serve the meal. For example, if you are serving a family-style dinner on long banquet tables, then you probably shouldn't do big, bushy garlands that will take up a large amount of real estate. Once you identify a basic footprint, think about composition. Like the ingredients on the menu, keeping the floral elements on your table seasonal and local is ideal. A good place to start is by looking up the state flower where you are getting married, or finding out what grows naturally in the area. Ask your florist or a local gardener what will be available at the farmers' market during that time of year. Importing lilacs in the fall, peonies in the winter, or another out-of-season bloom from a foreign country is counterintuitive—and needlessly adds cost. Foodies will also insist that a centerpiece shouldn't consist of highly fragrant blooms as the smell will compete with the gustatory experience of the meal, but most people don't mind having their dinner with, say, a few beautiful stargazer lilies in front of them.

RECYCLE YOUR FLOWERS If your wedding festivities are going to be spread out across a weekend or longer, repurposing your flowers for multiple events is good for the environment and your budget. After the wedding, you can also arrange to donate the flowers to a local hospital or hospice center (through a company like Repeat Roses), or take them home and hang them to dry (if you are short on space, you might want to do this with just the bridal bouquet).

Delicate white blooms and greenery in classic polished silver vessels are elegant and timeless. Larger vessels were spaced farther apart while smaller chalices were grouped together, the result of which was that each guest had a unique point of view and the extremely long banquet tables felt more dynamic.

CLASSIC SHAPES

Low, midsized centerpieces work for both round and rectangular tables and are the most traditional. They can be separated with a few bud vases or fruits—and remember, centerpieces don't have to be identical if you want a more varied look.

SOFT AND FEMININE

KEY INGREDIENTS: Koko Loko garden roses, flannel flowers, bunny tail, abelia foliage, begonia foliage

WHY IT WORKS: A whimsical, flower-filled arrangement in a feminine, blush palette is perfect for an outdoor summer wedding. Big, lush blooms anchor the display at the base while a few squirrelly stems at the top make it feel light. Space out a few containers along the table and add bud vases in between to help connect the larger arrangements.

DUTCH MASTERPIECE

KEY INGREDIENTS: Garden roses, hydrangea, berries, dahlias

WHY IT WORKS: Inspired by the super-romantic Dutch Old Master paintings of the 1600s, these arrangements are filled with big, heavy blooms and are perfect for autumnal weddings where they can reflect the darker, moodier colors of the season. Here, blooms and wild blackberries (along with other fruits of the season) spill onto the table to create a warm still-life moment. Make sure to use flowers that are fully open, or even slightly past their peak.

CLEAN AND WHITE

KEY INGREDIENTS: Lilac, spirea, hellebore

WHY IT WORKS: Instead of a tightly packed dome, this organic, straight-from-the-field-style centerpiece has a low and wide footprint so that guests can easily converse with one another. With branches of small blooms that gently touch the table, it is natural and unfussy, yet the traditional color palette makes it timeless.

GARDEN VARIETY

KEY INGREDIENTS: Lace cap hydrangea, forsythia foliage, anemones, cafe au lait dahlias, porcelain berry, clematis, lisianthus, spray roses

WHY IT WORKS: Clean white vases raised this nuanced arrangement slightly, allowing guests to take in a range of pastels (the purple ties in with the napkin) against a backdrop of maroons and dark greens.

UNEXPECTED STYLES

Beyond low, round centerpieces, there are many different ways to experiment with the structure and dimension of your centerpieces. If you stick with classic blooms (like white roses), these new shapes will feel less surprising.

SATELLITE VESSELS

KEY INGREDIENTS: Billy balls, Dutch hellebores, freesia

WHY IT WORKS: Instead of large, identical centerpieces, consider deconstructing an arrangement into multiple small vessels (called satellite or cluster arrangements). Use a single variety of blooms for the whole table, or let each container hold something different. Similarly, the vessels can be uniform, or you could incorporate a mix of silver julep cups, glasses, ceramic containers, and/or planted flowerpots. If you can part with them, encourage guests to take these home as favors.

HIGH-LOW

KEY INGREDIENTS: Asparagus ferns, roses

WHY IT WORKS: A hallmark of tropical destination weddings, an elevated green arrangement can also work well on a more formal tablescape. Here, long and lean glass vessels were placed in groups of three with simple bud vases holding roses below. On a long banquet table, this arrangement adds big drama without taking up a lot of room. Plus, working with greenery, branches, and foliage is always much less expensive than using cut flowers.

IKEBANA-INSPIRED

KEY INGREDIENTS: White nerine, lunaria

WHY IT WORKS: *Ikebana* translates to "the way of flowers," and these sculptural arrangements are guided by ancient principles of form often associated with a scalene triangle. Use a shallow dish or bowl with a flower frog in the center to anchor a few singular stems, and be sure there are an odd number of elements in the display (traditional ikebana artists believe an even number inspires conflict). The result is an unexpected, wabi-sabi moment of calm, and possibly a more cost-effective treatment for a minimalist table.

GARLAND

KEY INGREDIENT: Silver dollar eucalyptus

WHY IT WORKS: Garlands can be flower-filled (which sometimes resembles a hedge) or they can be green. Leafy garlands are a wonderful idea for those getting married in the wintertime, when not much is in season. They have an androgynous feel and are usually easy on the budget. Some of the best varieties for a green garland include salal leaves, baby-blue and silver dollar eucalyptus, and Grevillea foliage.

PLACE SETTINGS

Depending on where you get married, you may have access to your venue's in-house supply of china, flatware, and glassware. If it's sufficiently in line with your style, then no need to overthink things. If not, you may want to supplement with individual rented pieces (a special dinner plate, for example, or a decorative charger) or by dipping into a friend's china cabinet. If the venue's inventory is too generic for your taste (and you have the budget), or if you are getting married somewhere off-site where you are responsible for bringing in everything, you'll need to curate the entire look of your tabletop items. At a good rental outfit, the number of different style options can be staggering.

Look at the big picture before making any specific decisions. This is a good time to get reacquainted with your mood board (see page 17). Is your style modern or vintage? What hues from your color story do you want to appear here? And, more important, which specific pieces will you actually need for your meal? Beyond the essentials (dinner plate, water glass, wine/Champagne glass, fork, knife, and spoon), here are extra items to consider.

- Charger (the decorative base under the plate)

- Bread plate

- Butter knife

- Demitasse spoon (usually used for coffee drinks)

- Individual salt and pepper cellars with spoons

- Salad fork

- Soupspoon

- Steak knife

- Chopsticks

COST CONTROL   Here are a few creative ways to curb tabletop spending without sacrificing style.

- Opt for vintage porcelain or glass plates over fine china.

- Use fewer, higher-quality pieces instead of populating your table with many decorative or unnecessary elements.

- Use simple stemware made of clear glass (such as Riedel glasses) instead of ornate cut-crystal glassware.

- Incorporate personal pieces (make sure you have a system to keep track of what's yours).

- Get elements such as your flatware or plates from a secondhand source.

With an exposed wooden farm table as the foundation, handmade white speckled ceramic plating accented by linen napkins, hammered silverware, and stemless glasses is low key but elevated.

Next, select the plating, as this will be the focal point of the setting. If you are covering your plate with a napkin treatment (see pages 210–211) or if you have a printed tablecloth, you may want to choose a neutral-colored plate with clean, simple lines. If not, you may want a more elaborate plate (i.e., one with scalloped or raised-pattern edges, or a hand-painted print). Don't be afraid to experiment with different ideas to make your setting more interesting, whether by opting for a colored or opaque glass on a neutral table or by adding heirlooms, such as antique platters and candelabras, to offset more modern elements.

Your choice of silverware should complement the dinner plate in tone. Consider how to style your flatware—if you have a basic setting, you may want to lay out the cutlery in an unexpected way, such as placing the forks and knives in aggregate heights instead of right next to each other or turning the forks and spoons so that they are facedown on the table.

Once you narrow down your tabletop selections, ask the rental company and your florist to do a mock-up where you can see how all the different elements will interact with one another, and adjust as needed. (Ideally, this would take place at your venue, but you can also do it at the vendor's location; the florist may charge a fee for the centerpiece, but your rental company should provide a couple of table setting choices for free if it's just for a few hours, though they may require a deposit.) Take pictures of your mock-up so you can mull it over before making a final decision (you can always schedule another mock-up, if needed).

GLASS

Glass plates and chargers are wonderful building blocks for a formal tablescape, especially when they feature a gold rim, as seen here. Glass is usually the least expensive option out of all the plating choices (not including plastic or paper).

MODERN

With a clean white tablecloth and the vellum menu, this matte black place setting feels simple, streamlined, and perfectly in sync with the couple's avant-garde style.

CLASSIC WHITE

The easiest way to elevate a standard white plate is with the addition of modern flatware—whether gold, silver, or another color. The use of stemless water glasses and wineglasses here also lends a modern touch. A simple setting like this can skew either formal or casual and works in any season.

POLISHED EARTHENWARE

Paired with modern white flatware and rose-tinted glassware, this matte ceramic plate set is contemporary, feminine, and cohesive and ties back to the wedding's color story.

PRINTS

Printed plates can instantly enliven a tablescape; just be sure to keep the rest of the elements simple and classic. When going for the mismatched look, stick within a certain theme (e.g., vintage floral or blue-and-white prints).

VINTAGE INSPIRED

These intricate lace-detailed dinner plates have an old-world sensibility but are modernized when paired with colored glassware and gold cutlery. Individual salt and pepper cellars add a refined touch.

CANDLES

If your reception is taking place in a hotel, a restaurant, or another public space, ask if they allow open flames—many won't due to fire codes, and others may insist that candles be protected in a glass hurricane.

If and when you have the green light for candles, decide if you want to incorporate a mix of heights (tea lights, votives, pillars, and tall tapered candles) or if you want to use just one style. Also consider floating candles, which may be placed in bowls or special candleholders. Another thing to keep in mind is color. While white or ivory wax is the default choice (and sometimes the best option), candles in neutral colors like black, gray, beige, and soft pastels can be more thoughtful and cohesive. All-natural beeswax candles come in various hues depending on the shade of the seasonal pollen and give off a sweet honey smell. Most florists will be able to help you source the actual candles, or you can do this yourself.

TEA LIGHTS

TEA LIGHTS AND VOTIVES

Tea lights have a burn time of four to five hours, while slightly larger votives can burn for up to fifteen hours. It's lovely to see them grouped in clusters along the table, providing unexpected pockets of light—although they will probably be too dim to serve as a primary light source. Vessel options include clear, opaque, frosted, and colored glass; cut crystal; and mercury glass in cylindrical, fluted, flared, and round shapes—or the tea lights can be placed in small dishes (like the unique bronze dishes pictured at right). If you are using tea lights in a transparent container, make sure the candles don't have a metal wrap around them.

TAPERS AND VOTIVES

PILLARS

PILLARS

Taller and wider than votives, pillar candles are usually associated with more casual events. When paired with votives or tea lights, they are a great way to aggregate candle heights while keeping the lighting low—for example, group tea lights and votives around a pillar candle to create individual moments along the table. Vessel options include simple glass hurricanes, wooden or glass pedestals, and lanterns, which are great for outdoor events.

TAPERS

Tapered candles have become a trademark of black-tie parties, but they can really be used for any style event. They range in thickness and in length: A standard taper (also called a dinner candle) is 8 or 12 inches long and ⅞ inch in diameter and fits into most candleholders.

For a round table, a candelabra filled with tapers and encircled with flowers and low tea lights is always elegant. Rental outfits will typically carry silver candelabras, but don't confine yourself to their inventory. It's often less expensive to buy them if you are having a small wedding (especially if you plan to use them afterward).

For rectangular tables, you can place low lights (tea lights or low pillars) between individual tapered candles. If you are going for a more organized look, line up the tapered candles along the center of the table; if you want something a little more organic, place the tall candles in clusters of twos or threes. The vessel options for individual tapered candles are seemingly endless: Glass hurricanes and marble, brass, ceramic, and wooden stands can sit at table level or be elevated a few inches. You may also create custom candleholders with a ceramicist, carpenter, or welder. Small shallow dishes can also be used to hold tapers, secured to floral frogs. And if you don't like the look of a vessel, you can embed tapers in your centerpieces so that the base is hidden. At the end of the evening, there's something so romantic about seeing wax that has dripped down onto the table and flowers.

TAPERS

TABLE MARKERS

The classic table marker (a silver stand holding a white card with a number printed on it) has given way to a bevy of personalized, nonnumeric interpretations. This detail is the perfect DIY project for someone who wants to be a little more hands-on without having to spend an inordinate amount of time at the craft table. Consider identifying tables with an illustration of a favorite flower or animal, or with the name of a place that has special meaning to you as a couple. More creative types can try painting and mounting numbers on tiles or carved wood—you can place these flat on the table or on an easel. If you are sticking with traditional numbers, consider displaying them in a nontraditional way, like on a clipboard, in a frame, or even in a flower frog.

VERSATILE VESSEL
Place a sticker over a wine label, or hire a calligrapher to pen the number onto glass water bottles. If you wanted to get fancy, you could create leather sleeves for bottles with the number printed on them.

CLEAR CUT
Similar to the idea of placing a table number in a picture frame, this modern acrylic sign makes a discreet yet modern statement on the table. It also echoes the table's translucent ghost chairs (not pictured).

SELF-STANDING

This traditional table number is printed on a tented card in an elaborate script (most people use machine printing for the table numbers instead of hand-calligraphy, especially if there are a lot of tables).

NATURAL OBJECTS

Whether you source objects from a craft store or they are indigenous to the area (think shells, rocks, or smooth stones, like the one pictured), unexpected surfaces make your tablescape feel earthy, organic, and a bit unconventional.

FESTIVE HERALDRY

A textured deckle-edged card is displayed in a rustic log-like stand. If you created a custom crest for your invitation, this is a great place to repurpose it.

ECCENTRIC ICONS

Remember, table markers do not necessarily need to be numbers. Instead they can be more creative (and even cheeky) and feature images that are meaningful to your relationship.

A FOREST FAIRY TALE

Under a canopy of ancient redwood trees, a maximalist bride carried out
the wedding of her dreams, leaving no stone unturned.

As someone who delights in the pomp and circumstance of a wedding, Annabel Mehran found that eight months was hardly enough time to piece together all the details for her wedding to writer Josh Eells. A photographer by trade, Annabel had a highly conceptualized vision for the day, akin to watching a short film unfold against the backdrop of an enchanted redwood forest. Scenes were lush and layered with florals and decor that felt indigenous to the space. Nods to both her Persian heritage and his Mexican roots were beautifully woven into the storyline, as was their shared passion for food and wine. And while many components were grand in scale (Annabel's cascading bouquet and horsehair veil from Monique Lhuillier, for starters), nothing ever felt out of character or overly formal.

To help bring it all to life, the couple turned to planner Maggie Wilson of Shelter Co. and some of Annabel's bridesmaids: artist Becca Mann hand-painted the invitations; designer Jaclyn Hodes of the eco-conscious fashion label Awaveawake designed the bridesmaids' dresses; and Joanna Newsom, a harpist, performed just before the ceremony and also helped with the calligraphy. Not surprisingly, the wedding's most cinematic moments were all Annabel's doing. As the couple leaned in for their first kiss, a cannon erupted with a plume of biodegradable confetti just as the band, hidden behind the stage, burst into song. "I got the idea from watching the fireworks scene in *To Catch a Thief*," Annabel remembers. Dinner afterward was held under a dramatic clear-frame tent that had been strung with fairy lights and verdant chandeliers that cast a magical glow onto the farm tables below. After dinner, the couple arranged for the dancing to take place at the River Theater in nearby Guerneville.

On the way there, Josh asked the driver to pull over so he and Annabel could practice their first dance one more time. He cued up "Lovely Day" by Bill Withers on his iPhone and twirled his bride under the moonlight on the country road—another beautiful scene, if a little off script.

A GREENHOUSE GALA // The redwood chips beneath the oak cross-back chairs and the long wooden tables were indigenous to the site. The florist created leafy hanging chandeliers of fragrant stephanotis plants, and the ceiling of the clear-frame tent and the trees above it were strewn with magical twinkle lights.

ABOVE:

KEEPING IT LIGHT // The band that came with the venue had a limited number of songs in their repertoire. Nothing seemed to be a great fit for the ceremony, so the couple embraced the quirkiness of it all and chose a song they hoped would lighten the mood. As confetti spewed into the air, the band played "I Gotta Feeling" by the Black Eyed Peas. "It worked!" says Annabel.

OPPOSITE, CLOCKWISE FROM TOP LEFT:

SLEIGHT OF HAND // Annabel wanted the tabletop flowers to be abundant but styled in a way that felt natural and in line with the magical forest setting. Centerpieces arranged on a mossy base of manzanita and ferns seemed to be growing right from the table, and pomegranates foraged from her grandmother's garden were scattered along the tables.

IN THE NUDE // The four-tier "naked" strawberry shortcake was made by San Francisco pastry shop Miette. In honor of Josh's heritage, the couple also served Mexican wedding cookies and a tres leches cake by Tartine Bakery.

COURSEWORK // "The most important thing to me was that there was always food and drinks on offer, no matter what time it was," says Annabel. For dinner, Componere Fine Catering served a family-style meal that featured some Persian dishes—including carrots that had been pickled by Annabel's grandmother. The mural surrounding the menu was lifted from a frame that artist (and bridesmaid) Becca Mann had found at a thrift store.

ANIMAL INSTINCTS // Instead of using traditional table numbers, Annabel had the cards printed with Inuit wood-block-print-inspired animal drawings she found on Pinterest.

Paul Filo

Josh Eells

Menu
October 24, 2014

First Course

Caramelized Kabocha Squash,
Beet Pickled Cauliflower, Crispy Quinoa
Spiced Yogurt, Brussels Sprout Leaves,
Pepitas

Second Course

Grilled Whole Churrasco Steak, Preserved Orange Chimichurri

Pollo al Mattone: Chicken Cooked Under a Brick

Slow Cooked Salmon, Blistered Red & Gold Cherry Tomatoes

Persian Rice

Componere Farm Vegetables a la Plancha

Dessert

Campfire Kulfi
Wedding Cake

Wine

Chateau Clos du Marquis, St. Julien — Bordeaux 2005
Henri Boillot Meursault — White Burgundy 2013
Kistler Pinot Noir Sonoma Coast Estate 2013
Crocker and Starr Sauvignon Blanc 2014

Champagne

Bollinger Brut Special Cuvée

ABOVE, LEFT:

BENCHMARKS // Long wooden benches were lined with programs for the ceremony. At the end of each bench was a nest that held lace flowers (which Annabel sourced from a famous Austrian lace maker), dried bachelor buttons, and white daisies for guests to toss during the recessional.

ABOVE, RIGHT:

AN ARTFUL WELCOME // The welcome bags were designed by Annabel's friend Su Barber, art director for the fashion company Opening Ceremony, and emblazoned with a word-based graphic designed by another friend, artist Marc Hundley. The bags were filled with Have'a Corn Chips, crab-claw pens, poppy seeds to plant (poppies are one of Annabel's favorite flowers), a map of the area for the wedding weekend, and small bottles of Maker's Mark bourbon and Patrón tequila (baby sequoia trees from Muir Woods were substituted for teetotaling guests).

ABOVE, LEFT:

RED, WHITE, AND BLUE // The bridesmaids wore white silk dresses designed by fellow bridesmaid Jaclyn Hodes of Awaveawake. The look was completed with white block-heeled sandals by designer Maryam Nassir Zadeh, Tom Ford "Carnal Red" nail polish, a flower crown, and a small, textured arrangement of lamb's ear and blue wildflowers.

ABOVE, RIGHT:

SITTING PRETTY // Annabel found her dramatic Monique Lhuillier horsehair veil in Los Angeles. Though she didn't have her dress to try it on with, she decided to purchase the veil anyway, hoping that the two pieces she loved would complement each other. When she tried them on together just before the wedding, it was exactly what she'd had in mind.

FOLLOWING PAGE:

WILD AND WOOLLY // Annabel wanted a cascading, untamed, presentation-style bouquet— like something that might have been foraged from a clearing in the forest. Florist Grant Rector wrapped the stems with a white silk ribbon to make it feel a bit more polished.

THE REGISTRY

Here's a look at some of the items that topped Annabel and Josh's wish list.

ATLAS PASTA MACHINE

AVAILABLE FROM

SurLaTable.com

**SANTA MARIA
NOVELLA CANDLE**

AVAILABLE FROM

Buy.SMNovella.com

**WEBER SMOKEY MOUNTAIN
COOKER SMOKER**

AVAILABLE FROM

CrateandBarrel.com

CHEMEX COFFEEMAKER

AVAILABLE FROM

Williams-Sonoma.com

DURACLEAR TUMBLERS

AVAILABLE FROM

Williams-Sonoma.com

JOSEF HOFFMANN CRYSTAL

AVAILABLE FROM

Shop.NeueGalerie.org

**FRANCES PALMER POTTERY
PLATTER**

AVAILABLE FROM

FrancesPalmerPottery.com

**NESPRESSO AEROCCINO4
MILK FROTHER**

AVAILABLE FROM

Nespresso.com

**HEREND INDIAN
BASKET CHINA**

AVAILABLE FROM

HerendUSA.com

5 FOOD & DRINK

Certain meals are meant to be elevated, and an elaborate, multicourse plated dinner is guaranteed to evoke a sense of importance and gravitas. But complex recipes and fancy ingredients are not the only ways to impress. Today more and more couples approach the choices for their wedding menu in a way that is closer to how they entertain at home, with family-style preparations that encourage guests to linger at the table for hours. However you decide to serve the meal, nourish your loved ones with dishes that work to connect your past, present, and future.

HIRING A CATERER

Many hotels and event spaces will work only with their in-house restaurant or a team from their list of approved caterers, so make sure you are happy with their choices before you commit to a venue. If you are hiring an outside vendor, the most common approach is to reach out to a few catering companies for itemized quotes, then schedule tastings. You could also ask your favorite restaurant if they would be able to do an off-site event, or you could think about having a food truck or different food stations. Here are a few things you will want to go over when you meet with potential caterers.

- What is included in the cost per person (rentals, decor, staff, etc.)?

- Is there a fee for the tasting before you select the full menu?

- Will they be able to create a custom menu for your event, or do you have to select dishes from predetermined menus? Furthermore, can they make personal recipes, like your grandmother's famous meatballs?

- Can they handle making appetizers, dinner, *and* dessert?

- Are they committed to using high-quality, organic ingredients and do they have relationships with local farmers and producers?

- If you are inviting guests with dietary restrictions (vegan, kosher, gluten-free, etc.), can they accommodate those needs?

- Will guests be required to preselect entrée choices? (If so, you'll need to include a selection card with the wedding invitation; see page 44.)

- Are they able to provide bartending services, stock the bar, and suggest wine pairings?

- What is their approach to food styling (ask to see examples) and will they assist with table styling?

THE COCKTAIL HOUR

The cocktail hour is a great way for guests to connect with one another and recap the ceremony, but it is a bit of a misnomer. Cocktails should really be about forty-five minutes, and definitely not longer than one hour, or guests tend to get hungry and restless. Also, the cocktail hour should not include just mixed drinks—there should be wine, beer, and some bubbly (see page 242 for more on stocking the bar). Oftentimes the couple will take a few pictures after the ceremony while their guests are enjoying their drinks. Ideally, the location of the cocktail reception is close to where you are having dinner, so you can keep the same bar setup. To avoid the bar getting swarmed after the ceremony, ask your reception staff to offer tray-passed drinks.

AT THE BAR

While it needs to be functional, the bar is often an overlooked opportunity to make a statement. Beyond the standard rectangular box, there are more design-forward options, like a beautiful antique table or a bar topped with a slab of salvaged wood. If your venue has a generic structure that doesn't enhance the design of your wedding, consider disguising it with a large cascading floral arrangement and/or a tablecloth. You may want to keep hard alcohol and wine in their original containers so guests can easily identify them, but consider finding some pretty vessels for garnishes and mixers. Don't forget about the back of the bar, where bottles, supplies, and glasses might be stored; this area should be tidy and well designed as it will be in guests' view. And it might go without saying, but under no circumstance should you ever do a cash bar or allow a tip jar on the bar at a wedding (if your venue does this, you should request to have it removed).

To kick off cocktail hour, consider greeting your guests with a Champagne tower. Ask an experienced professional to handle the pouring—especially if you want the bottles opened with a saber, which is an old French tradition.

BAR STRUCTURES

Chances are, your guests will spend a fair amount of time at the bar, so consider a setup that will connect with your event's overall aesthetic.

CURVED APPEAL

In addition to being visually stunning, a circular or semicircular structure helps prevent a crowd of people from bottlenecking.

MAXIMIZING SPACE

If you are short on space, a display case behind the bar can hold additional glassware and bottles. Make it an intentional design moment by styling it with candles, greenery, and florals.

THE COVERED BOX

A soft gray tablecloth is the perfect solution to conceal a generic bar. This minimalist setup was topped with napkins, an ikebana-style flower arrangement, and votives. Behind the bar was an assortment of alcohol on draft.

SELF-SERVE

This elegant, all-ages buffet included bottles of Champagne for the adults and Martinelli's for the little ones (and for those who prefer something nonalcoholic). Glass flutes were displayed alongside cups of mixed nuts.

STOCKING THE BAR

When it comes to selecting what kind of alcohol to serve your guests, pick things that you know people will drink. Ana Alvarez, the director of special events at Wolfgang Puck in Beverly Hills, advises to start the reception with Champagne: "It's definitely the most celebratory, especially when it is served out of a large-format bottle, like a magnum or double magnum." If budget is a concern, prosecco is a perfectly acceptable alternative to Champagne—"Most people are just looking for a celebratory moment, and that usually means bubbles. Plus, there are some amazing proseccos to pick from, and even Blanc de Blanc sparkling wines are totally acceptable," says Alvarez.

As for the wine that's served during the cocktail hour, Sauvignon Blanc and a Pinot Noir are the most popular wines. For dinner, the most popular choices are Chardonnay and Cabernet Sauvignon. Alvarez notes that in terms of service, it's helpful to offer the same wine varietals throughout the evening to avoid glassware confusion, *but* it is a nice treat for your guests when you can elevate the evening by offering more of a "pairing" experience with a meal.

Beyond your signature cocktail (see below), the choices for hard alcohol will depend on whether you are having an open bar or a limited bar selection. If you need to narrow your choices, the most-requested liquors are whiskey, vodka, and tequila, followed by cordials, rum, gin, and brandy. As a general guideline, each mixed drink contains about 1.5 ounces of liquor, so a 750 ml bottle will make about 16 drinks. For mixers, make sure to have club soda, tonic water, fresh juices (cranberry, orange, grapefruit, etc.), cola, and plenty of lemons and limes on hand.

When it comes to beer, you really need only two or three choices: a light beer (like a pilsner), a heavier beer (like an IPA), and maybe a domestic lager.

SIGNATURE COCKTAILS

Creating a drink menu is a fun way to personalize the cocktail hour, and it can also cut down on lines at the bar, as certain drinks can be premixed. Develop unique concoctions (aka your signature cocktails), or offer drinks reflective of the season—for example, spiked apple cider and eggnog for winter weddings, Moscow mules and mojitos in the summer. This is also a great opportunity to serve something with a personal connection, such as a local beer or a liquor in honor of the bride's or groom's heritage (Russian vodka or a bottle of scotch, for example). And if the colors of the drinks align with your color story, even better!

BAR MATH Your caterer will be able to help you stock the bar, but if you want a general sense of what to expect in terms of staffing and consumption, here's a quick tip sheet.

Bartenders: One for every 75 to 100 guests (or every 120 to 150 guests if they won't be mixing cocktails)

Barbacks: One for every 120 to 150 guests

Wine: At least three glasses per guest (just over half a bottle). During the cocktail hour, have twice as many bottles of white than of red. During dinner, expect your guests to drink more red.

Champagne: At least one glass per person (one bottle of Champagne fills six to eight glasses), especially if you are doing a Champagne toast. It's always a good idea to order an extra case of Champagne for good measure.

Cocktails: Two or three per guest

STATIONS
Guests always appreciate knowing there is a place where they can find food and not have to wait to be served. Here, hemstitched linen napkins weighted down with kumquats were placed next to an oversized crudités board featuring artisanal bread, olives, vegetables, dips, and cheeses. You might consider keeping the station up beyond the cocktail hour, too.

RIGHT:
PASSED
Elevated and unexpected appetizers are a nice way to kick off dinner. Here, shucked oysters were topped with edible star-shaped borage blossoms. Oysters can be tray passed on ice or set up as a raw bar with other local seafood.

APPETIZERS

Whenever you serve something to drink, you should always offer something to nibble on. If you have a large budget, this could be formal tray-passed appetizers or delicacies such as a raw bar with sushi or oysters on ice. Otherwise, you might want to set up a table or two with classic ideas like a cheese board, crudités, an assortment of charcuterie, or meze.

THE COCKTAIL-STYLE RECEPTION   In an effort to cut down on costs or simply to upend the traditional seated dinner, many couples opt for an informal cocktail-style reception. This might be a good choice if your venue has an early cutoff time or if you are getting married in the middle of the afternoon between lunch and dinner. In addition to tray-passed appetizers, food stations and food trucks both work well for this type of reception. If you aren't serving enough food for dinner, don't expect guests to hang around for a night of dancing. Be sure to make clear on the invitation that there will not be a seated meal.

COCKTAIL AREAS

Whether your cocktail hour will take place indoors or outdoors, you'll want to design spaces near the bar where guests can mingle with their drinks. Most times, a few high-top tables are sufficient, but you may want to include seating as well, either with bistro tables or small dining tables, or by creating an outdoor living room with sofas, chairs, poufs, and stools. Seating is especially important if guests will continue to use the space during the reception. For a more casual gathering, you can even throw out some Persian rugs or blankets and pillows for guests to sit on on the ground.

OPPOSITE, CLOCKWISE FROM TOP LEFT:

CLASSIC HIGH-TOPS

On a sunny day in Napa Valley, high-tops draped in white fabric were lined up near the outdoor bar. Each was paired with an umbrella and accented with a small flower arrangement. For the reception, the umbrellas were taken down. You could also mix in a few bistro tables with chairs so that guests have the option to sit down.

BUILT-IN BANQUETS

If your cocktail area doesn't have much room to bring in furniture, take advantage of existing structures—whether a pathway (like the one pictured), steps, or a garden wall—by adding cushions, candles, and small cocktail tables.

DESIGN-SAVVY RENTALS

In an ideal world, your venue would have furniture that perfectly aligns with your wedding aesthetic, though you may want to add small accents (like throw pillows and blankets) to make it feel more cohesive. If your venue doesn't have existing furniture, look for elegant rentals (which you can use during the reception, too).

THE OUTDOOR LIVING ROOM

Under tents, leather butterfly chairs, antique rugs, and a modern coffee table provided a perfect place for guests to retreat with a drink. The setup would work without the tent, too, and for more seating you could add a few sofas to the mix.

CUSTOM DETAILS

Little details can add a personal flair to your event. Custom cocktail napkins or matchbooks, for example, can be inscribed with your and your partner's initials, icons, or family crests, or the location and date of your wedding. You can commission independent vendors on Etsy to create these, or ask your stationer.

NAPKINS

These custom cocktail napkins with gold foil featured the couple's names, the wedding date, and a series of icons organized within a compass that spoke to the wedding's elevated, campy vibe.

MATCHBOOKS

Customized matchbooks are sweet takeaways for guests and, of course, are not just for smokers. If possible, get the strike-on-box style instead of a flip book; it feels more substantial.

COASTERS

One of this wedding's specialty cocktails was an Aperol Spritz. Guests who ordered the drink also received a colorful coaster with its list of ingredients: 209 gin, Aperol, lemon, seltzer, and orange wheels.

TEMPORARY INK

One of the bridesmaids created illustrations for these New York City–themed temporary tattoos, including images of the stained-glass water tower where the couple got engaged. Bowls were placed on the bars, along with application instructions.

THE ESCORT DISPLAY

Unless you are doing open seating, you'll need to direct guests to their tables before dinner (typically, everyone picks up escort cards during the cocktail reception). And if you want guests to sit in a specific seat at the table, you'll also need to provide place cards at each setting.

FASTENED TO A WALL

To save space and make use of a beautiful ivy-covered wall, escort cards were loosely organized in alphabetical order and hung from yellow and green tassels secured to the leaves.

SIGNAGE

A chalkboard, a mirror, an old-school letter board, a paper scroll, or another kind of sign where all the names are printed together is usually more ecofriendly and oftentimes less expensive than creating individual cards. The most important thing is that it's easy to read!

INDIVIDUAL CARDS

Traditional cards can either be laid flat or tented (if they will be outdoors, be sure they won't get blown away with a strong breeze!). Unlike with large signs, it's easy to make last-minute adjustments with individual cards.

LITTLE FAVORS

If you want the escort cards to serve as a small token of appreciation for your guests, choose something unisex, such as a frame with a pressed flower or picture, or a little bundle of flowers, sage, or palo santo wood (pictured) with a name tag attached.

DINNER

There is no substitute for sharing a meal with those you love. Even in the most informal settings, it's a chance to slow down and engage with your guests, rest your feet, and—this is important—eat something. Whether you are experimenting with new gastronomic techniques or gathering over a simmering pot of paella, the goal is simple: serve food that you want to eat—and serve a lot of it.

Convention tells us to offer entrée choices of chicken, fish, and steak, with a vegetarian option upon request, but consider instead simply serving what you love according to what's local and in season, whether it's one choice or four. Los Angeles–based caterer Annie Campbell says, "Begin by brainstorming a fantasy meal: In a world where budgets, dietary restrictions, and logistical issues didn't exist, what are the dishes you would be most excited to share with your loved ones? The only stipulation is that it should be authentic to you!"

If your caterer is open to it, try to incorporate a drink or a dish that has special significance to you, whether it's inspired by your favorite restaurant or location, or a recipe that's been passed down in the family.

Once you have your ideas and wish lists, you can get into the logistics of what is possible with your actual budget. A big part of your catering budget should be allocated to staff, both servers and the people in the kitchen. As Campbell rightly points out, it won't matter how exciting and beautiful everything is if guests are waiting around for a drink or dinner comes out slowly or cold. For a sit-down dinner, you need at least one server per ten guests, in addition to bartenders and a service captain; for a fancier affair, you'll probably want additional food runners; for a buffet, you need about one server for every fifteen to twenty guests. Ultimately, trust your caterer's or coordinator's recommendations on proper staff numbers.

After the wedding, ask your caterer for the recipes from your wedding so you can make these dishes again and again. For that matter, you may want to order a few extra cases of your wedding wine and Champagne to help bring you back to the day whenever you are feeling a little nostalgic.

ACCOMMODATING DIETARY RESTRICTIONS

Chances are, someone attending your wedding will need a dietary accommodation that is more specific than vegetarian, whether they are gluten-free, dairy-free, nut-free, kosher, or something else. Create a space on your wedding website or on your RSVP cards where guests can inform you of any dietary restrictions. Then try to offer an option on the menu that satisfies all sensitivities (work with your caterer to create a dish that is still interesting and flavorful), or deal with these meals individually with your catering team.

COST CONTROL Food and wine can easily take up half the overall wedding budget (particularly once you factor in a 20 percent gratuity), but there are a few things you can do to bring down the total cost:

- Determine which serving style will be most cost effective (family-style and plated meals are typically more expensive than a buffet).

- Have a lunch, brunch, or cocktail-style reception (see page 243) with heavy appetizers instead of dinner.

- Limit the menu options.

- Use lower-cost ingredients— but not lower-*quality* ingredients (for example, serve salmon instead of lobster, or hanger steak instead of filet mignon).

- Offer wine, beer, and a signature cocktail instead of a full bar.

- Do a self-serve bar.

- Buy some or all of the alcohol yourself (if allowed).

PLATED SERVICE

Plated courses delivered by a fleet of white-gloved waiters are an elegant touch at any style of wedding. Caterers may request that your guests make their entrée choice in advance. If you wish to give your guests the option of ordering on the spot (which is called "tableside selection"), you will need to purchase enough food so that you don't run out of options if everyone ends up ordering the same thing. As this can be expensive and wasteful, if you go this route, you may want to consider offering fewer choices. Alert the chef to food sensitivities so they can prepare special meals for those guests.

And when it comes to the number of courses, stick to two. As caterer Annie Campbell points out, "People want to get up and dance, and if there are too many courses, the momentum is often lost. Instead, let your hors d'oeuvres and the limited plated courses be especially amazing."

Make a strong impression with the first course, especially if you are sticking with more traditional entrée choices. Here, an elegant beet salad with whipped goat cheese, "beet dirt" (aka dehydrated beet powder), and edible flowers.

FAMILY-STYLE SERVICE

This is perhaps the most natural way to serve a meal, and most like the way you entertain at home. Platters are placed directly on the dining tables and guests serve themselves. This is typically viewed as less formal than plated dinners (although it is frequently the more expensive plating option because of the abundance of food needed). The best way to do it is to put out numerous small platters instead of a few bulky ones (smaller dishes minimize passing and feel more personal). Also, family-style service does not just apply to food; have a few bottles of wine and water open at each table so guests can refill their own glasses, too.

BUFFET AND FOOD STATIONS

Buffets are great for large weddings and require the least amount of staff. This serving style is an easy way to accommodate food sensitivities, since you'll be offering a variety of dishes. Use this setup to serve traditional-style menu items or more exotic options, like ramen or tacos. Make sure everything is clearly marked and that the table is styled with flowers and candles. Keep cutlery and napkins at the tables where guests are sitting so they will have less to carry back from the buffet. If possible, have a server at each chafing dish or station. Waitstaff should also refill drinks and clear dining tables. A buffet is not the best option if you've asked people to wear black tie—it's not only viewed as less formal, but it also seems inappropriate to ask guests in long gowns to walk around with plates of food.

TOASTS

Toasts traditionally occur between dinner courses (when it's easiest to get everyone's attention, and people are still relatively sober) and are given in the following order: the best man, the maid of honor, the couple, and finally the couple's parents (usually the bride's first if they are hosting the party, then the groom's). That said, pick a format that works with your unique set of circumstances. If the idea of standing up in front of your guests gives you anxiety, ask your new spouse to do the honors solo (you can visit the different tables during the dinner hour to thank your guests for attending). For the sake of your guests, be cognizant of time: an average toast is between three and five minutes (if you are having fewer speakers, you can invite them to speak for a bit longer). In an effort to save time, many couples request that just their parents speak during the wedding and save the friends' and siblings' toasts (which tend to be more informal) for the rehearsal dinner.

SILVER SERVICE (OR ENGLISH SERVICE) This serving style is a hybrid between a formal plated meal and family-style where waiters bring the courses to the table on platters and serve each guest individually from the left-hand side. Butler service, which is slightly different, is when the waiter holds the platter as the guest serves him- or herself.

MIDNIGHT SNACK With a few hours left on the dance floor and no curfew in sight, keep the party going with a midnight snack. Sliders, truffle fries, grilled cheese, and pizza rule the night—serve them on a silver platter to dress them up a bit. Or consider bringing in a food truck.

MENUS

The menu should graphically tie in with your other paper goods with similar paper stock, fonts, and icons.

BUFFET

You can either include the menu at the beginning of the line next to the plates (as was done here) or, if you have a large number of dishes, put an individual card, with a description of the ingredients, next to each dish.

FAMILY STYLE

A casual meal appears more wedding-appropriate with a modern square menu weighted on each setting with a stone.

PLATED

This formal deckle-edged menu doubles as a place card, with each guest's name written at the top. Securing the menus to acrylic boards lends a sophisticated, restaurant-like touch.

PLATED–FAMILY STYLE COMBO

These playful, individual menus specify that the salad course will be plated, followed by a family-style entrée and dessert courses. The couple included their names and the wedding date, and the icons surrounding the menu were the images used for the table markers.

THE CAKE

By the time people are finished with their entrée, they are usually ready to stretch their legs and get another cocktail. That's why many couples wait until about forty-five minutes after the end of dinner service to offer dessert. Cake cutting usually signals the earliest acceptable time to leave for guests who need to make an early exit (such as people with young children), so don't make it too late.

For some couples, cutting the cake is a sacred rite of passage, as important as the first dance or the first kiss. For others, it's a fun photo op done without much fanfare. Whichever camp you fall into, the cake usually ranks high on a photographer's shot list, and, of course, you want it to be delicious. You may need to outsource the job to a local bakery instead of using your caterer or the hotel/restaurant's resident pastry chef—especially if you have special requests like a vegan tier or have a complex design in mind. One of the best parts of wedding planning is the cake tasting, which you should try to schedule two to three months before the wedding.

If you have a high guest count but don't want an oversized cake, make two cakes—one as a display and the other to have sliced in the kitchen (this will also help reduce costs). The truth is, most people don't eat a lot of cake, so you may want to err on the side of something smaller even if you are having a larger wedding.

FREEZING THE CAKE

If there are any leftovers, many couples embrace the tradition of freezing a slice of wedding cake to enjoy on their one-year anniversary. You may want to send it home with a bridesmaid so it's not forgotten at the end of the night.

On a low wooden stand, this traditional four-tiered cake is decorated with ribbed frosting and greenery, giving it movement and a less formal appearance.

WHITE DONE RIGHT

Whether it's swathed in buttercream, fondant, royal icing, cream cheese, or marzipan frosting, you can't go wrong with a traditional tiered white cake. It's a perfect foundation for adornment, and you don't have to commit to just one flavor—instead, you can do something unexpected at each level.

TONS OF TEXTURE

Mimicking the look of torn paper, these delicate shards of rice paper make for an edgy, romantic, and unexpected confection.

CUTTING-EDGE

This architectural five-tiered cake is unembellished save for a soft, pebble-textured tier in the middle and sculptural lunaria branches on top.

SHORT AND SWEET

Smaller weddings call for smaller cakes. This one, with just two tiers, is adorned with an edible magnolia bloom to match the florals on the table. (If you simply prefer the look of a small cake, you may have a larger sheet cake in the kitchen for plating.)

PRECIOUS PEARLS

Taking its cues from the décor on the stand, this cake featured pearl-like beading at each tier and was finished with simple green vines and flowers.

BEYOND THE WHITE CAKE

Some of the best cakes are not what you might typically envision as "wedding cake"—in fact, they may not even be cakes at all. Perhaps you have a family recipe for a Bundt cake that can be dolled up as a wedding cake. What about pies, tarts, doughnuts, cupcakes, crumbles, or cakes with colored frosting? And don't forget about unusual cake flavors (such as funfetti or matcha).

THE NAKED CAKE

Sans frosting (or perhaps very lightly coated with glaze, aka "semi-naked"), this type of cake is perfect for a more casual celebration. The best ones look effortless and can even be done in different flavors. When the cake is topped with seasonal fruits like sliced figs, blackberries, or raspberries, no one will miss all that sugar.

LOCATION-INSPIRED

Different countries have different versions of a traditional wedding cake. In France, for example, it's a croquembouche; in England or the Caribbean, it could be a fruitcake; in Greece, it's a flourless almond cake; and in Italy, a traditional wedding cake of filo pastry and vanilla cream is called a *millefoglie* (pictured).

A WORK OF ART

Pastry chefs love showing off their artistry with different kinds of decorative techniques, like hand-painting, airbrushing, and piping. You may want to provide a picture, color palette, or textile for them to translate.

COLOR-COORDINATED

The cake is a great opportunity to incorporate a hue from your color story (see page 17). With textured tiers decked with *Pieris japonica* blooms, this light-colored chocolate cake perfectly complemented the natural decor of the couple's wedding.

CAKE TOPPERS

Instead of crowning your cake with flowers or fruit, consider
using a cake topper. It's a great way to include an heirloom if you
have one in the family. If not, Herend makes adorable high-end
porcelain pieces, and there are more reasonable options on Etsy—
go for animal figurines or an old-fashioned bride and groom. You
can also place these beside the cake instead of directly on top of it.

On a simple, classic cake, an
heirloom topper like this one
featuring a couple underneath an
arbor lends a cute touch without
feeling too kitschy.

THE DESSERT TABLE

Include a range of options on the dessert table and, if possible, have an attendant on hand to replenish as needed. Here, in a clean green-and-white color palette, spinach mini cakes, lemon verbena almond cakettes, and a naked cake of Earl Grey, lemon buttercream, and matcha were presented alongside a pea-shoot wedding cake with vanilla buttercream.

A wedding cake and a dessert table don't have to be mutually exclusive. You can put the cake on the dessert table and surround it with other after-dinner treats, including some allergy-friendly options, more cakes (like a groom's cake, for example), cheese, fruit (watermelon slices for a summer wedding, figs and grapes to complement a cheese board), and dessert wines, coffee, and tea. The trick is not to go overboard with the number of choices—just pick two or three desserts and make them perfect. This type of setup allows guests to go at their own pace (and come back for seconds).

HIGHER GROUND

A pair of childhood friends make it official with a clean,
modern affair above the Pacific Ocean.

Emma Lim and Michelle Wang were busy planning a destination wedding in Big Sur when something serendipitous happened. A few months after they got engaged, Section 3 of the Defense of Marriage Act was voted down, which granted federal benefits to same-sex spouses. They decided to seize the moment and get married. So on a Wednesday afternoon in July during their lunch breaks (Emma is a lawyer and Michelle works in finance), they met at the New York City Clerk's Office to make it official. "We drew a line between being married and having a wedding, though," says Emma. "We considered our courthouse wedding just to be paperwork and always thought of Big Sur as the real thing."

Neither Emma nor Michelle, who met as children in Singapore, had ever been to a same-sex wedding. Planning one felt a bit like navigating uncharted territory. One thing they knew was that they wanted a small wedding on a cliff overlooking the ocean. Michelle recalled a beautiful trip she had taken to Big Sur, and the next thing they knew, they had found a San Francisco–based planner (Shannon Leahy) and an exquisite midcentury venue perched on the edge of the Pacific.

Their wedding the following spring was a balance of nontraditional and traditional elements—they spent the night before the wedding together but got ready separately with their bridal parties (Emma kept her gown a secret from Michelle); they both walked down the aisle separately and without an escort, but during the ceremony they incorporated the old Irish custom of hand-tying; the only speeches were made by Emma and Michelle themselves, but they did elect to do a first dance, to "The Moon Song" by Karen O, from the movie *Her*.

As fate would have it, Michelle's best friend (who was their officiant) realized that the date of their wedding was the ten-year anniversary of the legalization of same-sex marriage in Massachusetts, the first state to pass the law. "Many of our guests came from Singapore, and there is no gay marriage there, so it was a big deal," says Michelle. After the wedding, they stayed at the property for a few extra nights to let it all sink in.

JUST LIKE HOME // Under the open frame
tent with grass underfoot, warm wood details like
hexagonal pendant lights mixed with industrial
accents like the Tolix Marais A café chairs (the couple
has the same chairs in their dining room in New York).
Square tables were covered with cream linens, while
long rectangular tables featured gray runners.

ABOVE, LEFT:

KEEPING A LOW PROFILE // In keeping with the day's clean, modern visage, white rose petals were neatly scattered on either side of the aisle. Low decorative spheres from Elan Event Rentals flanked the entrance of the aisle. The benches were from Bright Events Rentals in San Francisco, and the altar was purposefully left bare, keeping the focus on Emma and Michelle and the dramatic seascape.

ABOVE, RIGHT:

A FULL PLATE // The long rectangular tables were 30 inches wide, so the centerpieces needed to have a small footprint. To make the bouquet-inspired arrangements, florist Atelier Joya tied bundles of hydrangea and peonies with raffia. The clear glass votives were also encircled with raffia ribbons. For dinner, the couple served a decadent three-course plated meal, and each course was paired with a different California wine.

OPPOSITE, CLOCKWISE FROM TOP:

THE OUTDOOR LIVING ROOM // Emma and Michelle had recently renovated their apartment, and they sent their planner, Shannon Leahy, a picture of their living room to inspire the wedding decor. A color palette of soft jade, white, and gray emerged. The natural woven couch was sourced from Elan

Event Rentals, and the sea-green votives were from Glassybaby in San Francisco.

FASHIONED TOGETHER // Both Michelle and Emma created custom looks for the wedding. Michelle worked with tailor Martin Greenfield in Brooklyn to design a shawl-collar tuxedo. "It was hard to find a good tailor who would make a men's-style suit for a woman," she says. Pattern maker Atelier Nicolas Caito in Manhattan created a custom gown for Emma that was feminine but not overly bridal. The silhouette was inspired by one of her favorite lace tops.

WRITTEN IN THE STARS // The couple created a welcome package for each guest room that contained local foods (cheese, nuts, and tapenade), the weekend itinerary, and a star finder. Emma came across the star finder idea on Pinterest and asked their stationer, Yonder Design, to customize one for them (Yonder even named a constellation after the couple). "You don't see the stars like you do in Big Sur anywhere else. People actually used it," says Michelle.

FOLLOWING PAGE:

CLIFFSIDE COCKTAILS // Woven rattan peacock chairs and stools were arranged beneath ancient Monterey cypress trees during the sunset cocktail hour. The escort table in the foreground featured heavy cement vases with sturdy almond branches (name cards were weighed down with pieces of sea glass).

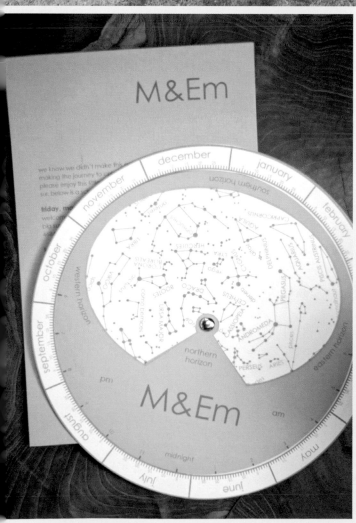

M&Em

we know we didn't make the
making the journey to
please enjoy the
sur, below is a

friday, m
wek
bla

december

january

november

february

southern horizon

october

western horizon

HERCULES

PEGASUS

ANDROMEDA

PERSEUS ARIES

september

northern
horizon

eastern horizon

pm

am

august

M&Em

july

june

may

midnight

THE REGISTRY

Here's a look at some of the items that topped Emma and Michelle's wish list.

**KITCHENAID PRO LINE
STAND MIXER**

AVAILABLE FROM
Williams-Sonoma.com

LUE BRASS SERVING SPOON

AVAILABLE FROM
HeathCeramics.com

**HEATH CERAMICS
CLOUDVIEW DINNER SET**

AVAILABLE FROM
HeathCeramics.com

DOMA FLATWARE

AVAILABLE FROM
WestElm.com

**WILLIAMS SONOMA PROFES-
SIONAL COPPER 10-PIECE
COOKWARE SET**

AVAILABLE FROM
Williams-Sonoma.com

**NESPRESSO CITIZ ESPRESSO
MAKER WITH AEROCCINO**

AVAILABLE FROM
Nespresso.com

**GLOBAL CLASSIC 10-PIECE
WOOD BLOCK SET**

AVAILABLE FROM
Williams-Sonoma.com

FRETTE BATH TOWELS

AVAILABLE FROM
Frette.com

**DYSON PURE HOT+COOL
LINK AIR PURIFIER**

AVAILABLE FROM
Dyson.com

6 THE PARTY

An unforgettable reception doesn't need to have a lot of bells and whistles. Unlike your tablescape, where every little detail matters, small elements at the reception tend to get lost in dim lighting. Instead, focus on the big-picture elements—music (whether you are hiring a ten-piece band or plugging in an iPod), a thoughtfully designed floor plan, and a stocked bar should be the foundation. After the essentials are in place, turn to nondancing activities for your guests (such as bonfires, fireworks, and live entertainment), lighting, and creating seating areas for reprieve.

LOCATION

The majority of couples utilize one space for both dinner and dancing. Using this kind of all-in-one setup is almost always more cost effective than hosting your event in two separate spaces, but having a second location (whether it's a tent or a different area of the property) for dancing provides a natural transition between events and a change of scenery after a long meal. Wherever you hold the after-dinner reception, be sure to ask if your venue has restrictions with regard to curfew and/or noise; at a certain time, they may require that you move the party inside or to a separate location altogether.

The ground usually doesn't have to be perfectly flat to erect a tent, but this uneven clearing sloped considerably toward the ocean, requiring a custom platform to level the surface. The sides of the oval Sperry tent were left open so guests could take in the view.

TENTS

Tents have become a hallmark of the wedding industry and allow couples to host their reception almost anywhere. Enclosing a space instantly makes a party feel more intimate and cozy; it's also a must for outdoor receptions if you are getting married somewhere with unpredictable weather. The rental company you work with will be able to calculate the size and number of tents you need (the general rule of thumb is 15 to 20 square feet per person, plus room for the dance floor, stage, bar, and lounge areas). Have your guest count and a floor plan (see page 274) in mind before meeting with them so you can get an accurate idea of cost. There are three kinds of tent styles to choose from.

1 Frame Tents: These are the most expensive, but they work on any surface and are better in tight spaces (and can even be modulated to make different shapes, like an "L" around a corner, if needed).

2 Pole Tents (or Sperry Sailcloth Tents): Set up in the same way as a circus tent, these are incredibly gracious, but they need to be staked to the ground and require more space than a frame tent.

3 Canopy Tents: The simplest option, canopy tents are smaller and can be joined together to create more coverage—note that most need to be staked to the ground, and they protect guests only from mild weather, since they are usually open on the sides.

Once you've chosen your tent(s), you'll need to decide whether you prefer the look of grass underfoot or would like to add flooring or carpeting. If you opt for the latter, which is very costly, subflooring will need to be added to level the floor and protect it from water that might seep up from the ground and make it damp. Construction of a large tent might also require a building permit (and sometimes even the need for a crane)—a good rental company will be able to handle all the permitting issues. A more formal tent will closely mimic a true indoor setting, with flooring (and subflooring), chandeliers, liners to conceal poles and the ceiling, and even artwork hung on the walls. A less formal tent might have grass underfoot, exposed ceilings and poles, and easy access to the outdoors. Whichever style of tent you go with, find ways to personalize it. Here are some additional things you'll need to consider.

Walls: Choices include solid, clear, cathedral (windows), fabric, or open (no walls).

Climate Control: Will you need to add heat lamps, fans, or air-conditioning?

Flooring: Is the existing groundcover (whether grass or hardscaping) sufficient, or will you need to add a dance floor and/or flooring to cover the whole area (see page 274)?

Liners: If you don't like the look of exposed framework inside the tent, consider concealing it with a draped fabric liner (but be warned that liners can often be more expensive than the tent itself).

Lighting: From chandeliers and pendants to twinkle string lights and wash lights, the options abound. See page 276 for a full review of the many ways to illuminate your space.

BRINGING THE OUTDOORS IN

Decorating the inside of a large reception space usually calls for big arrangements that everyone can see. Floral installations and strategically placed trees and plants will not only make the room feel more natural but can also help delineate spaces for dancing and lounging.

VINE-WRAPPED POLES

Many vine varieties are hardy enough to be out of water for a good amount of time. Add flowers for a fuller look—consider long-lasting varieties such as chrysanthemums, dahlias, and spray roses, or concealing delicate stems in flower tubes.

TREES AND POTTED PLANTS

Bringing in trees and potted plants is a cost-effective way to define different areas in a large space. They're also more eco-friendly than large floral arrangements because they can be rented from companies such as the Plant Library (see page 348) or purchased and replanted after the wedding.

VERDANT CHANDELIERS

Covering a chandelier in a swath of greenery is a great way to adorn an otherwise ordinary light fixture while saving space on the floor below.

INSTALLATIONS

Hovering above a dance floor, a large-scale green or floral installation adds an artistic wow factor. Keep the rest of the reception decor minimal to let this be the statement piece.

FLOOR PLAN

Mapping out where to place your reception tables, bar(s), dance floor, stage, and lounge areas will determine the flow of your party. If you are getting married at a venue that hosts a lot of receptions, the in-house team will be able to offer good suggestions of where to place things. If not, you'll need to work closely with your vendors to strategize the best layout (there are also quite a few websites, such as WeddingWire.com and AllSeated.com, that can help you determine the best way to configure these different elements).

The layout will be contingent on whether you will have one space for dinner and dancing or if you are utilizing two separate spaces. If you are using one space for both dinner and dancing, it's important to try to create a visual transition between the two events. Do this by clearing all of the dinner plates, turning down the lights, refreshing some of the spent candles, setting up some reception activities, and possibly incorporating some new furniture pieces (cocktail tables, couches, etc.). If the spaces are separate, the post-dinner reception area should ideally be within walking distance of the dinner setup.

THE DANCE FLOOR AND STAGE

The purposes of a dance floor are to protect the floor or grass beneath it, prevent people from tripping or slipping, and delineate a central space for dancing. If you are working with one shared space for dinner and dancing, the most common arrangement is to place the dance floor in the center with the dinner tables surrounding it in a U-shape, or to place it at the end of a rectangular room. The stage should always be next to the dance floor and should be placed against a wall or other natural end point. Ideally, the dance floor and the stage would be placed across from an exit (you don't want to see people leaving while you are dancing, plus it prevents congestion). As a general rule of thumb, when determining the size of your dance floor, allot 4 to 5 square feet per person, depending on the crowd. You should be able to source wood (either slabs or parquet), laminate, and acrylic tiles (usually used over a swimming

Above a glossy white dance floor, hanging phalaenopsis orchids and greenery dangled amid spherical pendant and twinkle lights designed to resemble the night sky, while bushy pampas grass hedges framed the stage.

pool) from a party rental company. If you want something more unique, you can source tiles and commission a flooring specialist to build a custom dance floor (and you can always use the tiles afterward).

On the other hand, some people don't love the look of a dance floor, claiming that it breaks up the continuity of the space and feels like a stage. If you don't expect people to be doing a lot of ballroom-style dancing and/or your reception is on some type of existing hardscape, you might not need to build an additional dance floor. It's also worth pointing out that not every reception needs to center around dancing, so you can forgo the dance floor altogether if you'd rather have a lounge-type environment where people can sit and socialize.

THE BAR

You should have one bar for every hundred guests. If you need to have two bar setups (it's always best to round up if you have more than a hundred people), you may want to place one closer to the dance floor and one farther away to avoid congestion. If you have only one, place it somewhere in between the dance floor and the seating area. A round bar placed in the midst of the dance floor is also a great way to keep the dance floor full—just make sure it is large enough to accommodate everything. Another good rule of thumb: place the bar away from the catering entrance and the bathrooms. For more information about bar structures, see page 241.

LOUNGE AREAS

Depending on the size of your party, you may want to provide cocktail tables and/or lounge seating around the perimeter of the dance floor (in addition to cocktail tables and/or lounge seating farther away from the action). This way, your guests can watch the dancing and have a place to rest their drinks.

For those who want to sit down and relax with a cocktail and a piece of cake and have a conversation, lounge areas farther away from the dance floor should feel like a comfortable living space with sofas, rugs, stools, end tables, coffee tables, etc. More whimsical structures like teepees and parked Airstream trailers add to the fun. As with your tabletop items, you may want to purchase select decor items if you can't find them available for rent.

And, last, consider creating a separate smoking area with cocktail tables and ashtrays on the outskirts of the party.

BATHROOMS

It's not a sexy subject, but creating a pleasant bathroom experience for your guests is important. If your venue doesn't have proper facilities, lavatory trailers can be parked on-site (but ideally not visible to the rest of the party). Figure about one stall for every fifty guests and get the nicest option you can afford—this is not the place to cut corners. Add bud vases, fragrant candles, fancy hand soap, lotion, and towels (personalized napkins are a nice touch here). Also stock them with baskets of necessities: gum, tampons/panty liners, mints, Tums, blotting papers, mouthwash, aspirin, deodorant, stain-remover pens, bobby pins, hair ties, hair spray, combs, lint rollers, safety pins, and Band-Aids.

LIGHTING

Since most receptions take place at night, lighting the party is a key design challenge. The goal with reception lighting is to illuminate the good and hide the bad, using strategically placed uplights and downlights to impart a glow. You don't need to hire a lighting designer unless you have a really large, complex layout; usually your rental outfit and/or your planner will be able to help you come up with good solutions. Try to schedule a walk-through of your venue at the same time of day (and, if possible, the same time of year) that your wedding will be held to come up with a strategy. Many venues will have lighting in place, so figure out if their existing setup will work or, if not, what you might be allowed to do instead of or in addition to it.

SPOTLIGHTS

A few strategically placed uplights will illuminate the landscape, larger arrangements, walls, and architecture. Here, candles cast a warm glow on the bar while a potted palm is dramatically uplit behind.

PAPER LANTERNS

Whether in varying or uniform sizes at different heights, paper lanterns are a great downlight solution and can be sourced from rental outfits or purchased online or from design shops and party supply stores.

DISCO BALLS

A disco ball works best when the rest of the room is dark, so if you are including one, keep your other light sources limited to candles and other forms of lowlights.

CANDLES

Add as many candles as you can: votives, lanterns, luminary bags (candles in paper bags), and/or hurricane candles will all help to create flattering ambient light (see page 222 for more on candles).

BISTRO LIGHTS

Also known as twinkle or string lights, these are an easy and affordable way to downlight a reception area (they can be rented, or purchased from big-box stores); when strung from trees or poles, they instantly impart a magical quality, and they can be used with other forms of lighting.

PENDANTS AND CHANDELIERS

Incorporating light fixtures that you might find in a well-appointed living or dining room will instantly make a reception tent feel like a more permanent structure. This crystal one was placed directly under the apex of a Sperry tent. You may also adorn simple wrought-iron fixtures with greenery (see page 273).

INSIDE
THE PARTY

Before you commit to any specific furniture pieces for your reception, put on your interior designer hat and make sure all of your preliminary choices are in line with your mood board (see page 17) and consistent with the style of the venue, and that the different pieces all support the same aesthetic. The after-dinner reception is a good time to play up a certain decor theme if you are so inclined. (Note: You don't need to hit it over the head; just a few special details will convey the message.) Options range from a camp theme with a bonfire, s'mores, and red plaid blankets and pillows to something more glamorous, like a masquerade party with masks, a disco ball, and Champagne sparklers. Regardless of whether your party has a specific theme, it should generate a sense of energy and be a place where you can finally let loose. In the following pages, you will see four different styles of receptions, each of which perfectly complements its unique setting, be it a polished indoor barn reception (page 284) or an alfresco affair in the desert (page 282). Details such as lounge setups, lighting, and unexpected activities for guests all work together to create environments that are cohesive and, most important, fun.

AU NATUREL

An all-in-one sailcloth reception tent seamlessly blended with the surroundings thanks to verdant hanging installations, playful custom accessories, and an easy indoor/outdoor flow.

BAR DECOR

In keeping with the lush green elements of this reception, the double-wide outdoor bar (just a short walk from the tent) featured a verdant trellis on its façade.

THE SIGN-IN BOOK

Instead of a traditional blank sign-in book, the couple used a favorite photography book. Guests left notes for the couple directly on the images and in the negative space.

LOUNGE SEATING

An outdoor lounge—complete with sofas, armchairs, a pouf, and a coffee table—was used for both the cocktail hour and the reception.

CUSTOM ACCESSORIES

Vibrant cocktails were served with napkins featuring an illustration of the couple along with their wedding hashtag.

DANCE FLOOR

A wooden dance floor was centered under a wild
hanging installation that made the space feel fresh and
a bit untamed. The rest of the flooring under the tent
was artificial turf.

MOROCCAN MINIMALISM

A narrow courtyard setting for dinner, dancing, and merriment called for neutral, thematic decor to create a clean, uncluttered space.

LAYOUT

Accented with a few discreet floor lanterns at the corners, the dinner space seamlessly transitioned to the dance floor.

EXTRA DETAILS

A cigar bar is a wonderful touch for an outdoor reception, whether you add a box to your party cart or actually have a professional on-site to hand-roll cigars. Make sure to supply lighters, cutters, and ashtrays.

LOUNGE SEATING

A warm modern sectional sofa with side tables created a natural boundary for the reception.

ADDITIONAL ACTIVITIES

A fire pit near the party added ambient lighting and a quiet refuge for tired dancers to rest their feet. Of course, if it's a chilly night, a fire pit or an outdoor fireplace is also a great heat source.

BAR DECOR

A Moroccan lantern, a simple arrangement of hellebores, and votives visually connect the standard wooden bar with the rest of the party. The lantern served as a design statement during daylight hours and at night provided ambient lighting.

A REFINED BARN DANCE

A cavernous barn was compartmentalized into different areas for dancing and lounging with a warm design treatment befitting the rustic setting.

LOUNGE SEATING
Brown leather tufted chesterfield sofas and ottomans created an inviting respite in front of the dance floor.

BAR DECOR

On the bar, a leggy arrangement of red and pink flowers was anchored by a few rosy pomegranates. A large-scale arrangement like this (either uplit or downlit to add drama) works better than something small that might get overlooked.

EXTERIOR

Outside the reception space, a pathway dotted with candles in hurricanes and greenery and twinkle lights above lent a dramatic touch.

COCKTAIL TABLES

As an alternative to lounge seating, a few strategically placed high-tops near the dance floor allowed people to take a break and rest but still be close to the action. The tables also made the large space appear fuller.

ADDITIONAL ACTIVITIES

This couple (who are both in the art world) commissioned performance artists the Bumbys to attend the reception. They used an analog typewriter to make personalized narratives that playfully described each guest's appearance.

OCEANFRONT ELEGANCE

An elevated structure next to the dining tent was custom-built for dancing and featured sheer pinstriped panels instead of solid walls to allow guests to enjoy the incredible surroundings.

A NATURAL SETTING

Just a few steps from the dining tent below, the party space was filled with muted, natural décor in a palette of cream and beige. The overhead lanterns gently swayed in the breeze and added a visual focal point.

BAR DECOR

The indoor and outdoor bars (as well as the DJ stand, inside the structure) were constructed out of a light beechwood in a custom herringbone pattern.

EXTERIOR

Potted palms wrapped in burlap concealed the base of the structure and were sturdy enough to withstand strong sea winds.

LOUNGE SEATING

In the corner of a seating vignette that featured a wooden coffee table and captain chairs, these elegant linen-covered benches adorned with pillows provided ample seating for guests to relax beside the dancing.

EXTRA DETAILS

The cocktail menu featured two favorite tropical libations: a classic daiquiri and a skinny margarita. The drink menu was placed in a simple white frame atop the bar and surrounded by ivory candles in hurricane vessels.

MUSIC

The much-debated question: Band, DJ, or iPod? If money is no object, having a band *and* a DJ is the best scenario (the DJ can play while the band takes breaks and after their last set). But in most cases, your budget will require choosing one or the other, as a full band is an extremely high-ticket item (in major cities, it can easily cost north of ten grand). With either a band or a DJ, you'll want to create a "do not play" list and a "must-play" list. Some bands and DJs will also act as emcees for the evening, so be sure you like their "on-air" personality. The safest thing to do is restrict their airtime to as few introductions and announcements as possible (if any!). Whether you end up with a band or a DJ, most of the questions you need to ask at the interview stage are the same.

- Can we see a live performance or a video reel?

- How many hours of playing time are included in the contract, and what's the overage cost?

- Can you play off a predetermined song list? If so, how long does it need to be?

- Can the band learn new songs (or, in the case of the DJ, source any songs you request)? How far in advance do you need the song lists?

- Will you take specific requests from guests?

- What happens in case of emergency or if the DJ or one of the band members can't make it?

- Do you have your own sound system?

- How big a stage is needed?

- How much time do you require for setup?

- How often do you need to take breaks, and what will you play during the breaks? (This primarily applies to bands, but some DJs will take breaks, too, if it's a long set.)

- What will you wear?

- Do you have any references?

Unless you are having a very small wedding (say, fewer than fifty people) where you don't need amplification, you'll want to use a sound system with speakers and microphones. If your venue isn't equipped with one, you can rent one from a full-service rental company. For the ceremony, you may want a pin-on microphone for the officiant, or a very discreet standing mic, and for speeches, you may need a handheld mic to pass around. If you are planning on showing a slide show or video during the reception, you may also need to rent a projector. Don't forget to have a check of all the equipment done before the event begins (ask if your venue has an A/V person to help with this).

LIVE BAND

When it comes to a band, as with anything else, you generally get what you pay for. But a common misconception is that hiring a top-tier wedding band is the only way to have live music, when in fact there are lots of other options. A great wedding band will be able to authentically cover a wide range of genres, from big band, rock 'n' roll, Motown, soul, and disco to '80s and contemporary hits. But you can opt for a more niche sound (depending on your taste, this could be something like a reggae or rock band), which can be great for a couple of hours. Don't limit yourself to traditional "wedding" bands, either. If you see an act at a local club that you think would be perfect, ask if they would be interested. You can also hire a vocalist for just the protocol dances (first, father-daughter, and mother-son).

The consensus among planners is, if you can afford a fabulous band, go for it. If not, you are better off with a great DJ than an okay band, or splitting the time between a more affordable live musician and a DJ. Know that even with a top-tier band, there will be cons: besides the cost (which can include transportation and housing if you are planning a destination wedding), musicians need to take frequent breaks, and they usually play only from a predetermined song list (most bands will learn new songs only for protocol dances).

DJ

Hiring a DJ might have once been the default choice for those who were priced out of having a live band (a DJ can be a fraction of the cost of a full band), but for many couples who want to hear the original songs or value a DJ's mixing style, it's now their first choice.

THE IPOD WEDDING

Those on a tight budget may need to rely on an iPod for some or all of their music. Many couples create playlists on their iPods for the cocktail hour and after the band or DJ has finished their last set. If you are using an iPod for the entire evening, you'll need to create multiple playlists (cocktail hour, dinner, dancing, after-party, etc.). Ask a friend to change playlists when necessary and make any announcements. Calculate how long each playlist is—you don't want to run out of music or have to repeat a song—and conduct a sound check to ensure that everything is compatible. To make things even easier, some rental companies stock iPods that are preprogrammed with music, or you can download a playlist from a music app like Spotify. If you're using a phone rather than an iPod, be sure to put it in airplane mode so the music isn't interrupted with calls or texts!

TRADITIONS

As with the ceremony, traditions abound at the reception, too. Here is a rundown of some of the most popular customs.

PROTOCOL DANCES

The first dance can be a nice moment, but only if you will actually enjoy it (same with the father-daughter and mother-son dances). If you want to uphold these traditions but are nervous about dancing in front of an audience, you can invest in lessons and choreograph a routine (you can do this even if you *are* a great dancer!) or ask other people to come up and join you (since many people think it's rude to dance before the bride and groom do, have your bandleader or emcee make some kind of announcement like, "The couple would like to invite everyone to join them for the first dance"). You may also want to ask the band or DJ to play an abridged version of the songs for your protocol dances to keep them short and sweet.

RETHINKING THE FIRST DANCE

Etta James's "At Last" will always be a classic, but couples today often want something less predictable for their first dance, be it reggae or even hip-hop. Here, Nikki Pennie, one of the country's most sought-after DJs, shares her favorite first-dance songs.

- "You Are the Best Thing," Ray LaMontagne

- "Real Love," Tom Odell

- "Sunday Morning," Maroon 5

- "Cheek to Cheek," Tony Bennett

- "Come Away with Me," Norah Jones

- "Coming Home," Leon Bridges

- "Moon River," Audrey Hepburn (from *Breakfast at Tiffany's*)

- "Stand by Me," Florence + the Machine

- "By Your Side," Sade

- "This Must Be the Place," Talking Heads

THE HORA

This Jewish dance is usually done at the beginning of the reception and starts with everyone holding hands or interlocking arms and moving around in a circle to "Hava Nagila." Eventually, the bride and groom are hoisted in the air on chairs while holding on to opposite ends of a handkerchief or napkin (sometimes family members and honored friends are also hoisted in the air after the couple). While the hora is rooted in Jewish tradition, raising couples on chairs is so much fun that it's becoming more and more popular at non-Jewish weddings.

THE GARTER TOSS

Pulling this off in a tasteful way is tricky, but it can be done. Save this moment until after your parents and grandparents have headed to bed and you are just among friends. And instead of tossing the garter to just the men in attendance, consider making it a coed experience.

THE BOUQUET TOSS

Superstition holds that the person who catches the bouquet will be the next to marry. If there are a lot of young single women in attendance, it can be a sweet gesture. And, if you want to be more inclusive, it's perfectly acceptable to invite the men to join, too. Brides who want to keep their bouquet should ask their florist to create a second arrangement to toss (some will even design one that will separate into a few bouquets in the air). If you aren't doing a big send-off, this can also be a nice way to signal the end of the party.

BEYOND THE DANCE FLOOR

Wish lanterns can be released into the sky or placed in a body of water. Encourage guests to light them while making a wish for the new couple. Get biodegradable lanterns and release them in an area that does not pose a fire risk.

Adding special performances and nondancing activities will help structure and diversify a lengthy reception. The options here are endless, but pick just one or two so your reception doesn't start to feel like a carnival. Here are a few ideas for entertainment.

Performances usually take the form of a musical act. A talented friend or family member could perform a special song for the couple, or a brave groom might serenade his bride. Your location can also inspire your entertainment: steel drums in the Caribbean, an opera or violin soloist in Italy, a gospel choir in the South (these performers could appear during the cocktail and dinner hours, too). Beyond music, you may consider something more unusual, such as a dance performance or synchronized swimmers.

Videos are an inexpensive way to entertain your guests. If you opt for a photo montage of your relationship, keep it short and sweet (no more than fifteen minutes). You could also project a classic black-and-white film (muted) or a piece of video art on a wall as a backdrop.

Fireworks have become a hallmark of high-end beach weddings. While they add instant drama, they are costly (and illegal in many places).

Activities are another wonderful way to engage your guests. Lawn games like bocce and croquet (for daytime weddings); photo booths; and cigar, scotch, and tequila bar carts are foolproof crowd-pleasers. Then there are the more unexpected ideas: falcon callers, piñatas, tarot card readers, gambling tables. Turn the page for a few fun ancillary ideas for adding a bit of dimension to your party.

FUN AND GAMES

SPARKLERS

Passing out handheld sparklers during the party is a festive way to break up the reception. Make sure this is done outside and, if possible, use smokeless 36-inch-long sparklers, which will burn for three to four minutes.

PHOTO BOOTH

Guests love a photo booth with props or a Hollywood-inspired "booth" with a red carpet–like step and repeat. This setup was inspired by black-and-white Cecil Beaton portraits.

THE ALTERNATIVE SIGN-IN BOOK

Instead of setting out the traditional blank book, ask people to take a selfie with a Polaroid and attach it with a note. You can also ask your guests to offer date-night suggestions or relationship advice.

HAPPY CAMPERS

For a beach wedding or a woodsy wedding, create a fire pit surrounded with pillows or benches. Add a fireside s'mores station with long wooden skewers, chocolate bars, graham crackers, and marshmallows.

SOMETHING MYSTICAL

Chances are, not many of your guests have ever had their aura read. At this wedding, guests were invited to stop by the Radiant Human dome tent and went home with a Polaroid souvenir from the wedding.

CARICATURE DRAWINGS

Sitting for a caricature artist, like the ones you see on a touristy boardwalk or in New York's Central Park, is a fun activity for adults and kids alike.

FLORAL CROWNS

A station where guests can create their own floral crown, whether it's a self-serve bar or staffed by a florist or artisan, is a particularly lovely idea for a daytime wedding. Plus, the crowns can double as favors.

ICE LUGE

A good old-fashioned ice luge is an unexpected addition to an upscale party. Just make sure it's kept as a peripheral event (it can also be used as an ice sculpture).

THE SEND-OFF

Whether or not you did a celebratory send-off after the ceremony (see page 188), you may wish to mark your exit from the reception with something for your guests to toss, or something for them to hold, like sparklers (your coordinator should hand these out as the party is ending and request that guests move outside and form a tunnel for you and your new spouse to run through).

It's also perfectly fine not to make a big to-do about your departure. Instead of interrupting the party, try to say good night to your family and very close friends before leaving, but by no means do you need to say good-bye to everyone at the party (especially if you are going to see them the next day for brunch).

There is something incredibly romantic about being whisked off in a classic car (or boat, if you happen to get married near the water). If you can't afford to hire a driver, ask a sober friend or family member to be your chauffeur.

THE AFTER-PARTY

Depending on your venue's cutoff time, you may want to make arrangements for an after-party. This might take place at a local dive bar, on a beach, or in someone's hotel room (it's best if it's not yours so you don't have to kick everyone out if you are tired). Information about the after-party is generally not included on the invitation, so designate a friend to spread the word or include the details in the welcome package. Make sure to have plenty of alcohol and an iPod with some speakers on hand.

These little squares with the after-party details on the back were passed out by a trusted friend at the reception.

THE NEW-FASHIONED COUNTRY WEDDING

Departing from the traditional rustic Napa Valley vibe, a design-forward
couple from Los Angeles infused a modern estate
with details that reminded them of home.

Dorianne Loshitzer and Jordan Passman first met through mutual friends when they were in high school. After college, their paths crossed again when Dorianne realized that her best friend and Jordan, who now runs a custom music company called Score a Score, lived in the same apartment building—and this time, sparks flew. While Los Angeles was the backdrop for their love story, they wanted their wedding to feel like a mini vacation within driving distance of home. At the end of a long scouting trip to Napa Valley with their planner, Beth Helmstetter, they came across a glass-and-cement estate at the top of a winding road and immediately booked it for a weekend in July.

Dorianne, who is a partner at Thea Home, an interior design firm founded by her mother, approached the wedding as if she were working on a new commission, creating clean, warm, and inviting spaces that weren't overly designed or fussy. "Jordan and I grew up in L.A. and didn't want it to feel like we were pretending otherwise," says Dorianne. To get the exact look she wanted, Dorianne collaborated with multiple rental

outfits to mix and match products—at one point, she even turned to a local welder to re-create candleholders she had found on Instagram.

The menu was also a priority. Before she became a designer, Dorianne attended Le Cordon Bleu in Paris and was a chef at some of L.A.'s top restaurants. The couple opted to serve the meal (braised short ribs, corn pudding, seared cod, and quinoa risotto) family-style: Dorianne knew from her experience as a chef that food keeps better when it's served this way, and she also wanted everyone to feel like they were actually sharing a meal together.

As the sun went down over the Valley, dinner seamlessly transitioned to dancing, with Jordan and Dorianne, in a silk Monique Lhuillier gown, twirling to oldies from Stevie Wonder, the Ronettes, and Van Morrison. At one point, Jordan even took the stage to serenade his bride with a rendition of the Beatles' "When I'm Sixty-Four." "I didn't want the night to end," says Dorianne. "But the wonderful thing about Napa is that we can come back every year."

CULINARY CENTRIC // The tables and black bentwood chairs came from Circa Vintage Rentals. Dorianne wanted to make sure people didn't have to wait to eat, so there were bread baskets, fresh seasonal fruit including grapes and figs, and cheese platters waiting at the tables.

LIGHTER THAN AIR // To fulfill the bride's wish for a hanging floral element, Studio Mondine sourced dried leaf skeletons for the chuppah and tied them to lengths of fishing wire that were weighted down with smooth river stones. "The leaves quietly floated back and forth in the wind," Dorianne remembers. "It felt like heaven."

ABOVE, LEFT:

THE "CAKE" // In lieu of a traditional wedding cake, the couple asked Jordan's mother to make her famous chocolate peanut butter balls, which were styled in the shape of a cake. They also had an ice cream bar, fresh Harvey's doughnuts from San Francisco, and pies from a local bakery.

ABOVE, RIGHT:

JAPANESQUE // For the centerpieces, Dorianne wanted something different and delicate. Studio Mondine created airy ikebana-style arrangements in low ceramic vessels that were custom-made for the occasion.

OPPOSITE, TOP:

PAPER TRAIL // Dorianne drew the map of the area by hand. Her grandmother, an artist, created playful drawings for many elements of the wedding stationery, including the welcome card, which features Dorianne and Jordan on a seesaw.

OPPOSITE, BOTTOM:

VALLEY HIGHS // Each phase of the party took place on a different level of the property. The planner was confident that they wouldn't need a backup plan for inclement weather, as it is very predictable at that time of year. After the ceremony, the chairs were quickly relocated to the dining tables.

FOLLOWING PAGE:

OUT TO DRY // Dorianne's grandmother also inspired the bridal and bridesmaids' bouquets. In her home in Tel Aviv, she always has dried flowers, which Dorianne photographed and sent to Studio Mondine as a reference. In the months leading up to the wedding, her florist foraged the meadows in Northern California and areas around San Francisco for dried elements that could be incorporated into the arrangements.

dorianne & jordan

CALISTOGA
CALIFORNIA
7.15.16 to 7.17.16

welcome to calistoga

THE REGISTRY

Here's a look at some of the items that topped Dorianne and Jordan's wish list.

SHELDON CERAMICS
SILVERLAKE DINNER SET

AVAILABLE FROM
SheldonCeramics.com

ALL-CLAD GOURMET
SLOW COOKER

AVAILABLE FROM
Williams-Sonoma.com

LSA INTERNATIONAL IVALO
CONTAINER AND LID

AVAILABLE FROM
www.LSA-International.com

FARMHOUSE POTTERY
OLIVE OIL BOTTLE

AVAILABLE FROM
FarmhousePottery.com

SHELDON CERAMICS
VERMONT BERRY BOWL

AVAILABLE FROM
SheldonCeramics.com

MATCH GABRIELLA
PLACE SETTING

AVAILABLE FROM
Match1995.com

SOL&LUNA ICE BUCKET

AVAILABLE FROM
SolxLuna.com

JIA CERAMIC STEAMER SET

AVAILABLE FROM
Nordstrom.com

BOROSIL GLASS TUMBLERS

AVAILABLE FROM
Food52.com

7 GIFTING

We should think about wedding gifts not in a material sense but in terms of how they nurture our relationships: What do they symbolize and how do they strengthen our connection? People always say that it is better to give than to receive, and while that might be true, couples today find themselves on both sides of this equation. Creating a registry is something that needs to be done carefully, as is purchasing gifts for your parents, your friends, and your beloved—they don't need to be big, but they should be from the heart.

FOR YOUR GUESTS

All of the elements of your wedding, from the stationery to the food and wine to the entertainment, are essentially gifts for your guests. If you have room in your budget (without having to sacrifice on more important things, such as music, flowers, or menu options), consider more direct forms of gifts such as a welcome basket or a party favor.

A WARM WELCOME

Welcome gifts are usually designated for guests who have traveled to attend your wedding and are typically placed in the guests' hotel rooms (the hotel might charge a small fee to distribute them, or they can pass them along at the front desk when guests check in). If you'd like to give your local guests a welcome gift, you should drop it off at their home. In addition to a note thanking your guests for coming, it's a good idea to include the weekend's itinerary, along with any transportation details, in the welcome package. Beyond these paper goods, focus on assembling a few high-quality items

rather than a hodgepodge of stuff. Here are a few ideas to consider.

- Local foods like fruits, nuts, crackers, and chocolates

- Something to drink, be it fancy bottled water and lemonade, or pricier options such as full or half bottles of wine and Champagne

- Hangover remedies such as packs of Emergen-C, Alka-Seltzer, and Advil

- Unisex beauty products like sunblock, hand lotion, ChapStick, hand sanitizer, bug spray, and foot soak

- Home products for your guests to enjoy during the weekend and take with

them when they leave, such as candles, room sprays, and potpourri

- A travel guide or local magazine if you are having a destination wedding

- Flowers, greenery, and herbs (dried or fresh)

- Custom apparel and accessories to wear for the weekend, like T-shirts, sunglasses, baseball caps, and playing cards

Package the assortment in bags (whether a simple paper bag, a drawstring cloth bag, or a canvas tote), decorative storage baskets (wire, wicker, or fabric), or boxes (which can be sourced from craft stores, Etsy, and Ikea).

UPON ARRIVAL

HOMEMADE FARE

Strawberry jam (made from scratch by the groom's mother) and fresh local bread were wrapped in customized pink paper bags that also included the weekend itinerary. A basket of local produce, cheese, or another kind of preserve is a lovely idea, too.

A BASKET FOR TWO

This natural woven basket housed information about the wedding (including a custom stargazer map), two bottles of Fentimans Victorian Lemonade, a bag of pistachios, a jar of olive tapenade, crostini, cheese, and six mini bars of TCHO chocolate in packaging that featured the couple's logo.

JUST THE THING

With a small budget or timeline, choose a single standout item, such as a bottle of wine (pictured), a bundle of flowers, or a bag of candied nuts.

FASHION-FORWARD

The motto for this destination wedding was emblazoned on the front of leather and palm market bags that were filled with *Vogue Italia*, a yoga mat, candy, a baseball cap, some local olives, and a peach.

PARTY FAVORS

This should be one of the lowest-priority items on your list, but guests always love a parting gift if you have the budget and energy to provide one. Find something unisex, reflective of your union, and relatively nonperishable—for example, a jar of rosemary-infused olive oil, a pot of wild honey, or handmade soap. Or pull inspiration from the surrounding landscape: If you were married in a rose garden, what about rose water for cooking or to use as a room spray? Etsy is a great resource for sweet and inexpensive favors. (Note: These gifts may be placed atop each setting at the dining table instead of at a table at the end of the party.)

APPEAL TO THE SENSES
At this wedding, the reception was infused with the scent of the bride's favorite candle, Diptyque's "Baies." For a party favor, the couple gave away individual votives in drawstring cloth bags.

PANTRY PROVISIONS
When gifting something that's homemade, include a tag that explains what's inside, how to use it (if necessary), and an expiration date (if it's perishable). Here, small glass bottles were filled with olive oil and *herbas Mallorquinas* (herbs of Mallorca).

SOMETHING SWEET

A regional delicacy from a local baker is always well-received (think saltwater taffy on the East Coast, beignets in New Orleans, etc.). Make sure it's easy to transport—like these boxes of chocolates.

KEEP THE PARTY GOING

Offer the secret ingredient to your evening's signature cocktail, along with the recipe. You may want to keep it under 3 ounces so that your out-of-town guests can bring it home with them on a plane.

THE SOUND TRACK

If you slaved over creating the perfect playlist for your dance party, create copies for each of your guests in a CD housed in a decorative sleeve. This throwback idea is easy on the budget.

BUNDLE UP

Consider this an egalitarian spin on tossing the bouquet: place a basket of fresh or dried flowers such as these lavender bundles at the exit for everyone to take.

FOR THE BRIDE

Beyond the engagement ring, the bride typically won't receive any other gifts from the groom during the engagement period, although some lucky ones might receive another piece of jewelry to wear at the wedding. That said, many brides are gifted family heirlooms and other smaller gifts by close friends (often at the bridal shower). Typically, these items are meant to be worn or used during the wedding, whether it's a piece of antique lace, a veil, jewelry, or serving pieces. Of course, some of these gifts are intended to be passed on to the next bride in the family (making them your "something borrowed").

MONOGRAMMING 101 Monogramming something like a handkerchief or a white button-down is perhaps the easiest (and most economical) way to transform a simple gift into an instant heirloom. Many companies offer in-house monogramming services for a fee, but there are also independent monogramming and engraving outfits that can personalize almost anything (see page 349). If there isn't an embroidery specialist in your area, you may want to send your pieces in the mail to a trusted brick-and-mortar store or find an independent vendor on Etsy.

On a scalloped lace handkerchief (a gift from a bridesmaid), the bride's initials and the wedding date were inscribed in baby-blue thread. Many brides wrap a monogrammed or vintage hankie around the stems of their bouquet and use it after the wedding as a decorative item on their dressing table.

FOR THE GROOM

It's traditional for the bride to gift the groom a watch before the wedding. If it's within budget and he needs/wants one, this is a nice idea. If your man already has a timepiece or doesn't like wearing one, or if it's not feasible with all the other wedding expenses, there are plenty of other options, including cuff links, a piece of artwork, monogrammed travel accessories (suitcases, luggage tags, a Dopp kit, a passport holder, etc.), or even some sporting equipment. The most important thing is that it's something he will actually use.

SARTORIAL SELECTS

If your groom will be wearing a formal tuxedo for the wedding, consider gifting him something to finish his look (here, a set of vintage onyx and diamond studs and cuff links).

JUST FOR FUN

Find something that speaks to his unique interests, be it an out-of-print book, tickets to a special concert, or a new grill. For a wedding in the Caribbean, the bride monogrammed a fishing reel with her husband's initials.

TIME-TESTED

A luxury watch, like this Rolex Submariner, is a generous gift that will last a lifetime. If you would like him to wear it for the wedding, give it to him in advance in case he needs to adjust the fitting.

FOR THE WEDDING PARTY

Even if you don't have designated "bridesmaids" or "groomsmen," it's nice to honor your close friends with a little something on your wedding day. It's a way of thanking them for all their support and friendship over the years. Also, it symbolically acknowledges the sacrifices they have made to be a part of your wedding. Whether you give each person something unique or the same item, be sure to include a handwritten card expressing your love and appreciation.

BRIDESMAIDS

Most brides will gift their bridesmaids something to wear, whether it's a dress for the wedding or something to get ready in—or both. A small piece of jewelry (like a pair of earrings, a pinkie ring, or even a barrette) is lovely but can be pricey if you have a big group. You may want to distribute the gifts during the bachelorette party so your bridesmaids know they will be part of the wedding look and have enough time to attend to any sizing issues.

If their wedding look is already complete, nonfashion gifts are great, too—think beauty products (a DIY perfume to wear to the wedding, or a mirrored compact) or an accessory for the home. A book about friendship or one set in a place that holds special meaning to you both, inscribed with a handwritten note, is always a good idea.

GROOMSMEN

The groom usually gives his groomsmen something to wear to the wedding, too: a tie or bow tie, a fabric belt, cuff links, a pocket square, and the like. It's a gentle way of ensuring that everyone wears something to your taste. Give these items in advance (at the bachelor party, for example), or let your groomsmen know what you will be providing. Of course, there are plenty of options outside the sartorial realm, too, like books, art prints, or beautiful vintage pocketknives.

LITTLEST ATTENDANTS

Gifts for your flower girls, ring bearers, and junior bridesmaids should be age-appropriate and ideally something that has longevity. For younger children, books, handmade wooden toys that can double as a decorative object when they outgrow them, or art prints are always nice. For an older girl, consider a purse or a small piece of jewelry to wear to the wedding; for an older boy it could be a compass or a watch. A gift can also take the form of something for you to do together, such as a trip to the zoo or the movies, or lunch at their favorite restaurant. It's best to give these gifts before the wedding to get your recipients excited about their role.

WABI-SABI WEDDING PARTY GIFTS

Los Angeles–based gifting guru Simone LeBlanc curated some of her favorite ideas for bridesmaid and groomsman gifts. Whether you give one or two items or everything pictured, remember that presentation is important—a delicate cloth gift bag or a wooden birch box, for example, will make any gift instantly feel more special.

FOR HER

In a hand-washed-linen drawstring gift bag:

- A freshwater pearl cuff to wear to the wedding

- A dried floral bundle to brighten up her home

- A Lady Grey Haute Chocolate bar

- Saipua vetiver with French green clay soap

- S/L Studio masala chai tea

FOR HIM

In a reusable birchwood box:

- Hudson Baby Bourbon whiskey

- A Postalco notebook

- A Gentlemen's Hardware nail kit by Wild & Wolf

- Monarch playing cards

- A Skultuna tray

- A House of Naive porcini chocolate bar

- An air plant

- Jack Rudy Cocktail Co. aromatic bitters

- A horn-handled knife

- A Makr leather key fob

THE REGISTRY

As a general rule of thumb, gifts that you select for your registry should be things you would eventually get around to purchasing yourself, and should be in line with the spending habits of your attendees. As the wedding approaches, check the registry every few weeks to make sure enough gifts remain in a range of prices. Guests sometimes send gifts years after the wedding, so continue to check the site every few months. To see examples of the type of items to include on your wedding registry, see pages 65, 147, 195, 233, 265, and 303.

REGISTRY WEBSITES

Since registries are no longer limited to kitchen and dining items, most couples use aggregate sites (aka universal registry sites) so they can register with multiple sources. Most of these sites will also facilitate group gifts (perfect for more expensive items such as furniture pieces or artwork), charity donations, cash funds, and experiences; they also have the ability to track who gave what to streamline the thank-you-note process (see opposite). If you are including requests for cash gifts, make sure to choose a wedding website with low processing fees (ideally under 3 percent). Some sites, such as Blueprint.com and Honeyfund.com, offer the option to pay by check, which is free. Note that not every registry offers password protection—some offer no protection, while others allow users only to turn off the search engine capability. Here are some of the best aggregate sites (all of which are free to set up, allow users to pull gifts from virtually anywhere, and offer password protection for privacy).

MyRegistry.com: This straightforward platform will sync registries from individual retailers into one master list. You can also add gifts by uploading your own photo and a caption.

Blueprint.com: This site's features include the ability to add gifts by room, turn expensive gifts into group gifts, and register for cash-based gifts (with a low credit card processing fee).

Zola.com: This company has a well-edited selection of items to pull from, a thank-you manager, a low processing fee for cash gifts, and the ability to control when gifts are shipped.

A WORD OF ADVICE FOR THE ANTI-REGISTRY COUPLE
Couples often dismiss the idea of registering for gifts entirely—they might philosophically reject the concept of "asking for things" or they may be older and already have their home essentials in place. No matter how justified the reason for not doing a registry, people will still want to give you something. For their sake, consider creating a small registry with gifts in a low price range or providing the names of a few charities to which guests can make a donation in honor of your wedding or anonymously. Otherwise, you'll likely end up with a lot of stuff you don't want and, in the process, deny your loved ones the pleasure of getting you something to commemorate your union.

THANK-YOU NOTES

PARENTS AND VENDORS Beyond the de rigueur note for your beloved and wedding party, don't forget to pen a handwritten letter to your parents expressing your excitement, gratitude, and love (whether they are paying for the wedding or not). This can be given before or after the wedding (or both).

After the wedding is also a good time to send thank-you notes to the vendors who went the extra mile to ensure that your day was perfect. This may be accompanied by a small gift (for example, a gift certificate for a massage for your wedding planner), but they will be most grateful for your referral.

You can expect to receive gifts during the time just after your engagement until up to a year after your wedding (sometimes even longer). When you meet with your stationer to design your save-the-dates and invitation suite, you may also want to design a coordinating set of correspondence/thank-you cards and order extra stamps. These cards can include both of your last or first names, your new shared surname (if applicable), your initials, or a symbol that appeared on your wedding stationery. Record any off-registry gifts (assuming your registry has its own tracking system) and all thank-you notes once they have been sent in the spreadsheet with your guest list (see page 24). In most circumstances, etiquette rules say to send thank-you notes a day or two after receiving a gift, but wedding thank-yous are an exception. If the gift is received before the wedding takes place, a thank-you note is expected within two weeks. If the gift is received after the wedding, it's okay to send a thank-you within three months of receipt. Try to stay on top of them so they don't pile up, but don't bring them on your honeymoon either—even if it means they will be delayed another week or two. By the time you get back, you may have even received your photos from your photographer, and you can include a picture of your recipient from the wedding with the thank-you note. And yes, you should thank your guests for making a donation to a charity if you are notified that they did so.

SOUL MATES

With references to both of their backgrounds, a couple
starts their next chapter with a down-home celebration
in their beloved Brooklyn neighborhood.

Solange Franklin, a fashion stylist, and Brian Reed, a
radio producer, are both professional storytellers,
albeit in very different capacities. So it's not entirely
surprising that at their wedding, there were many
different narratives at work—they were inspired
by 1930s African American art and literature,
jazz, soul, the Harlem Renaissance, the groom's
Jewish background, and the historic charm of their
home in the Bedford-Stuyvesant neighborhood of
Brooklyn. "We wanted something that reflected
us and not a preordered celebration or something
cookie-cutter, which created a lot of work for us,"
says Solange.

They structured the day around a few key
elements that could be found within a ten-
block radius of their apartment. Their venue, the
Akwaaba Mansion, an 1860s Italianate villa that
has been converted into a bed-and-breakfast, is
on a quiet tree-lined street. They called on their
favorite Sunday-night take-out joint, Soul Food
Kitchen, to prepare Southern family-style dishes
that were served on long banquet tables. And they
booked singer Boncella Lewis, whom they had
heard at a jazz concert in their neighbor's parlor.

Solange tapped into her Rolodex of fashion
industry friends to help assemble her look. She
also worked with a stylist friend, Kevin Ericson,
who "side hustles" as a florist. Meanwhile, Brian
sourced elements for the vintage party cart,
including scotch, rum, and cigars.

While the months of planning were not
without the drama that comes with a hands-on,
hyperpersonal wedding, the day unfolded without
a hitch. Simultaneously as they were pronounced
husband and wife, Solange jumped over a broom
(an African American tradition) as Brian crushed a
glass with his foot (a Jewish tradition). Dinner and
dancing ensued—the music was mostly Motown
and old-school hip-hop, save for a rowdy hora
and when Brian and his a cappella group from Yale
serenaded Solange.

"In the beginning, we said, 'If there is anything
we don't like at this wedding, it's going to be our
fault because everything came from us,'" Solange
remembers. Thankfully, it was exactly the story
they intended to tell.

ABOVE, LEFT:

TALL AND SMALL // Averse to large, tightly packed centerpieces, Solange found gilded candleholders to display arrangements of red and white dahlias, ranunculus, and greenery. Not pictured are the ten different varieties of hot sauce that were placed on each table.

ABOVE, RIGHT:

WELL READ // The custom Eric Lundquist rings were carried in a carved-out copy of the book that Solange had recommended to Brian at the beginning of their relationship, *All Aunt Hagar's Children* by Edward P. Jones. As a wedding gift, Brian gave Solange a copy that had been signed by the author with well wishes for their wedding.

ABOVE, LEFT:

PAPER CHASE // After half the save-the-date postcards got "lost in the U.S. post office ether," the couple went to the post office to get each invitation (pictured) hand-canceled. "I think that's when I realized I'm type A-minus," says Solange.

ABOVE, RIGHT:

GILTY PLEASURES // Floating on a cloud of baby's breath, the three-tiered dessert from Brooklyn cake studio Nine Cakes featured hand-painted gold trim and a lavender filling.

OPPOSITE, TOP:

LUCKY CHARMS // During their courtship, Brian gave Solange a key that was eventually used to unlock a box containing her engagement ring. For the wedding, they sourced old-fashioned skeleton keys and attached them to escort cards, Solange's baby's-breath bouquet, and Brian's boutonniere. They also had an address stamp made in the shape of a key that they used on all correspondence.

OPPOSITE, BOTTOM:

ELEVATED LOW COUNTRY CUISINE // Gold-edged plates provided a formal setting for a menu of traditional Southern fare. With so many details to attend to before the wedding, the couple almost forgot about printed menus. Thankfully, Brian's best man took the initiative and had them printed at a copy shop just a few days before the wedding.

FOLLOWING PAGES, LEFT:

IN THE ABSTRACT // To bring Solange's vision for an impressionist chuppah to life, braided garlands were hung from the end of the tree branches in the Akwaaba Mansion courtyard. The effect, she says, was like standing under a weeping willow.

FOLLOWING PAGES, RIGHT:

RETRO REDUX // Solange found her Alessandra Rich dress on Net-a-Porter, and Gianvito Rossi gifted her a pair of white leather pumps. Her veil, inspired by a James Van Der Zee photo of a bride from the 1930s, was sourced from New York Vintage in Chelsea.

8 PUTTING IT ALL TOGETHER

Whether you are hiring a full-service professional or doing much of the planning yourself, there are certain things every couple must know before they get to the "I dos," like understanding the general order of what needs to get done when and calculating how much everything is really going to cost. For couples trying to balance their everyday lives with the business of wedding planning, here is the essential, step-by-step guide to managing all the logistics.

TIMELINE & BUDGET

A year, give or take, is an ideal length of time in which to put a wedding together—you can simply enjoy being engaged for a while, and still have enough time to research and make discoveries. Since people start the planning process at different stages and have different needs and timelines, edit and condense the sample timeline that follows as needed. (Refer to page 123 for a list of beauty to-dos.)

Once you are ready to begin planning, start with something small, figure out what you can outsource, and just do a little bit at a time. Your wedding budget will influence almost every other decision, so put that at the top of your priority list. It's traditional for the bride's parents to pay for the wedding and the groom's parents to pay for the rehearsal dinner, but nowadays most weddings are a group effort, with contributions from both sets of parents and the couple themselves. However you split it, the best thing to do is deposit your wedding fund into a joint account (open one if you don't have one already) so you have everything in one place. If you link this checking account to a new credit card, you can accrue points with your wedding expenses.

Allocating your wedding budget is a valuable exercise in understanding your financial compatibility. The most important thing is to have an open line of dialogue about costs so that no one feels apprehensive. Wedding budgets vary greatly, and hopefully this book has shown that a wedding can be beautiful and meaningful without costing a small fortune. Whatever you do, don't get in over your head—an over-the-top wedding is not a good reason to max out credit cards or take out loans. (That said, for all the negotiating and penny-pinching, most couples will exceed their wedding budget. To avoid last-minute out-of-pocket expenses, create an emergencies-only cushion that amounts to 5 to 10 percent of the overall budget.) See pages 332–333 for sample budget breakdowns.

QUOTES AND CONTRACTS Vendors will typically have standard pricing packages, but if you really want to work with someone and you are on a strict budget, ask what they can do within your price range and if you can receive a quote for a *range* of services and prices. When requesting a quote, whether from a planner, a florist, or a rental company, make sure it's itemized so you can edit it.

If neither you nor your future spouse is a lawyer, don't sweat it; there is no need to seek outside counsel when it comes to signing vendor contracts. Most are pretty standard and straightforward, but that doesn't mean they are unchangeable. Read the fine print and don't be shy if you want to make reasonable adjustments.

SAMPLE TIMELINE

AT LEAST 9 MONTHS BEFORE

○ Determine your budget and open a joint bank account.

○ Create a new email address if you are planning on changing your name and/or create a joint email account for all wedding correspondence.

○ Insure your engagement ring.

○ Start creating your mood board and thinking about your color story (see page 17): follow potential vendors on Instagram, look at collections online, and make Pinterest boards.

○ Make preliminary guest lists (see page 24) for the wedding and all wedding-related events.

○ Set a date (and clear it with important guests and must-have vendors).

○ Find and book the ceremony and reception locations (see pages 154 and 270).

○ Reserve room blocks at nearby hotels for guests.

○ Hire a planner (see page 334).

○ Book an officiant (see page 182).

○ Book any must-have vendors.

○ Draft and sign a prenuptial agreement (see page 338).

○ Attend your engagement party.

○ Complete any religious conversions.

6 TO 9 MONTHS BEFORE

○ Create a wedding website (see page 56).

○ Order your dress (see page 70). Note that if you are planning on buying a ready-to-wear dress, you can do so closer to the wedding date.

○ Schedule all your trials: caterer (see page 238), cake maker, hairstylist (see page 114), makeup artist (see page 118), and florist; book the people you want to work with.

○ Hire a stationer (see page 28) and start designing the wedding invitation suite (see page 29) and save-the-dates (see page 46).

○ Book entertainment (DJ/band/ceremony musicians/etc.; see page 288).

○ Register for gifts (see page 316 for registry basics, and sample registries on pages 65, 147, 195, 233, 265, and 303).

○ Book a photographer (see page 336).

○ Book or help organize other wedding events, including the rehearsal dinner and day-after brunch.

3 TO 6 MONTHS BEFORE

○ Finalize guest lists.

○ Book a videographer.

○ Mail save-the-dates.

○ Assign wedding roles (reader, usher, member of the wedding party, etc.) to friends and family and ask specific people to prepare speeches.

○ Buy wedding rings and get them engraved (see page 93).

○ Book transportation (shuttles, cars, etc.) and/or valet parking.

○ Book rentals (tents, linens, furniture, tabletop items, and lighting).

- ○ Shop for gifts and favors (see chapter 7).

- ○ Send in the application for your wedding announcement to run in the newspaper of your choice.

- ○ Plan your honeymoon (make sure your passports, visas, and vaccinations are up to date).

- ○ Order bridesmaid and flower girl dresses and ring bearer ensemble (see pages 96–100).

- ○ Buy the groom's ensemble and any accessories for the groomsmen (see pages 126–138).

- ○ Attend the bridal shower.

- ○ Get a ketubah (for Jewish weddings).

- ○ Sign off on the final proof of the invitation suite.

2 MONTHS BEFORE

- ○ Finalize your wedding look (shoes, hair accessories, clutch, coat, etc.), including a reception dress and outfits for other wedding events.

- ○ Review the guest list and give venues, caterers, etc., the final head count.

- ○ Take dance lessons.

- ○ Call all wedding vendors and confirm arrangements.

- ○ Schedule dress fittings.

- ○ Mail invitations 6 to 8 weeks before the wedding.

- ○ Finalize all day-of stationery items (menu, programs, table numbers, escort cards, etc.).

1 MONTH BEFORE

- ○ Organize the music: Choose songs for the ceremony and for protocol dances (see pages 182 and 290); make playlists (and a "do not play" list) for the cocktail hour and the reception. (You may also want to create a day-of playlist to listen to while you are getting ready with your bridesmaids.)

- ○ Check your registry every few weeks to make sure there are enough gifts available for guests to buy in a range of prices.

- ○ Order catering for the day-of lunch.

- ○ Get your marriage license.

- ○ Print or write out your vows on nice card stock.

- ○ Create a shot list with your photographer (see page 336).

- ○ Do a site visit with your photographer to scout portrait locations and setups.

- ○ Follow up with anyone who hasn't RSVP'd.

- ○ Make a seating chart (see page 205).

- ○ Attend your bachelor/bachelorette parties.

- ○ Make a list of all the things you need to bring to the wedding venue and start gathering them together. This may include your vows, marriage license, ceremony accessories, tip envelopes, menus, party favors, iPods, speakers (for getting ready), guest book and pen, framed pictures, place cards and seating cards, programs, monogrammed cocktail and bathroom napkins, matches, baskets for the bathrooms (see page 275), cigars and cigarettes, sparklers, ring boxes, the day-of bag (see page 122), and any vases, candleholders, and platters you are bringing from home.

- ○ Meet with your officiant to go over the ceremony.

- ○ Draft a schedule of events (including delivery and pickup times) and give it to your day-of planner, all your vendors, your officiant, and your wedding party.

- ○ Practice your vows and first dance (do this regularly until the wedding).

1 WEEK BEFORE

- ○ Make any last-minute adjustments to the seating chart.

- ○ Give all the things that need to be brought to the wedding venue to your planner (or whoever is responsible for putting them in place).

- ○ Assemble welcome baskets (see page 308).

2 DAYS BEFORE

- ○ Deliver welcome baskets.

- ○ Pick up rental tuxes.

1 DAY BEFORE

- ○ Rehearse the ceremony.

- ○ Pick up food and drinks to have while getting ready the following day (if you aren't having it catered).

WEDDING DAY

- ○ Steam your dress.

- ○ Clean your rings.

- ○ Be sure to eat breakfast and lunch and stay hydrated.

- ○ Review your vows one last time.

- ○ Do something to relax and calm your nerves.

AFTER THE WEDDING

- ○ Send thank-yous to guests and vendors.

- ○ Arrange for rental returns and pickups of anything left behind.

- ○ Take your wedding dress in for cleaning and preservation.

- ○ Make the wedding album and order prints from your photographer for framing.

- ○ Change your name at the Social Security office, DMV, and other places like the post office, bank, and passport office.

- ○ Send a wedding announcement card to friends and family.

- ○ Ensure that your vendors have been paid in full.

- ○ Take down your wedding website (do this a year after your wedding—guests may continue to send gifts until that time).

BUDGET BREAKDOWN BY CATEGORY

Whether you itemize every dollar you spend on your wedding or just keep track of the big-ticket items (like venue, food, and drink), it's important to understand where and how your money will be spent. It will help alleviate stress down the line and set expectations for what you can and can't afford. As the wedding date approaches, the last thing you want is to quibble about money.

Each couple will have their own priorities and unique circumstances (maybe you aren't hiring a planner, or your venue is free, or you need extra rentals, etc.), so take this breakdown with a grain of salt. Also, take into account other expenses not listed below, such as additional wedding events, travel, lawyers for your prenup negotiations, pre-wedding beauty treatments, and the honeymoon.

CATEGORY	PERCENTAGE OF TOTAL BUDGET
Reception (venue, food, alcohol, staff, and rentals)	45 to 50%
Planner	4 to 20%
Photographer/videographer	10 to 12%
Attire and beauty (bride's dress, groom's formalwear, looks for the wedding party, hair, and makeup)	9 to 12%
Entertainment/music	7 to 9%
Flowers	6 to 10%
Stationery	2 to 3%
Wedding rings	2 to 3%
Parking/transportation	2 to 3%
Welcome gifts/favors	1 to 2%
Cake (if you are not using your caterer)	1 to 2%
Miscellaneous (officiant, marriage license, permits, hotel room, etc.)	3 to 5%

TIPPING A few weeks before the wedding, assemble all the tips that will need to be distributed to your vendors. Make sure the gratuity will not be included in the bill. For vendors who own their own business, a personal gift or a card can be given in lieu of a cash tip. Of course, the amount of the tip is always subject to the quality of the job. You may want to ask a parent or someone else you trust to decide the final tip amounts at the end of the evening. Here's a guide to industry standards.

Bartenders: 10% of the total bar bill

Bathroom attendants: $1 to $2 per guest

Coat check attendants: $1 to $2 per guest

Hairstylist: 15 to 20% of the total bill

Makeup artist: 15 to 20% of the total bill

Musicians: $25 to $50 per musician

Valet: 15% of the total bill

Bus/limo drivers: 15% of the total bill

Waiters: $20 and up (each); more for the headwaiter

BUDGET BREAKDOWN IN DOLLARS AND CENTS

Sometimes it's helpful to itemize expenses in terms of dollars instead of or in addition to looking at the percentages. Here's a realistic breakdown of how a $35,000 budget might be allocated (the average wedding in the United States costs just over $30,000 and has around 150 guests).

ESTIMATED COST	ITEM/SERVICE
$10,000	Food and beverage, including staff (about $67/per person)
$4,500	Venue and rentals (this can be reduced by having the wedding on a weekday or during the off season)
$3,500	Photographer
$3,500	Flowers
$2,500	DJ
$1,500	Planner (a day-of planner might cost as little as $800, while a full-service planner might take 20 percent of the total budget; see the following page)
$2,000	The bridal look (dress, shoes, clutch, hair accessories)
$1,500	Stationery and calligrapher
$1,500	Miscellaneous (officiant, marriage license, hotel room, etc.)
$1,100	The groom's tux
$800	Valet parking
$900	Hair and makeup for the bride and bridal party
$800	Two wedding bands (assuming you've chosen basic gold bands; obviously this could be much more)
$400	Wedding cake
$500	Gifts for the wedding party, supplies for DIY favors

HIRING A PLANNER

You can almost always tell the difference between a wedding that has been executed by a professional planner and one that hasn't—transitions are flawless, details are cohesive, and there's an effortless quality to the event. The scope of a planner's role can range from full-service expert who designs and orchestrates the entire wedding to "day-of" coordinator who just handles the logistics—and everything in between. Keep in mind that planners will have their own preferred vendors whom they want to collaborate with, and chances are they will do their best work with a team they are familiar with. Here's a breakdown of costs and responsibilities to help you decide whether to hire a full-service planner or just a day-of coordinator.

FULL-SERVICE PLANNER

If you are hiring a full-service planner, they will either work off a flat rate or a commission of up to 20 percent of the wedding budget. Many of the big-name planners will only work off a percentage of the total budget, but whenever possible, you want to negotiate a flat rate, especially if you are planning to research and select many of the

vendors yourself. This is always preferable so there aren't any surprises down the line and you take away any incentive for them to up-sell. If you are considering hiring a full-service planner, make this one of the first priorities on your to-do list. Not only will they handle every detail of the wedding, but if you can afford it, they can manage the rehearsal dinner, brunch, and your honeymoon, too.

DAY-OF COORDINATOR

An alternative to hiring a full-service planner is for the couple to do all the planning and design themselves, then leave it to the day-of coordinator to execute their vision. (In addition to day-of services, many planners can customize a package to include hourly, week-of, and month-of consultation services depending on the couple's needs and budget.) A few weeks before the wedding day, the couple may meet with the day-of coordinator to review the timeline and go over details. One week prior, the coordinator will confirm final details with vendors and make sure they have all their instructions and the timeline. They usually attend the rehearsal the day prior to help choreograph the ceremony.

FULL-SERVICE PLANNER RESPONSIBILITIES	DAY-OF COORDINATOR RESPONSIBILITIES
• Help devise a wedding budget with the couple. • Find locations for all wedding-related events. • Assemble all other vendors, negotiate contracts to fit the budget, and act as the liaison between the couple and the vendors. • Design and style all aspects of the wedding, from invitations to ceremony structure. • Attend every design meeting, trial, dress fitting, etc. • Make sure legal/religious obligations are taken care of (facilitate the acquisition of the marriage license, order the ketubah, book the officiant, etc.). • Make playlists. • Field all guest correspondence: mail invitations and track RSVPs, answer guests' questions. • Create and execute a wedding day timeline. • Create a wedding website and social media hashtag. • Assist with the registry • Assemble and deliver welcome baskets. • Organize all wedding-related events, including the rehearsal dinner, brunch, and honeymoon. • Handle all day-of responsibilities (see list at right).	• Coordinate and set up day-of lunch for the wedding parties. • Steam the wedding dress. • Set up the ceremony and reception (including ceremony accessories, escort table, guest book, table numbers and menus, favors, etc.). • Make sure everyone has their personal flower arrangements (flower crowns, boutonnieres, and bouquets). • Help guests find their names and seats. • Set up the guest book, table numbers, menus, and place cards. • Facilitate the on-time arrival of vendors, show them where to set up, and make sure their work goes according to schedule. • Make sure transportation runs according to schedule. • Make sure the groom and groomsmen are on time. • Coordinate the couple's first look with the photographer. • Wrangle the wedding party and guests for photos. • Communicate with everyone in the wedding party and the couple regarding where they should be at any given time during the ceremony. • Be at the bride's beck and call (with the emergency bag in hand). • Deliver microphones to people making speeches. • Move guests between different locations. • Cue the band for different songs. • Coordinate the cake cutting. • Make sure the photographer gets everything on the shot list. • Distribute final payments and tips. • Coordinate all departure transportation. • Pick up anything that was left behind and coordinate rental break-downs and returns.

HIRING A PHOTOGRAPHER

Most photographers put their wedding portfolios on their websites, and that's where you should start (see pages 367–369 for a list of recommended photographers). Consider how they capture light, if they shoot film or digital or both, if they work in black-and-white or color, if their style is more artistic or commercial, if they offer drone photography (yes, this is a thing), if they interact with guests or blend into the background. Once you narrow down your choices to two or three photographers, contact them to find out if they are within your budget. You don't necessarily have to set up an in-person meeting before you hire them, but you should speak with them about your expectations and make sure you are compatible. An engagement shoot can double as a test run for the wedding, where you can discuss the different shoot styles and angles you prefer (it may be helpful to schedule your makeup and hair trials on this day, too). You should also speak with your photographer about their emergency plan should they not be able to come at the last minute (if your photographer isn't part of a collective or doesn't shoot with a partner who would be able to cover with an assistant, this is especially important). A typical wedding photographer will provide eight hours of shooting and, depending on the size of the wedding, may need to bring an assistant. If it's within budget, consider hiring the photographer for the rehearsal dinner and the brunch, too.

Once you find your photographer, invite them to visit your venue to scout portrait setups and assess lighting. If there are specific things or people you want captured, have a conversation with your photographer beforehand or give them a shot list to check off (but don't make it too long or your photographer might miss some of the more beautiful, off-the-cuff moments). This is especially important if your photographer is not accustomed to shooting weddings. Here are a few examples of the kinds of things that might appear on a shot list.

- Grandmother's handkerchief with wedding rings

- Front page of the newspaper on your wedding day (it's fun to look back on the headlines)

- Bride with high school friends

- Groom dancing with his goddaughter

- The dinner table after everyone has finished the meal—messy, with melted candle wax

- A few landscape pictures as the sun is setting

If your photographer shoots with a digital camera, after the wedding they will be able to send your photos in an online gallery that you can use to download images, order prints, and forward to your friends—expect the turnaround time to be at least a month. For film photography, you'll need to meet with the photographer to look at negatives and make selections. Some photographers will also be able to help you create a wedding album—ask about this before you sign the contract.

HOW TO GET THE BEST WEDDING PICTURES POSSIBLE

Here are ten pointers on what to do and what not to do when it comes to wedding photography.

1. Scout portrait setup locations with your photographers in advance to test for the best background and lighting. Natural light always makes for the best images. Choose clean, uncluttered outdoor spaces if possible. If you are getting married indoors, then try to take all or some of the portraits outside.

2. After the sun goes down, add as many candles as possible to your reception venue to create a glow.

3. Make a shot list and be sure to include a bridal portrait (many brides regret not having one).

4. Keep your still-life shots in their natural setting. For example, shoot the wedding dress in the dressing room, not dangling from a tree outside.

5. This is not a fashion shoot—this is your wedding. Instead of traditional lineups, think about more natural, relaxed portrait positions—sitting on a blanket on the ground with your bridesmaids, having a candid conversation with your husband, laughing with your mother . . . these always feel like the most authentic portraits. Above all, don't forget to smile!

6. If you are unsure if your brother's new girlfriend should be in the official family portrait, take two versions, one with family only and one with dates.

7. Ask your guests to put away their cell phones for the ceremony. It's distracting and can ruin your ceremony pictures if everyone is fiddling with their phone.

8. Ask your officiant beforehand to step out of the frame when you lean in for your first kiss. It makes for such a prettier, cleaner photo when it's just the bride and groom in this frame.

9. The only way to get truly candid photos is to capture truly candid moments, so ignore your photographers and be yourself. If they want you to smile for a photo, they will direct you.

10. Invest in actual prints, whether you create an entire album or frame just a few photos (your photographer will be able to Photoshop out any stray hairs, blemishes, or background imperfections).

MAKING IT LEGAL

The process of becoming legally married in the United States varies greatly from state to state, so check with your local government to see what rules apply. It's a two-step process that goes something like this: Make an appointment to get a marriage license at your local marriage license office or county clerk. You'll both need to appear in person and bring your IDs, and it will cost about $35. You'll fill out an application asking for information like your officiant's name, previous marriages and divorce dates, Social Security numbers, and where your parents were born. It will ask if the bride will be changing her surname, so think about this in advance (traditionally the bride replaces her middle name with her maiden name and adopts her husband's surname, but you are also allowed to hyphenate the two surnames or drop your maiden name and keep your middle name with your husband's surname; or your husband can change his name). The license will be processed while you wait. You'll bring the license to your ceremony and give it to your officiant.

After the ceremony, your officiant will sign the document (you'll also need a witness to sign it, usually a sibling or a close friend) and send it off to the office of the county clerk, recorder, or registrar. A few weeks later, you'll receive an official marriage certificate (request a few additional copies).

Destination weddings performed abroad may be honored in the United States, but the legal requirements aren't always easy, and it can be expensive. For example, you may be required to submit blood tests and an affidavit of eligibility to marry. In France, for example, one person must have been a resident of that country for a specific period of time before the marriage. In Mexico, you need to have a certified translator translate an original copy of your birth certificates. Each country has different requirements, so check with the embassy or tourist information bureau where the marriage is to be performed for more information. You'll also need to confirm that your destination wedding will be recognized in the United States. Contact the office of the attorney general of your state of residence to find out what documentation you'll need to submit. To avoid going through all this rigmarole, most couples simply choose to legally marry at home (i.e., at a courthouse) before or after having a symbolic destination wedding elsewhere.

PRENUPS If you and your partner decide you'd like a prenuptial agreement, you'll each need to hire a lawyer (this might need to be factored into your wedding budget) who will negotiate the terms of the agreement. Prenuptial agreements should be done as far in advance as possible. No matter how easy you anticipate the process will be, it usually takes longer than you think, and you don't want this encroaching on your day. If you don't think you can reach an agreement before the wedding, there is always the option of doing a postnuptial agreement, which can enforce all the same terms as a prenup.

RESOURCES

Sorting through the vast amount of content on Pinterest boards and Instagram accounts, plus the stratosphere of wedding blogs, magazines, and portfolios, can easily become a full-time job—and not an entirely enjoyable one. To help streamline your search for people and products to bring your vision to life, here's a vetted list of professionals. Some exclusively deal with weddings, while others might take on only one wedding per year. Remember that wedding vendors don't work alone—sometimes if you find just one person you'd love to work with, they will be able to help fill out the rest of your team. If you aren't able to work with these sources directly, glean ideas from their portfolios, Instagram accounts (included in their listings below), and Pinterest boards and challenge your local vendors to re-create them or be inspired by them.

BAKERIES & CONFECTIONERS

CAKE BLOOM
Sonoma, CA
cakebloom.com | @cakebloom

The ingredients that Susan Williams uses in the kitchen change with the seasons (for example, stone fruits and almonds in the summer, figs and honey in the fall), but she does have one evergreen rule: no fondant. Instead, she exclusively uses Swiss meringue buttercream.

CARISSA'S BREADS
East Hampton, NY
carissasthebakery.com | @carrisas_breads

All of Carissa Waechter's custom cakes have white or chocolate layers and a fresh, seasonal fruit filling.

Decorations are unique and hand-designed by Carissa, and they typically involve an artistic sprinkling of colorful fresh-cut fruits and flower petals.

JASMINE RAE CAKES
San Francisco, CA
jasmineraecakes.com | @jasmineraecakes

Jasmine Rae's elevated sensibility pushes the boundary between art and confection. Think sophisticated flavor combinations (jasmine flowers, matcha green tea, black sesame, and coriander) housed within highly textured, architectural forms.

LUCKYBIRD BAKERY
Brooklyn, NY
luckybirdbakes.com | @luckybirdbakes

Amy Berger Roy has perfected naked cakes (and semi-nude cakes) at her charming brick-and-mortar store in East Williamsburg. A formal tasting is $75 per couple and usually lasts thirty to forty-five minutes; delivery is available in Brooklyn and Manhattan.

MEGAN JOY CAKES
Eagle, CO
meganjoycakes.com | @meganjoycakes

Megan Joy trained at the French Pastry School in Chicago before setting up shop over 6,000 feet above sea level. Cakes begin at $1,500, and since her focus is on taste, she doesn't offer any sculpted designs, just beautifully textured (think tiers of hand frilling) and delicious cakes.

NINE CAKES BROOKLYN
Brooklyn, NY
ninecakes.com | @ninecakes

Betsy Thorleifson's cakes are renowned for their smooth, modern silhouettes with a twist. Thorleifson recommends meeting at her boutique studio three to nine months before the big day to start the collaborative design process.

PERFECT ENDINGS

Napa, CA

perfectendings.com | @perfectendingscakes

There's something to be said for the fact that chef Thomas Keller orders his birthday cakes from Sam Godfrey. The sought-after baker can do large, elaborate, themed confections as well as simple, classic buttercream desserts.

SAINTE G. CAKE COMPANY

Portland, OR, and San Francisco, CA

sainteg.com | @sainte.g

The Sainte G. website's gallery is a testament to this bakeshop's creative range, from a ready-to-order fondant cake inset with real geodes to one that's delicately hand-painted and another that's decorated with a garden of sugar dogwood blossoms and poppy appliqués.

SWEET LADY JANE

Los Angeles, CA

sweetladyjane.com | @sweetladyjanebakerycafe

For over thirty years, this establishment has been turning out high quality desserts using imported chocolate, fresh butter and cream and in-season fruits without mixes or preservatives. In addition to traditional cakes, they offer everything for the dessert table including pies, cheesecakes, cupcakes, cookies, and tarts. Delivery is available nationwide.

SWEET LAUREL

Los Angeles, CA

sweetlaurel.com | @sweetlaurelbakery

Claire Thomas and Laurel Gallucci are behind this health-conscious cakery where everything on the menu is grain-, dairy- and refined sugar–free. Delivery is available, and they can also decorate your cake with flowers upon request.

VALERIE CONFECTIONS

Los Angeles, CA

valerieconfections.com | @valerieconfctns

Valerie Gordon, a self-trained chocolatier, launched this artisan confection house along with her husband, Stan Weightman Jr., in 2004. They now offer highly customized dessert tables, à la carte dessert options, and boxed chocolates that make great favors.

CATERERS

ANNIE CAMPBELL CATERING

Los Angeles, CA

annie-campbell.com | @anniecampbell

Annie Campbell is beloved among L.A. tastemakers for her crowd-pleasing (and often health-conscious—it is California, after all) cuisine. In addition to creating truly Pinworthy crudités boards and naked cakes, her team also helps with overall planning and event styling.

BIRCH TREE CATERING

Philadelphia, PA

birchtreecatering.com | @birchtreecatering

Operating out of an old dye factory outside that's home to small businesses and artist studios, this women-owned company sources ingredients from small, local vendors (they also compost waste and opt for sustainable when possible). The team works with couples to build customized events, with day-of-coordination built into the menu price.

CLOUD CATERING AND EVENTS

Queens, NY

cloudcateringny.com | @cloudcateringny

Founder Will Keh, whose father is credited with having brought Sichuan cuisine to the Big Apple, has a squad of Michelin-trained chefs proficient in a range of culinary styles (including ventures into the gastronomic).

COMPONERE FINE CATERING

Emeryville, CA

componerefinecatering.com | @componerefinecatering

With a progressive business philosophy (employees are required to take three weeks of vacation and are served daily organic lunches from the farm in Marin that supplies many of the company's eggs, nuts, honey, and produce), this experienced team headed up by husband-and-wife duo Ethan and Tisa Mantle also offers custom cultivation for unique menu ingredients.

FRANKIES SPUNTINO GROUP

Brooklyn, NY

frankiesspuntino.com | @frankies.pm

Chefs, co-owners, and friends "the Franks" (aka Frank Castronovo and Frank Falcinelli) grew up together in

Queens before launching their culinary empire, which now includes products, books, restaurants, a coffee shop, and a top-notch catering arm.

HAMBY CATERING

Charleston, SC

hambycatering.com | @hambycatering

Serving the Southeast for nearly forty years, this family-run operation excels at lowcountry staples with a twist, such as an elegant Carolina pulled pork BBQ station, gourmet-style shrimp and grits, and truffle deviled eggs. They book weddings around eighteen months in advance and can also assist with rentals and location scouting.

HEIRLOOM LA

Los Angeles, CA

heirloomla.com | @heirloomla

Co-owner Matt Poley cut his teeth with Gino Angelini of Angelini Osteria and a Michelin-starred restaurant in Italy while co-owner Tara Maxey trained at Spago and Cake Monkey Bakery. They are known for their "lasagna cupcakes," individual portions of lasagna that are meant to be eaten with your hands.

HOSPITALITY COLLABORATIVE

Los Angeles, CA

hospitalitycollaborative.com | @hospitalitycollaborative

This umbrella corporation founded by Steven Fortunato is home to catering company Roomforty, two event spaces (the Fig House and the Harper), and Pharmacie (an elevated beverage catering company).

HUNGRY BEAR CATERING

Los Angeles, CA

hungrybearcatering.com | @hungrybearcatering

Founded by husband-and-wife team Jennie Trinh and TJ Holgado, Hungry Bear creates custom menus focused on simple, flavorful preparations of local, high-quality ingredients.

LIMELIGHT CATERING

Chicago, IL

limelightcatering.com | @limelightcatering

The first "green" caterers in the Windy City, Rita Gutekanst and Marguerite Lytle have been committed to fresh, local, and sustainable cuisine for over twenty-six years. They are also now part of the Revel Group, an agency of indie event companies based in Chicago.

LORI A. STERN

Brooklyn, NY, and Los Angeles, CA

loriastern.com | @loriastern

A personal chef, caterer, cake designer, and artist, Lori Stern excels at presentation (think abundant use of edible flowers) and can whip up everything from the appetizer cheese board to the red velvet wedding cake (made with real beets, by the way). Menus are customizable and cakes can be made vegan, gluten-free, or refined sugar–free upon request.

LRE CATERING

San Francisco, CA

lrecatering.com | @lrecatering

Founded by two pedigreed chefs, Living Room Events specializes in pretty and inventive dishes that are often served family-style. While catering is their bread and butter, they can handle everything from the flowers and decor to entertainment, staffing, and photography.

MARY GIULIANI CATERING AND EVENTS

New York, NY

marygiuliani.com | @mgcevents

Eight years after launching her boutique catering concept in 2005, Mary Giuliani started Mario by Mary, executing Italian menus and recipes designed by Mario Batali.

OLIVIER CHENG CATERING AND EVENTS

New York, NY

ocnyc.com | @oliviercghengcatering

Olivier Cheng has been in business for over fifteen years and caters events for a range of clients (including brands like Hermès) who share an appreciation for creativity and attention to detail. The events team now offers event design and production services in every capacity.

PAULA LEDUC FINE CATERING

Emeryville, CA

paulaleduc.com | @paulaleduc

The grande dame of the NorCal catering scene, Paula LeDuc has been honing her craft since 1980 and, in the process, has gotten to know the ins and outs of some of NorCal's best venues. She's so well respected that planners often use her for their own weddings.

PEARL CATERING
Portland, OR

pearlcateringpdx.com | @pearlcateringpdx

Named after the Portland's up-and-coming Pearl District, this full-service company can do fully custom off-site events or events at Urban Studio, their partner event space. They also have a food truck with a range of menu themes from tacos to Cajun, bento boxes, and burgers.

PHARMACIE
Los Angeles, CA

pharmaciela.com

Need help deciding on a signature cocktail? Or choosing a wine to pair with dinner? Talmadge Lowe, founder and "drinkist" in charge, will handle all of your wedding-day bar needs, from staffing to garnishes.

POPPY'S CATERING AND EVENTS
Brooklyn, NY

poppyscatering.com | @poppysbrooklyn

Jamie Schmones Erickson, a proud alum of City Bakery's Catering and Events team, is a go-to source for health-conscious, elevated basics that you'd want to eat every day.

SALTBOX KITCHEN
Concord, MA

saltboxkitchen.com | @saltboxfarm

Chef Ben Elliott runs this award-winning café, craft brewery, cooking school, and full-service catering company that serves seasonal dishes with ingredients like honey, vegetables, eggs, and lamb sourced from a ten-acre organic farm in Concord that once belonged to his grandparents.

TASTE CATERING AND EVENT PLANNING
Millbrae, CA

tastecatering.com | @tastecateringsf

With experience at venues such as the Legion of Honor and Bently Reserve, the team at Taste has a wedding-specific arm where designers work with couples on everything from custom menu planning and floral and tabletop design to full-service event planning.

TRÈS LA GROUP
Los Angeles, CA

tresla.com | @treslacatering

Alan Dunn's experience as the food and beverage director at the iconic Chateau Marmont Hotel prepared him to open his own business in 2003. In addition to offering full-service off-site catering, the company runs two historic event spaces (the Carondelet House in L.A. and the Ebell in Long Beach), as well as a bar program, Mama's Medicine.

TRUFFLEBERRY MARKET
Chicago, IL

truffleberrymarket.com | @truffleberrymkt

In a culinary capital like Chicago, the team at Truffleberry stands out from the crowd with a clean, modern presentation style and customized menus, whether re-creating a family recipe or taking inspiration from a trip to Paris.

URBAN PALATE
Los Angeles, CA

urbanpalate.com | @urbanpalatela

This company is frequently asked to do editorial collaborations because their work is so pretty—and unexpected. For example, instead of sliders and fries for a late-night snack, the team here might come out with a plate of chicken sausage, French toast, and maple bourbon syrup.

WHOA NELLY CATERING/LITTLE NELLY CATERING CO.
Burbank, CA

whoanellycatering.com, littlenellycatering.com | @whoanellycaters, @littlenellyla

Stephanie Bone and Elizabeth Griffiths initially met in the kitchen at A.O.C. restaurant before starting Whoa Nelly. They launched Little Nelly with weddings in mind, offering simplified package pricing ($70 per person for food and dinner service) and fixed menus. (If you want something more custom, Whoa Nelly is still your best bet.)

FLORAL DESIGNERS

ARIEL DEARIE FLOWERS

Brooklyn, NY

arieldearieflowers.com | @arieldearieflowers

Ariel Dearie's work feels like the collaboration of a seventeenth-century Dutch Old Master painter and a modern organic farmer. Her elegant compositions have graced the pages of countless editorials as well as high-fashion ads for Dior and Balenciaga.

ARIELLA CHEZAR

New York, NY

ariellaflowers.com | @ariellachezardesign

The mentor to many other distinguished florists, Ariella Chezar is a pioneer of the loose, organic movement in the industry. She's also begun farming her own flowers in a plot in the Hudson Valley.

ASRAI GARDEN

Chicago, IL

asraigarden.com | @asraigarden

Elizabeth Cronin runs her fifteen-year-old business out of a fairy-tale-like retail space that showcases her edgy, eclectic style. Full-scale weddings start at $5,000, although personal arrangements are available for pickup.

ATELIER JOYA

San Francisco, CA

atelierjoya.com | @atelierjoya

They can do a traditional white wedding, but the team at Atelier Joya loves a creative challenge; think ombré floral installations or an escort board made out of vintage window shutters. In addition to floral design, they offer planning services.

BLOOM & PLUME

Los Angeles, CA

bloomandplume.com | @bloomandplume

Maurice Harris's larger-than-life personality translates into arrangements that are full of movement—some of his centerpieces extend so far horizontally that they seem to defy gravity.

BLOSSOM + VINE FLORAL DESIGN

Washington, DC

blossomandvine.com | @sophiefelts

The Blossom and Vine team, helmed by Sophie Felts, operates out of Daphne Hill, a 1,700-square-foot barn that is also available for rent. Full-service wedding packages start at $5,000, though in-studio pickup is generally available without a minimum.

BOWS AND ARROWS

Dallas, TX

bowsandarrowsflowers.com | @bowsandarrowsflowers

In the land where bigger is better, Alicia Rico and her husband, Adam, subscribe to more whimsical, just-picked-from-the-garden-style arrangements.

BRRCH

Brooklyn, NY

brrch.com | @brrch_floral

Though Brittany Asch was raised in the Hudson Valley and her studio is now in Brooklyn, her arrangements of exotic, rainbow-hued flora often conjure an otherworldly place. She's also the on-call florist for fashion brands like Mansur Gavriel.

CHARLOTTE AND DAUGHTERS

Oakland, CA

charlotteanddaughters.com | @charlotte_and_daughters

Charlotte Cox's passion for flowers began in her grandmother's English garden. Today her style has evolved to reflect the laid-back, rustic spirit of California, where everything from wildflowers, vines, grasses, branches, and colorful Dutch Master–like blooms are all part of the harmonious mix.

CHERRIES FLOWERS

San Francisco, CA

cherriesflowers.com | @cherriesflowers

Specializing in custom builds (escort tables, chuppahs, bars, floral ceilings), Cherries has also published a black book of all of their favorite vendors to work with on their website.

CHICKADEE HILL FLOWERS

Bar Harbor, ME

chickadeehillflowers.com | @chickadeehillflowers

Operating as both a design studio and a sustainable flower farm on Mount Desert Island, Chickadee Hill Flowers is known for its super-romantic, wild arrangements that are 100 percent seasonal.

CORNELL FLORIST

Chicago, IL

cornellflorist.com | @cornellflorist

Part floral studio and part retail shop (offering an incredibly elevated assortment of accessories, including Cécile Daladier raku vases), Cornell's museum-worthy portfolio ranges from sculptural, ikebana-style arrangements to dense asymmetrical centerpieces.

EMILY THOMPSON FLOWERS

New York, NY

emilythompsonflowers.com | @emilythompsonflowers

With an MFA in sculpture from UCLA, Emily Thompson makes use of unexpected flowers, seed pods, branches, and undergrowth to "achieve design that creates desire for the obscure and love for the hard-to-love."

EOTHEN FLORAL

Santa Cruz, CA

eothenfloral.com | @eothen_

Eothen is Greek for "from the East," which is fitting since Katie Chirgotis grew up on a small organic farm in Virginia before moving to California and studying under the team at Studio Choo. "Big energies, loud music, holding ritual and seeing the signs" all inspire her sculptural, nature-inspired work.

FARMHAND FLOWERS

Hudson, NY

farmhandflowers.com | @farmhandflowers

On eleven bucolic acres in the foothills of the northern Catskills, Sarah Monteiro cultivates flowers for cut arrangements without the use of chemicals or pesticides, then styles them in the most natural, organic compositions.

FIELDWORK FLOWERS

Portland, OR

fieldworkflowers.com | @fieldworkflowers

Modern oversized terrariums, woolly eucalyptus garlands, and a moody bouquet of bearded iris . . . the team at Fieldwork takes a design-forward approach to everything they do. Check out their nursery, the Magic Garden, to see choices, and to pick up some potted honey for your welcome baskets.

FLORET FLOWERS

Mount Vernon, WA

floretflowers.com | @floretflower

With a background in landscape design, Erin Benzakein grew her floral business literally out of her own backyard. Today she is a leader in the farmer-florist movement whom many call on for her heirloom seeds.

FLOWER GIRL

New York, NY

flowergirlnyc.com | @flowergirlnyc

Step inside Denise Porcaro's store on the Lower East Side (or the shop-in-shop within Marché Maman) and you are immediately charmed by the buckets of farm-fresh-cut flowers and branches, unusual vases, and exclusive candles.

FÔRET DESIGN STUDIO

Somerville, MA

foretdesignstudio.com | @ladies_of_foret

This "seed-to-table" floral and event styling company was founded by best friends Rose Mattos and Erin Heath, who previously created visual displays for Anthropologie. Their unique and inspired arrangements utilize everything from seasonal flowers and fruit-filled branches to foraged berries and acorns.

FOX FODDER FARM

New York, NY

foxfodderfarm.com | @foxfodderfarm

Taylor Patterson was trained as a painter (Dutch landscape designer Piet Oudolf is a big source of inspiration) before getting into floral artistry. Her company is named for her family's Delaware farm.

THE FOXGLOVE STUDIO

Chicago, IL

thefoxglovestudio.com | @thefoxglovestudio

Caitlin Kerr is a student of flowers and frequently brings up matters like sustainability and the people who inspire her (Saipua and Papel SF's paper flowers, for example). She also helped start a cut-flower farm in the city called Avium Flowers that grows unique and specialty blooms

HART FLORAL

Bend and Portland, OR

hartfloraldesign.com | @hart_floral

Hanging gardens, fragrant lilac arches, abstract dogwood backdrops . . . Madison Hartley's beautiful portfolio is also a testament to her technical skill. The floral designer, who was trained as a painter, splits her time among Oregon, Korea, and China, where she teaches floral workshops throughout the year.

HOLLYFLORA

Los Angeles, CA

hollyflora.com | @hollyflorala

Whether they have been commissioned to do a traditional all-white wedding or the most eclectic bash, Holly Vesecky and Rebecca Uchtman always infuse original, surprising little details with just the right amount of edge.

HONEY & POPPIES

Long Beach, CA

honeyandpoppies.com | @megan_gray

Since 2009, Megan Gray's studio has almost exclusively focused on weddings, curating whimsical designs for discerning hipsters across California—think kumquat boutonnieres, foxtail fern bouquets, and a tropical bouquet of palm leaves, jasmine, anthurium, and cut-open fruit.

HONEY OF A THOUSAND FLOWERS

Salt Lake City, UT

sarahwinward.com | @sarah_winward

Sarah Winward is a modern visionary in the floral industry. Unexpected ceremony structures, sculptural hanging arrangements, and compositions all feel fresh, classically beautiful, and never too loud.

INTERTWINE

Chesterton, IN

kellylenard.com | @kellylenard

Kelly Lenárd is a destination floral designer who travels across the country (from Big Sur to North Carolina) for weddings big and small. No matter where she is, her sophisticated, European style and clean palette always feel just right.

ISA ISA FLOWERS

Los Angeles, CA

isafloral.com | @isaisafloral

This chic, high-concept studio founded by Sophia Moreno-Bunge was born out of her desire to bring "weird and wonderful inspiration into our daily lives." Rest assured, your weddingscape will be unique.

JACKSON DURHAM EVENTS

Atlanta, GA, and Dallas, TX

jacksondurham.com | @jacksondurhamevents

Founders Heath Alan Ray and Charles Vance have expanded their full-service event planning company with a focus on lush floral design from its original location in Atlanta to Dallas. Think ginger jar centerpieces packed with colorful roses and banisters and entrances clad in magnolia garlands.

JENN SANCHEZ

Los Angeles, CA

jennchez.com | @jennsanchezdesign

Drawn by the tangible, multidimensional qualities of floristry, Jenn Sanchez traded in her paintbrushes to work with flowers when she was a teenager. She specializes in romantic installations and has a sizeable inventory of vases, linens, and candles/lighting available to purchase or rent.

KATHLEEN DEERY DESIGN

San Francisco, CA

kathleendeerydesign.com | @kathleendeerydesign

Kathleen Deery is a legend in the S.F. wedding world. Her style tends to be polished over wild, but she does prim and pretty in a way that feels natural and never too heavy-handed.

LAMBERT FLORAL STUDIO

San Francisco, CA

lambertfloralstudio.com | @lambertfloralstudio

Founder and artistic director Sammy Go graduated from UC Berkeley with a degree in landscape architecture. His artistic pieces "breathe and flow, honor the changing seasons, and carry the richly romantic spirit of the natural world."

LILY LODGE

Los Angeles, CA

lilylodge.com | @lilylodge

Ariana Lambert Smeraldo is known for styling hard-to-find, pesticide-free stems that you definitely can't source at a grocery store (parrot tulips, French lilacs, and Dutch hydrangeas, to name a few).

LOUESA ROEBUCK

Ojai, CA

louesaroebuck.com | @louesaroebuck

Louesa Roebuck is a true floral artist who has (literally) written the book on honest, high-integrity "arrangements" with *Foraged Flora*. Her unconventional style is the result of a slow, instinctual process that fundamentally rejects engaging with agribusiness or any kind of flower farm.

LOVE 'N FRESH FLOWERS

Philadelphia, PA

lovenfreshflowers.com | @lovenfreshflowers

Jennie Love, a trained professional horticulturist and an experienced, lifelong farmer, runs this sustainable, urban flower farm, creating superfresh textural arrangements from its own bounty and from other local growers.

MAX GILL DESIGN

Berkeley, CA

maxgilldesign.com | @maxgilldesign

Max Gill has been the floral designer at Chez Panisse for over a decade. His work is distinguished by his use of specialty blooms and rare flowers that he sources from local growers and his own backyard cutting garden.

MCKENZIE POWELL DESIGNS

Seattle, WA

mckenziepowell.com | @mckenzie_powell

Beyond traditional centerpieces, McKenzie Powell encourages couples to use "an approach that considers the entire table, the entire environment." To that end, she also helps with decor, whether it be swag-adorned banisters or candle-filled mantels.

METAFLORA

New York, NY

metafloranyc.com | @metafloranyc

Marisa Competello has the design world's attention with the museumworthy abstract arrangements (think painted palm leaves, ostrich feathers, and anthurium) she creates in her Chinatown studio.

MINDY RICE DESIGN

Los Olivos, CA

mindyrice.com | @mindyricedesign

Mindy Rice might be the busiest florist on the West Coast, and for good reason. Since opening her business in 1993, she's worked with all the best vendors and venues and always overdelivers—and twenty-five years later, she's as creative as ever.

MOON CANYON

Los Angeles, CA

mooncanyondesign.com | @mooncanyon

Working out of her Silver Lake studio, Kristen Caissie considers herself a storyteller of seasons. Whether it's a delicate ikebana centerpiece or an aisle filled with stalks of pampas grass, her style embodies the West Coast's fine casual sensibility.

MOONFLOWER DESIGN

Athens, GA

moonflowerdesign.com | @moonflower_design

Moonflower Design is the floral studio of 3 Porch Farm, Mandy and Steve O'Shea's entirely solar- and water-vegetable-oil-powered farm, where they grow cut flowers and organic fruits and mushrooms.

NICOLETTE CAMILLE FLORAL DESIGN

Brooklyn, NY

nicolettecamille.com | @nicamille

Nicolette Owen has an incredible eye for space and composition, consistently delivering romantic, perfectly imperfect designs that celebrate the essence of each stem.

PARK FLORAL DESIGN

Denver, CO

parkfloraldesign.com | @parkfloraldesign

Ashley Swapp loves working with feminine, soft colors, whether creating a series of adorable ikebana-style arrangements for an installation wall or traditional centerpieces.

PEARTREE FLOWERS

Brooklyn, NY

puravidapeartree.com | @peartreeflowers

From a wedding tent turned into a smilax dreamworld to the daintiest flower frog arrangements, Liza Lubell's poetic work is marked by the occasional tropical streak (once a year she decamps to the jungle in Costa Rica to lead a creativity workshop).

THE PLANT LIBRARY

Berkeley, CA

theplantlibrary.com | @theplantlibrary

As the name suggests, the Plant Library allows you to rent, enjoy, and simply return the plants after your big day. Choose from a range of sizes, varieties, vases (terra-cotta, white, stone), and toppings (moss, limestones, lava rocks). They also do custom work.

PUTNAM & PUTNAM

New York, NY

putnamflowers.com | @putnamflowers

One of the most buzzed-about florists in the city (with over 270K followers on Instagram), husband duo Darroch and Michael Putnam deftly mix wild and formal, with a preternatural knack for elaborate, large-scale installations.

REPEAT ROSES

Available nationwide

repeatroses.com | @repeatroses

This company repurposes wedding displays into bedside bouquets for those in hospices and cancer treatment facilities and victims of homelessness and domestic abuse at local shelters. After the bouquets have wilted, the company collects them and locally composts them so that they don't end up in a landfill and contribute to greenhouse gases. Service fees begin at $1,500.

ROSEGOLDEN

Birmingham, AL

rosegolden.com | @hollymcarlisle

Holly Carlisle, who has a fine art background, conjures the romance of the Deep South from a modern perspective—think foraged boutonnieres and the most exquisite doorframes and banisters.

SAIPUA

Brooklyn, NY

saipua.com | @saipua

Along with her partner, Eric Famisan, Sarah Ryhanen, a visionary of the natural arrangements movement, has helped cultivate a generation of new floral artists through her awe-inspiring work, which often incorporates rare blooms culled from her upstate flower farm.

SOIL AND STEM

Salt Lake City, UT

soilandstem.com | @soilandstem

Nicole Land is a leading member of Salt Lake City's cadre of inspiring wedding vendors. As evidenced on her well-archived website, she offers a wide range of beautiful work, from artsy editorials to natural weddingscapes of indigenous ingredients.

STEEL CUT FLOWER CO.

Baltimore, MD

steelcutflowerco.com | @steelcutflowerco

Sourcing blooms from local farms to overgrown alleys around the city, Mary Ellen and Matt LaFreniere launched this boutique floral company in 2016 with a shared love for "garden roses and velvet, patina on copper, and late afternoon light." Don't expect any boring arrangements here.

STUDIO CHOO

Middletown, RI, and Novato, CA

studiochoo.com | @studiochoo, @studiochooeast

Best friends, business partners, and creative collaborators Jill Rizzo and Alethea Harampolis refer to their wild and lush arrangements as a "garden in a vase."

STUDIO MONDINE

San Francisco, CA

studiomondine.com | @studiomondine

Amanda Luu and Ivanka Matsuba's design practice is largely inspired by Japanese principles. Flowers grown in their studio's cutting garden or foraged from the side of the road are artfully arranged and possess a quiet, graceful beauty.

SULLIVAN OWEN

Philadelphia, PA

sullivanowen.com | @sullivan_owen

Sullivan Owen's own wedding was the catalyst she needed to get into the flower biz. Today, operating out of a tony studio in the Fishtown neighborhood, she delights clients with her sense of playfulness and use of color, or what she describes as "controlled wildness."

TINGE

Salt Lake City, UT

tingefloral.com | @tingefloral

Ashley Beyer apprenticed for Sarah Winward of Honey of a Thousand Flowers (see page 346) before setting out on her own. With dozens of weddings under her belt, she artfully transforms negative space into lush, feminine compositions.

TULIPINA

San Francisco, CA

tulipina.com | @tulipinadesign

Kiana Underwood's signature garden-style designs hearken back to classic Dutch Old Masters. You can watch the artist make things like "music-inspired centerpieces" or a fern arbor installation on one of her Vimeo series.

WATERLILY POND

San Francisco, CA

waterlilypond.com | @waterlilypond

Combining their backgrounds in engineering and architecture, husband-and-wife duo Daniel Schultz and Natasha Lisitsa are able to design and fabricate challenging, abstract hanging installations in addition to traditional centerpieces—think a cloud of baby's breath hovering over a dining table or a ceiling of effortlessly draped wisteria.

YASMINE MEI

Los Angeles, CA

yasminefloraldesign.com | @yasminemei

Yasmine Mei's retro, romantic style incorporates colorful blooms and citrus and berry branches, but her signature element is mushrooms.

MONOGRAMMING SERVICES

ETSY

etsy.com | @etsy

Not surprisingly, Etsy is home to many talented monogrammers. Most will send digital mock-ups with different font and thread combinations based on the client's selection. Favorite shops include Linen Whites, Southern Linen, and The Southern Baby.

MONOGRAMMIT

Beverly Hills, CA

monogrammitbeverlyhills.com | @monogrammitbeverlyhills

This little gem has been in business for over twenty-five years. They offer a selection of wedding gear like getting-ready robes, pajama sets, handkerchiefs, and makeup bags, but they will also monogram items purchased outside of the shop.

THE MONOGRAM SHOP

East Hampton, NY
themonogramshops.com |
@themonogramshopeasthampton

A darling shop for monogrammed wicker and lacquer trays, custom handkerchiefs, and cocktail napkins. They can also do orders over email.

SASHA NICHOLAS

Saint Louis, MO
sashanicholas.com | @sashanicholas

This company monograms virtually anything that you can find in a china cabinet: dinnerware, platters, chargers, bowls (which make for really cute bridal party gifts), Champagne buckets, etc. Use their custom design service or upload your own design (like your wedding crest).

PERFORMERS & RECEPTION ACTIVITIES

DART COLLECTIVE

Los Angeles and San Francisco, CA
dart-collective.com | @dartcollective

With the goal of offering a more customized approach to wedding music, Dart Collective is a group of supercool DJs and live musicians—including a tiki-inspired vibraphone trio, a gypsy jazz quintet, and "the funkiest" dance band.

ÉLAN ARTISTS

Nationwide
elanartists.com | @elanartists
A national talent agency with a deep bench including fire dancers, water ballerinas, and some of the best cover bands out there. They can also help you book a celebrity act.

MAGBOOTH

Available in seven cities nationwide
magbooth.com | @magbooth

A portable photo booth that comes with an attendant to help guests take an unlimited amount of crisp, clear photo favors. Currently serving Austin, TX; Chicago, IL; Los Angeles, CA; Louisville, KY; New York, NY; San Francisco, CA; and Seattle, WA.

POEM STORE

Los Angeles, CA
yoursubjectyourprice.com | @jsuskin

Jacqueline Suskin brings her old-fashioned typewriter to your event and composes personalized, improvisational poetry for guests.

RADIANT HUMAN

Portland, OR
radianthuman.com | @radianthuman_

Christina Lonsdale operates this mobile aura photography lab, setting up a dome tent where she takes Polaroid photographs of you and your aura (a fun and unusual way to keep guests entertained at the reception).

WEST COAST MUSIC

Beverly Hills, CA
westcoastmusic.com | @westcoastmusicbevhills

WCM has live videos on their website of high-caliber bands (the Midnight Special and JB Project are great for weddings) and can handle all the A/V and sound components. With a talent pool ranging from dance groups to orchestral acts, they can also book big celebrity talents like John Legend, Lionel Richie, and Bruno Mars.

PLANNERS & DESIGNERS

42° NORTH

Ipswich, MA
42northweddings.com| @42_north

A trustworthy full-service planning and design firm founded by Francie Dorman and Britt Cole, 42° North specializes in high-end weddings at private estates and nontraditional venues around New England (and farther afield). They take on only a handful of weddings every year, and each one is nearly perfect.

ALEXANDRA KOLENDRIANOS

Santa Barbara, CA
alexandrak.com | @alexandrakr

With highly personalized, one-on-one service, Alexandra Kolendrianos is just as adept at throwing a formal and traditional dinner party in a Montecito lemon grove as she is an edgy, modern fete in Palm Springs. She also has relationships with some of the most coveted vendors in the SoCal wedding market.

ALISON AND BRYAN
Santa Barbara, CA
alison-bryan.com | @alisonandbryan

After moving from Michigan and putting down roots in her native Santa Barbara, this eponymous husband-and-wife team have been planning incredibly elegant destination events around the world (sometimes traveling for months at a time) for over ten years.

ALISON EVENTS
San Francisco and Sausalito, CA
alisonevents.com | @alison_events

Alison Hotchkiss Rinderknecht and her design-savvy team take on six to eight incredibly customized weddings each year. Having planned over four hundred events in her career, she says her favorite clients are "up for doing something that's never been done."

AMY OSABA DESIGN
Atlanta, GA
amyosaba.com | @amyosabaevents

After a successful career as a ballet dancer, Amy Osaba is now one of the most sought-after event and floral designers in the South thanks to an innate sense of grace and a small but mighty team of inspiringly talented women.

BASH PLEASE
Los Angeles and San Francisco, CA
bashplease.com | @bashplease

The team at Bash Please is behind some of the most design-forward weddings on the West Coast (and some truly ingenious escort table ideas). They are a full-service creative event production company and pride themselves on forging their own path.

BETH HELMSTETTER EVENTS
Los Angeles, CA
bethhelmstetter.com | @bethhelmstetter

Couples can work with either girl boss Beth Helmstetter herself or one of the team's seasoned event producers, depending on their level of design and production demands. Helmstetter also launched the

Good Beginning, an online registry where couples can register for donations to charities in lieu of or in addition to traditional gifts.

BLUEBIRD PRODUCTIONS
Aspen, CO
bluebirdproductions.com | @bluebirdproductions

Virginia Edelson's team expertly tames the Wild Wild West with touches of glam and civility, and collaborates with top-shelf talents like florist Mindy Rice and Casa de Perrin rentals.

BROWN PAPER DESIGN
Los Angeles and San Francisco, CA
brownpaperdesign.com | @brownpaperdesign

Danielle Rowe's business began as a floral design studio, eventually evolving into a full event design company. She is based out of a by-appointment-only studio in Berkeley.

CAIT & JULES
Brooklyn, NY
caitandjules.com | @caitandjules

This up-and-coming boutique planning and design firm was started by Caitlin O'Hara and Julianne Austin, who met as event producers for the legendary planner David Monn. They have no shortage of fresh ideas for cool, fashion-forward clients—and they execute them with classic, well-developed techniques.

CALDER CLARK
Charleston, SC
calderclark.com | @calderclark

Working out of a nineteenth-century Charleston home, Calder Clark's boutique firm specializes in destination weddings. Her mantra: "Parties can be relaxed and chic without being trendy."

DAVID REINHARD
New York, NY
davidreinhard.com | @davidreinhardevents

Ann David and Nicky Reinhard started their full-service events company in 2000, and their years of experience show in the well-oiled events they produce, from complete backyard transformations to European destination fetes.

A DAY IN MAY

Traverse City, MI

adayinmayevents | @adayinmayevents

Alicia Caldecott's team brings a polished reverence to events along the shores of Lake Michigan (and beyond). She explains, "There is a difference between trying to impress someone and resonating with one's soul—we work for the latter."

DUET WEDDINGS

Los Angeles, CA

duet-weddings.com | @duetweddings

With an eye for creating festive environments, be it a colorful fiesta or an elegant European fete, this boutique firm exclusively offers full-service planning (they also share studio space with Moon Canyon—see page 347).

DUKE + VAN DEUSEN

East Hampton and New York, NY

dukevandeusen.com | @dukevandeusen

If you are planning an event in the Hamptons and want to work with a local team, Duke + Van Deusen has plenty of experience transforming country homes into magical wedding venues.

EASTON EVENTS

Charleston, SC, and Charlottesville, VA

eastonevents.com | @eastonevents

Lynn Easton's operation may be based in the South, but the team is hired for luxury events near and far. They've even designed an online portal where clients can check in on the logistical elements of their wedding, such as vendor schedules, guest lists, budgets, and task lists.

ESTERA EVENTS

Chicago, IL

esteraevents.com | @esteraevents

With Estera, couples work with a lead planner in addition to an in-house conceptual stylist to handle all the design elements. They are experienced in working with a range of venues, from country clubs and summer homes to converted manufacturing lofts and Chicago's Art Institute.

FIREFLY EVENTS

Jackson Hole, WY, Los Angeles, CA, and New York, NY

firefly-events.com | @fireflyevents

When being bicoastal simply wasn't enough, founder Teissia Treynet, who is based in New York, and Alia Wilson, who heads the L.A. office, opened their latest branch in Jackson Hole.

GATHER EVENTS

Los Angeles, CA, and Seattle, WA

gatherevents.com | @gatherevents

Since 2003, Sarah Tivel has "gathered" inspiration, experiences, and a small army of creative women in Seattle, joining forces with Maris Events to throw playful, never-too-stiff events up and down the West Coast.

GATHERIST

San Francisco, CA

gatheristco.com | @gatherist_

Emmily Jones describes her coveted aesthetic as "clean, intentional, and natural." She offers everything from hourly advice for the bride who needs just a little guidance to soup-to-nuts planning and design.

JACIN FITZGERALD

Atlanta, GA

jacinfitzgerald.com | @jacinfitzgerald

With satellite offices in New England and Napa Valley, Jacin Fitzgerald specializes in destination and private estate celebrations (floral design, which isn't included in her planning package, starts at $10K). She doesn't offer partial or day-of planning, and she takes on only four weddings per year—each one in its own way perfect.

JESSICA SLOANE

Nashville, TN

jessicasloane.com | @jessicasloane

As a creative director, event planner, florist, designer, and stylist, Jessica Sloane is something of a Renaissance woman when it comes to weddings. She has a minimalist sensibility and loves working within a textured palette of creams, grays, and olive green.

JOVE MEYER EVENTS

Brooklyn, NY

jovemeyerevents.com | @jovemeyer

Jove Meyer launched his company after planning and designing his best friend's wedding in 2008. Meyer is a passionate advocate for marriage equality, and all of his weddings are modern, laid back, and fun.

JOY PROCTOR

Santa Barbara, CA

joyproctor.com | @joyproctor

Joy Proctor's feminine sensibility plays out in romantic scenes with vintage getaway cars, ruffled gowns, and pastel tablescapes. She offers more affordable design aid through the Wedding Template, which you can access through her website.

JOY THIGPEN

Serenbe, GA

joythigpen.com | @joythigpen

The cofounder of If I Made (an online learning site for wedding professionals) and the creative director for Once Wed, Joy's philosophy is: "I've never wanted to make art to hang on walls—I want to make art people live in."

KG EVENTS & DESIGN

Martha's Vineyard, MA

kgeventsdesign.com | @kgeventsdesign

Dreaming of a quintessentially cool wedding on the Cape? Kristen Gosselin's team puts a sophisticated touch on traditional green, blush, and white weddings in the northeast (and Caribbean). Best of all, she's a certified green planner.

LAURIE ARONS SPECIAL EVENTS

San Francisco, CA

lauriearons.com | @lauriearons

If anyone can throw a perfectly polished wedding in a wild redwood forest, it's Laurie. As one of the most respected planners in the biz, Laurie has amassed a Rolodex of some of the best vendors and even hosts her own master class workshops to share her expertise.

LISA VORCE CO.

Santa Ana, CA

lisavorce.com | @lisavorce

Lisa Vorce has become the go-to planner for exquisite destination fetes that feel authentic and timeless. Vorce says planning a wedding "takes a general's strategy, a diplomat's negotiation, a concierge's direction, a confidante's comfort."

LOLI EVENTS

New York, NY, and Paris, France

lolievents.com | @lolievents

Lauren "Loli" Fremont hails from Paris and honed her hospitality skills planning events for Daniel Boulud and Thomas Keller. With her own events company, it's her goal to ensure that "every last detail strikes a balance between approachability and luxury."

LOVE THIS DAY EVENTS

Denver, CO

lovethisdayevents.com | @lovethisdayevents

The team at this boutique firm specializes in rustic elegant Colorado weddings using elements such as burlap tablecloths, barn doors, and antlers in elevated ways. They offer month-of and full-service packages.

MERRIMAN EVENTS

New York, NY

merrimanevents.com | @merriman_events

Since launching her business in 2015, Serena Merriman has thrown dozens of intimate and imaginative Manhattan nuptials and become an expert planning resource for publications including *Domino*.

MICHELLE LEO EVENTS

Sandy, UT

michelleleoevents.com | @michelleleoevents

Michelle Leo's guiding principle is that establishing a heartfelt connection with clients is the key to producing a memorable event. Her ten-person team can do everything from full-service planning to hourly consultations.

MICHELLE RAGO DESTINATIONS

New York, NY

michelleragodestinations.com | @michellerago

Michelle Rago specializes in destination weddings and deftly blends a couple's personality with the culture and history of where they are getting married, whether it's the Côte d'Azur or the Caribbean. Beyond the actual wedding weekend, team Rago can help coordinate the proposal and the honeymoon itinerary.

MODERN KICKS

Kingston, NY

modern-kicks.com | @modernkicksny

This boutique planning firm specializes in beautiful, relaxed upstate New York weddings, although they plan events in the city and the Hamptons, too. They offer several different planning packages depending on where couples are in the process.

THE NOUVEAU ROMANTICS

Austin, TX, Los Angeles, CA, and New York, NY

thenouveauromantics.com | @thenouveauromantics

A close working relationship is so important to this team's process that many of their clients turn into lifelong friends. They produce fewer than five weddings a year to give each their undivided attention.

OREN CO

Los Angeles, CA, and New York, NY

orenco.co | @orenco.co

Yifat Oren has been planning high-end events for decades, and unlike many other household names in the biz, she is personally on-site for every event to ensure that each detail is up to snuff.

RHIANNON BOSSE CELEBRATIONS

Grand Rapids, MI

rhiannonbosse.com | @rhiannonbosse

Formerly Hey Gorgeous Events, the company's recent rebrand encompasses all of founder Rhiannon Bosse's lifestyle passions, along with an archive of well-documented wedding celebrations. (Hint: She books up far in advance.)

ROSEMARY EVENTS

Los Angeles and San Francisco, CA

rosemaryevents.com | @rosemaryevents

Rosemary Hattenbach's background as a film producer helped prepare her for a career staging some of the most polished fetes across Napa Valley and Sonoma.

RYE WORKSHOP

Brooklyn, NY

ryeworkshop.com | @rye_workshop

An experiential agency producing edgy, cool, and elegantly undone events for creative companies and couples. They also have a "no monograms" policy.

SARAH PARK EVENTS & DESIGN

Los Angeles, CA

sarahparkevents.com | @sarahparkevents, @sarahparkdesigns

Before jumping into wedding world, Sarah Park got a degree in Architecture/Landscape/Interiors from Otis College of Art and Design. Couples can choose from one of three packages: partial, design and styling, or full-service planning and design. She also has a charming Etsy shop selling custom bouquet paintings (etsy.com/shop/SarahParkDesigns).

SHANNON LEAHY EVENTS

Los Angeles and San Francisco, CA

shannonleahy.com | @shannonleahyevents

Shannon Leahy's range is a testament to her truly client-centric approach. She can deftly handle everything from the perfect autumnal Napa wedding to a romantic seaside reception in Croatia, a modern gallery party to a black-tie ceremony on a riverboat.

SINCLAIR AND MOORE

San Francisco, CA, and Seattle, WA

sinclairandmoore.com | @sinclairandmoore

Steve Moore has been obsessed with weddings since he was a young boy (he baked his first wedding cake when he was twelve and made a wedding dress for his sister when he was sixteen). Now, with his wife, Jamie, he designs weddings (including florals) with a classic pared-down approach.

STEFANIE COVE AND CO.

Los Angeles, CA, and New York, NY

stefaniecove.com | @stefcoveco

Indisputably one of the best planners on the West Coast (repeat clients include GOOP and Molly Sims), Stefanie Cove has a rock-solid reputation for incorporating supremely elevated and creative ideas into approachable and fun environments—big and small, near and far.

STEFANIE MILES EVENTS

Dallas, TX

stefaniemiles.com | @stefaniemiles

Stefanie Miles's belief is that "beautiful events are more than details coming together; they are works of art coming to life." She does many destination weddings and has an impeccable eye for designing well-balanced tablescapes.

TARA GUÉRARD SOIRÉE

Charleston, SC, and New York, NY

taraguerardsoiree.com | @taraguerard

Tara Guérard's two books outline her spin on the Southern weddings—think table lamps instead of traditional candelabras, or a chinoiserie-inspired bar on Kiawah Island. She's also partnered with an eco-friendly stationery line, Lettered Olive (LetteredOlive.com).

TOAST EVENTS

Atlanta, GA, with satellite offices across the Southeast

toast-events.com | @toast_events

For over fifteen years, Lindsay Sims and her seasoned team have perfected the art of Southern hospitality with large-scale events that are packed with personality (think custom installations, monogrammed accessories, and exquisitely curated welcome bags).

TWINE EVENTS

Santa Monica, CA

twineevents.com | @twineevents

Erica España of Twine Events offers a complimentary consultation to determine a customized planning package. Her sweet spot is planning events in wineries, open fields, historical landmarks, and unique venues that showcase the beauty of the California landscape.

UNION JANE

unionjane.co | @unionjaneco

This online-only service (which employs a team of design professionals) walks couples through every step of wedding planning, from assembling a mood board to finding vendors and creating a floor plan, all for $300 (the average wedding planner costs $3,200).

VAN WYCK & VAN WYCK

New York, NY

vanwyck.net | @vanwyckvanwyck

With a flair for the dramatic, this family-run firm loves creating whimsical, fantastical environments with a focus on fun.

RENTALS

ARCHIVE RENTALS

Locations throughout California and in Cancún, Playa del Carmen, and Tulum, Mexico; ships throughout North America

archiverentals.com | @archiverentals, @archivemexico

In addition to the wide selection of canopy structures, table linens, and perfectly distressed vintage rugs, the Archive collection boasts a 1955 Airstream. Owners Regina Crosby Atkins and Krista Jon are also available for full event design and coordination through Crosby + Jon Design (crosbyandjon.com).

ARK

Glendale, CA; ships nationwide

thearkrentals.com

As self-described "modern archaeologists digging daily for uncommon tabletop pieces and other beautiful objects," the team at Ark offer an edited assortment of items, from beautiful crinkle linen napkins to custom upholstered escort boards.

BORROWED BLU

Culver City, CA, New York, NY, and West Hartford, CT

borrowedblu.com | @borrowedblu

This luxury tabletop company houses a mix of antique and new pieces, including an exclusive stash of earthy ceramic Russel Wright plates. Browse their extensive presentation styles to help inspire your scape.

BRIGHT EVENT RENTALS
Locations throughout California
bright.com | @brighteventrentals

If you are throwing a Wine Country wedding and need to bring in everything, Bright is a great place for basics, with an extensive rental catalog featuring everything from catering kitchens and heating to Riedel glasses.

CASA DE PERRIN
Los Angeles, CA; ships worldwide
casadeperrin.com | @casadeperrin

This site is a must-visit for tablescape inspiration. Diana and Josh Perrin, a husband-and-wife duo, have set the standard with a cache of curated settings with a collection that includes Heath Ceramics and perfectly mismatched vintage patterns. They now even produce their own in-house line in Italy.

ELAN EVENT RENTALS
Santa Barbara, CA; ships nationwide
elaneventrentals.com | @elaneventrentals

Founded by a surfer and longtime Santa Barbara resident, this company offers a warm, modern collection of items that feels more like what you'd find in an interior design showroom than at a rental business. Think teak cups and bowls, wooden loungers with crisp white cushions, surfboards, and tons of custom, weathered pieces you'll want to bring home.

FOUND VINTAGE RENTALS
Fullerton, CA
foundrentals.com | @foundrentals

Jeni Maus's assortment of antique and reimagined pieces grew from her quest to fill her own home with distinct furnishings. Culled from the California coast, Texas, the Mid-Atlantic region, Hungary, and France, her assortment is distinguished by authentic, well-made, one-of-a-kind items.

GOODWIN EVENTS
Greensboro, GA
goodwinrentals.com | @goodwinevents

Margie and Drew Sorrel stumbled into the rental industry after opening a bed-and-breakfast called Goodwin Manor. Don't be fooled by the mom-and-pop front—they can handle big Southern extravaganzas (like pitching a 10,000-foot sailcloth tent with 1,300 square feet of dance floor, 400 square feet of staging, and over six hundred chairs).

LA MAISON FÊTE
Bedford, NY, and Boston, MA
lamaisonfete.com | @lamaisonfete

La Maison Fête is a full-scale wedding and event planning company founded by Brett Cameron and Deanna Maranon. They are also well-known for a beautiful collection of tabletop decor that's available for rent.

LA TAVOLA
Locations nationwide
latavolalinen.com | @latavolalinen

From their Napa-based warehouse, La Tavola offers options that are not your standard rental-grade textiles; instead they source fabrics from the same manufacturers used by the fashion and design industries. Beyond tablecloths, they offer aisle runners, chair covers, and lace for chuppah canopies.

PATINA
New York, NY
rentpatina.com | @rentpatina

Patina's expertly curated modern furnishings are broken down into different style collections to help organize your look—or you can mix and match items from different collections. Moroccan floor pillows, teepees, and pink velvet sofas are some of the most popular finds.

SHELTER CO.
Austin, TX, and San Francisco, CA
shelter-co.com | @shelterco

In addition to being able to provide all of the rentals for an outdoor event (they are renowned for their stylish Meriwether tents), Shelter Co. can handle all the planning needs. There's a $2,000 rental minimum for in-state rentals and a $20,000 rental minimum for rentals outside of California and Texas.

SKYLINE TENT COMPANY
Charleston, SC, and Charlottesville, VA; ships throughout the South and the Mid-Atlantic region
skylinetentcompany.com | @skylinetentcompany

Skyline is here to make a tented wedding the first choice, not a backup, with authentic Sperry sailcloth tents and signature pennant flags. This is the go-to place for all things tents in the Southeast. They will also help with venue consultations.

SMALL MASTERPIECE
Los Angeles, CA, and New York, NY
smallmasterpiece.com | @smallmasterpiece

With a "white-glove" approach to table setting, Jason Murakawa has assembled a collection that includes thousands of pieces produced in the eighteenth and nineteenth centuries. Think David Haviland & Co. Limoges porcelain sets, Christofle knife rests, and sterling silver flatware.

THEONI COLLECTION
Beverly Hills, Napa, and San Francisco, CA; ships to many parts of California
theonicollection.com | @theonicollection

Planners love pulling from Theoni's design forward collection of furniture and tabletop (dinnerware options, for example, include Haviland, Heath Ceramics, Vietri, Juliska, and their own in-house line), but they also stock things like lighting and heaters.

TOWN & COUNTRY EVENT RENTALS
Pasadena, Santa Barbara, and Van Nuys, CA
tacer.biz | @tacer_losangeles

This company has setting up and striking down to a perfect science. And with a massive inventory (think tents, china, lawn games, linens, etc.), they can also easily handle more than one party at a time.

YEAH! RENTALS
Los Angeles and San Francisco, CA
yeahrentals.com | @yeahrentals

The modern, urban pieces curated by Michael Antonia, who got his start in the design world working with Alex Calderwood of Ace Hotels, make events instantly feel cool (think Moroccan poufs and Herman Miller modular sofas).

SPECIALTY FASHION & BEAUTY

Chances are, you are already aware of some, if not all, of the big names in bridal design: Amsale, Carolina Herrera, Dolce & Gabbana, Elie Saab, Jenny Packham, J Mendel, Lela Rose, Monique Lhuillier, Oscar de la Renta, Reem Acra, Valentino, Vera Wang, Viktor & Rolf, etc. On the men's side, there's Burberry, Dolce & Gabbana, Giorgio Armani, Ralph Lauren, Tom Ford, Yves Saint Laurent, etc. Then there are the department stores that carry some of these brands, including the Saks Fifth Avenue bridal departments in Los Angeles and New York, Bergdorf Goodman's bridal department, and the Neiman Marcus bridal salon in Dallas—and let's not forget David's Bridal, which is the largest bridal-store chain. Beyond these well-known designers and distributors, there are a handful of under-the-radar specialty boutiques and wedding salons offering indie and emerging designers, vintage pieces, custom suiting, one-of-a-kind items, and smaller, tightly edited selections of luxury brands. Then there are the hair and makeup professionals who will bring together your whole look. Here is a curated list of those less conspicuous names to have in your back pocket.

LITTLE ONES

BONPOINT
Locations nationwide
bonpoint.com | @bonpoint

This classic and luxurious European children's clothing (think cashmere sweaters, silk dresses, and tailored suits) and accessories boutique has locations in the following cities: Bal Harbour, Beverly Hills, Chicago, Houston, New York City, Palm Beach, and Short Hills.

ETSY
etsy.com | @etsy

Etsy is a wonderful resource for handmade smocked dresses and linen suits. Many independent vendors will also create custom pieces. Favorite sources include Patricia Smith Designs (etsy.com/shop/PatriciaSmithDesigns), Itty Bitty Couture (etsy.com/shop/IttyBittyCouture), and Chasing Mini (etsy.com/shop/ChasingMini).

HIP! HIP! HOORAY!
Dallas, TX
hiphiphooraydallas.com | @hiphiphooraydallas

This family-owned boutique has become a Dallas institution since opening its doors in 1999, stocking high-quality smocked clothing and heirloom pieces from birth to children's size 12. Popular brands include Anavini, Auraluz, Feltman Bros, Florence Eiseman, Kissy Kissy, and Ralph Lauren.

J. CREW
Locations nationwide
jcrew.com | @jcrew

While J. Crew may have folded its bridal collection, it is still a great place to find looks for your littlest attendants. The Crew Cuts line features a range of preppy staples including Italian wool suits and special-occasion chiffon dresses.

LOS ENCAJEROS
Bilbao and Madrid, Spain
losencajeros.es | @losencajeros

Charming high-quality European-made linen dresses for little girls and babies. Don't worry: the website translates all the ordering information into English.

SPRING FLOWERS
New York, NY, and Palm Beach, FL
springflowerschildren.com | @springflowerschildren

Since 1983, this Upper East Side establishment has sold the finest luxury European clothing, shoes, and accessories for babies and children up to age fourteen.

MEN'S

BILLY REID
Locations nationwide
billyreid.com | @billy_reid

Bill Reid is an American sportswear designer who describes his style as "lived-in luxury." His company, which is headquartered in Alabama with a Manhattan design studio, also offers a made-to-measure experience. Measurements and fittings can be done at one of their thirteen domestic retail locations.

J. MUESER
New York, NY
jmueser.com | @j.mueser

Jake Mueser got his training at the Fashion Institute of Technology before opening his own boutique on Christopher Street, where he designs bespoke suits (grooms-to-be can enjoy a glass of Balvenie scotch with each fitting).

KLEIN EPSTEIN & PARKER
Locations nationwide
kleinepsteinparker.com | @keprebels

Offering made-to-measure suits at department store prices (a custom two-piece suit is $698, tuxes start at $998) out of fabrics sourced directly from Italy, they can even duplicate your look for your groomsmen.

MARTIN GREENFIELD CLOTHIERS
Brooklyn, NY
greenfieldclothiers.com | @greenfieldsuits

Martin Greenfield has been called the best men's tailor in the United States. The Holocaust survivor—along with his two sons, who both work for the company—creates handmade suits in his factory near Williamsburg.

MILLER'S OATH
New York, NY
millersoath.com | @millersoath

Brothers Kirk and Derrick Miller opened the doors to Miller's Oath in Greenwich Village in 2007, proffering the finest-quality bespoke suits, coats, shirts, and accessories.

WOMEN'S

A&BÉ
Locations nationwide
aandbebridalshop.com | @aandbe_bridalshop

Book a ninety-minute appointment at one of these jewel-box boutiques and find an offering of emerging designers and a laid-back, no-fuss experience. Most dresses are made to measure and start at around $1,000.

BHLDN

Locations nationwide

bhldn.com | @bhldn

This Anthropologie sister brand has emerged as one of the most popular destinations for vintage-inspired wedding gowns. They also specialize in looks for the bridal party and bridal accessories and offer whimsical wedding-centric design objects such as candleholders, ring pillows, boxes and dishes, and pretty cake servers and stands.

CYNTHIA COOK BRIDES

San Francisco, CA

cynthiacookbrides.com | @cynthiacooksmith

Former *Vogue* staffer Cynthia Cook is the go-to stylist for fashion-forward brides-to-be. In addition to helping select the dress, she can curate the entire wedding look, from save-the-date to send-off.

THE DRESS THEORY

Nashville, TN, San Diego, CA, and Seattle, WA

thedresstheory.com | @thedresstheory

You won't find mermaid silhouettes or ball gowns here. Instead, these sister-owned bridal shops stock an edited range of rare and unique gowns that don't feel traditionally bridal.

GLAMSQUAD

Locations nationwide

glamsquad.com | @glamsquad

On-demand hair, makeup, and nail teams servicing New York City, Southern California, South Florida, Washington, DC, and Boston. They can schedule trials in advance, and bridal party hair packages include blow outs, updos, and braids.

HAPPY ISLES

Hollywood, CA

thehappyisles.com | @happisles_salon

Tucked away along Sunset Boulevard in Hollywood, this tony shop carries vintage designer gowns from the 1950s through the 1990s in addition to bridesmaid gowns, made-in-L.A. crowns and hair accessories, and a wide array of veils. Appointments are hosted one at a time and bridal parties are welcome.

HUSHED COMMOTION

Brooklyn, NY

hushedcommotion.com | @hushedcommotion

Designer Thea Bloch-Neal creates unique, hand-crafted veils, headpieces, and belts and consults with bohemian brides-to-be out of her jewel-box studio.

LE JOUR COUTURE

Lafayette and New Orleans, LA

lejourcouture.com | @lejourbridal

This upscale boutique has two locations and carries an elevated selection of dresses from New York Bridal Fashion week, including designs from Atelier Pronovias, Viktor & Rolf, and Reem Acra, along with a host of accessories.

LOHO BRIDE

Los Angeles and San Francisco, CA

lohobride.com | @loho_bride

LOHO offers a modern bridal experience for "women who don't identify with the mainstream aesthetic, but who seek an organic, comfortable, and easy alternative to dress shopping for their big day." The store carries made-to-measure designers, including Houghton, Sophie et Voilà, and Bo & Luca, in addition to accessories and off-the-rack pieces.

LOVELY BRIDE

Locations nationwide

lovelybride.com | @lovelybride

Having opened their first location in 2010, this company claims to be "the O.G. indie wedding dress boutique." They continue to stock under-the-radar, up-and-coming designers who also tend to be more cost-conscious than some of the traditional bridal maisons. Cities include Charleston, Chicago, Dallas, Houston, Los Angeles, Miami, New York City, Philadelphia, Phoenix, Rochester, San Diego, San Francisco, Seattle, and Washington, DC.

LUNA BOUTIQUE

Sewickley, PA

luna-boutique.co | @lunasewickley

The curated selection at this appointment-only boutique features original, nontraditional styles (think eco-friendly fabrics and vintage and bohemian silhouettes). Designers in the permanent collection include A la Robe, Lindee Daniel, and Daughters of Simone.

MARK INGRAM ATELIER

New York, NY

markingramatelier.com | @markingrambride

Since 2002, Mark Ingram's intimate midtown bridal salon has been a go-to source for brides seeking classic gowns from high-end designers like Vera Wang and Oscar de la Renta. Ingram is on the floor almost every day to offer advice, plus there's an in-house seamstress to handle all of your alterations.

THE MEWS

New York, NY, and Clifton and Notting Hill, England

themewsnewyork.com | @themewsbridal

Led by a mother-daughter team, this by-appointment boutique exclusively stocks cool French designers Laure de Sagazan, Margaux Tardits, and Rime Arodaky.

MODA OPERANDI

New York, NY, and London, England

modaoperandi.com | @modaoperandi

Brides can search online by style (sheath, embellished, off-the shoulder, etc.), event (wedding, honeymoon, rehearsal dinner, etc.), or designer, or shop one of the online trunk shows. The team here offers in-person appointments (fittings and styling) at their New York and London showrooms, special orders and custom gowns, head-to-toe looks for the bridal party, and even ring sourcing.

MONVIEVE

New York, NY, and Milan, Italy

monvieve.com | @monvieve

This haute couture bridal accessory company offers the finest quality bespoke veils from Italy and headpieces from France.

NAME OF LOVE

nameoflove.com | @nameoflove

A foolproof aid to finding the perfect bridesmaids' dresses, this site allows brides to create a digital showroom and then invite their maids to come shop. Modern dress styles come in complementary silhouettes and a color palette that's meant to be mixed and matched.

NET-A-PORTER

net-a-porter.com | @netaporter

If you don't mind skipping the in-person experience of shopping for your dress, this British website consistently has one of the best assortments for the modern bride, with a designated shopping tab filled with the season's white pieces. It's also a wonderful resource to find looks for other wedding events.

REFORMATION

Los Angeles and San Francisco, CA, and New York, NY

thereformation.com | @reformation

A go-to source for on-trend, superflattering, budget-friendly bridesmaids and bridal dresses, Reformation is committed to eco-fashion, creating sustainably made garments (many constructed of deadstock or Tencel).

SARAH SEVEN

Chicago, IL, Los Angeles, CA, New York, NY, and San Francisco, CA

sarahseven.com | @sarahseven

Designed for casual, effortless weddings, the classic collection is stocked with simple, body-hugging architectural gowns while the bride collection offers more ethereal, flowing silhouettes.

SHAREEN

Los Angeles, CA, and New York, NY

shareen.com | @shareenbridal

Shareen Mitchell's vintage emporiums have been a favorite source among top fashion editors. In addition to vintage wedding gowns, she offers a line of reworked and custom white gowns for a bride with a sense of nostalgia.

SPINA

New York, NY

spinanyc.com | @spinabride

This by-appointment-only boutique with two locations in downtown Manhattan carries an exquisite assortment of international designers including Luna Bea, A la Robe, and Lee Grebenau, with the majority of gowns in the $3,500 to $6,500 range. They are also offer floral design, full wedding planning, and day-of coordination.

STONE FOX BRIDE

stonefoxbride.com | @stonefoxbride

Molly Rosen Guy is leading the charge of unconventional brides looking for gowns that reflect a cool, modern, downtown vibe. In addition to custom-made dresses, the brand offers vintage gowns, rings, veils, tiaras, and headpieces.

ULTIMATE BRIDE

Chicago, IL

ultimatebride.com | @ultimatebridechicago

The buyers at this posh Oak Street establishment have an eye for picking the best-of-the-season gowns that are in line with the tastes of their fashion-forward clientele. Designers carried include Carolina Herrera, Mira Zwillinger, and Oscar de la Renta.

VÊNSETTE

The Hamptons and New York, NY, Los Angeles and San Francisco, CA, and Miami, FL

vensette.com | @vensette

Laura Remington-Platt's beauty concierge services allows users to book vetted on-location professionals online or through the app. Wedding packages include up to two hair and makeup trials for the bride, custom hair and makeup on the wedding day, and touch-ups for photos following the ceremony.

THE WEDDING DETAILOR

Napa, CA

theweddingdetailor.com | @theweddingdetailor

The team here goes far beyond alterations, providing brides with a range of day-of services including professional ironing and steaming, last-minute on-site alterations (for the bridal party too), and styling. Their monogrammed hankies made from lace from the bridal gowns are beautiful keepsakes.

WHITE ROSE COLLECTIVE

New York, NY

whiterosecollective.com | whiterosecollective

Teddi Cranford left her career as a hairstylist in the high-fashion world (think runway shows for the likes of Dior and Valentino) to work with brides and brought a team of experienced stylists (both hair and makeup) along with her, giving wedding parties around Manhattan cool, fashion-forward beauty looks.

STATIONERY

While there are a handful of wedding stationers with brick-and-mortar locations, the truth is that in-person meetings are not essential—phone, email, and snail mail are perfectly acceptable ways to communicate with your stationer. Keep this in mind as you decide on whom you'd like to work with—in this category, your vendor could live across the country. (If that's the case, you will need to build in time for the delivery of materials, particularly the day-of materials, such as the escort cards and table numbers.)

AERIALIST PRESS

Walnut Creek, CA

theaerialistpress.com | @aerialistpress

If you aren't able to make an appointment at their studio, you can design everything online based on their regular collection templates or their "couture" collection. What's also nice is their pricing transparency: there's a spreadsheet on their site laying out specific costs for each piece by quantity.

AMBER MOON DESIGN

Los Angeles, CA

ambermoon-design.com | @ambermoondesign, @pitbullsposies

An architect turned wedding planner turned paper designer, Amber Moon (who previously operated under "Pitbulls and Posies") is beloved by wedding industry insiders for her up-for-anything attitude, her love of creative collaborations among friends, and her raw talent.

ANNE ROBIN

Los Angeles, CA

annerobin.com | @annerobincallig

Anne Robin grew up doing calligraphy for friends' bar mitzvahs and her parents' grown-up parties. Today, in addition to traditional calligraphy, she's best known for the modern, streamlined fonts she's developed herself.

BE A HEART

Los Angeles, CA

beaheart.com | @beaheartdesign

Erica Tighe strongly believes that "beauty will save the world," and out of that ethos she runs her L.A. boutique, where she works with couples on custom suites and day-of goods. You can also order wonderful things from the online shop, like your vows written out in watercolor or printed on a linen scroll.

BERNARD MAISNER

New York, NY

bernardmaisner.com | @bernardmaisner

With over thirty years of experience creating bespoke invitations, master calligrapher and stationer Bernard Maisner is known for his distinct blend of Spencerian and copperplate writing categorized by Italian, French, and Americana scripts (his Italian font was originally created for Valentino).

BROWN LINEN

Atlanta, GA

brownlinendesign.com | @brownlinendesign

As seen in custom items such as dripped-wax seals and tissue paper wrapping, proprietor Abany Bauer's aesthetic balances modern minimalism with old-world European sensibilities. Call early, because the studio books well in advance.

BRYLO

Longmont, CO

brylostudio.com | @brylo_wed, @brylo_studio

Modern, minimalist, elegant, artistic, clean . . . these are some of the descriptors for Chaz Cole's letterpress work. Couples can choose from seven different collections and customize a suite with a two- to three-week turnaround time; a custom job usually takes four to six weeks, but she can accommodate rush orders.

CURLICUE DESIGNS CALLIGRAPHY

New York, NY

curlicuedesigns.com | @curlicuedesigns

Samantha Martin is known for applying her old-school technique in modern ways—think unexpected surfaces, such as leaves, or unique color combinations, such as gray on blush. Her signature font, the Curlicue, has "flourishes for days."

A DAY IN MAY

San Francisco, CA

adayinmay.com | @adayinmay

Lesley Hathaway and Eve Weinsheimer create impressive monograms and custom suites printed on an old-school letterpress. (Note: They work by appointment only and exclusively with clients represented by event planners.)

ELLEN WELDON

New York, NY

weldondesign.com | @ellenweldondesign

From her Flatiron studio, Ellen Weldon excels at crafting completely customized suites with supercreative envelope liners (marbled, splatter-painted, faux croc, etc.) and monograms.

EMILY J. SNYDER

Los Angeles, CA

emilyjsnyder.com | @gemtones

Emily Snyder has a BFA in drawing, painting, and jewelry design. She got into stationery working at Mr. Boddington's Studio. Today the multimedia artist is sought after for her bold, unconventional, slightly Tim Burton—esque script style.

A FABULOUS FETE

Orange County, CA

afabulousfete.com | @afabulousfete

Lauren Saylor turned her side hustle into her life's work. Now the self-taught designer applies modern, whimsical fonts and watercolors onto surfaces from classic kraft paper and vellum to place cards made out of acrylic, agate, or terra-cotta tiles. Couples can shop semi-custom suites or create something from scratch.

HAPPY MENOCAL

New York, NY

happymenocal.com | @happymenocal

It's hard to believe that Happy Menocal only opened the doors to her studio in 2012. Her oft-imitated watercolor emblems and playful hand-painted invitations paved the way for a new approach to stationery design that's approachable, relaxed, and bespoke.

HILLARY HAUSER

Pasadena, CA

hillaryhauser.org | @_hillaryhauser

A self-described "recovering florist and overall creative enthusiast," Hillary divides her calligraphy styles into two categories: fancy and fun. Both convey her clean, approachable, nontraditional style.

IDYLL PAPER (TARA SPENCER)

Vancouver, Canada

idyllpaper.com, tara-spencer.com | @taraspencer_

Many newcomers to the stationery space try to emulate Tara Spencer's delicate, romantic studies in muted palettes, with details like abstract brushstrokes, textured deckle-edged papers, and wax. Couples can find her original, refined stationery suites online, and she does bespoke work, too. Along with her husband, Spencer is also director and founder of August, a linen brand.

IRINA BIRDIE

irinabirdie.bigcartel.com | @irina.birdie

Almost everything on the Irina Birdie site features a delicate herbarium print, and all of her creations are lovingly handcrafted (kraft paper gift tags with pressed leaves and flowers make for especially wonderful additions to party favors and welcome bags).

JANELLE SING

Napa, CA

janellesing.com | @janellesing

Charming, colorful custom monograms adorned with fanciful flora and fauna are the focus of Janelle Sing's work, which has been featured in a number of high-fashion publications.

JONATHAN WRIGHT AND COMPANY

Los Angeles, CA

jonathanwright.com | @jonathanwrightandcompany

If the online stationery experience sounds too impersonal, or if you simply want to work with one of the best in the biz, Jonathan Wright's one on one approach focuses on quality and authenticity, whether the couple's taste is classic or totally avant-garde. (*See examples of his work on pages 34–41.*)

JOYA ROSE

Carpinteria, CA

joyarose.com | @joyarose

Hand-lettering artist and illustrator Joya Rose Groves abides by the spirit of the Danish word *hygge*, which "embodies the most cozy of cozy"—in other words, a sense of intimacy and authenticity in each brushstroke.

JULIE SONG INK

Oakland, CA

juliesongink.com | @juliesongink

Julie Song has created beautiful watercolor botanicals for individuals and companies such as BHLDN (you can also purchase prints on her Etsy shop). Couples can choose from one of the semi-custom invitation suites (which start at $1,060). She also takes on a limited number of custom projects each year.

KAELA RAWSON

Nashville, TN

kaelarawson.com | @kaelarawson

With a BFA in graphic design and a penchant for using unconventional mediums like pastels, Kaela Rawson takes a progressive approach that results in artful and understated stationery suites. She's known for using abstract cutouts and shapes, textured paper, negative space, and a muted palette.

KATIE FISCHER DESIGN

New York, NY

katiefischerdesign.com | @katiefischerdesign

Katie Fischer approaches wedding stationery as a branding exercise in which every element must be part of a cohesive whole. First, she creates an inspiration board for her client, then designs mock-ups, and finally unveils her custom-designed products, which include everything from the website to the day-of goods along with extras such as place mats, maps, and seating charts.

THE LEFT-HANDED CALLIGRAPHER

Dallas, TX

thelefthandedcalligrapher.com | @nicoleblackcalligraphy

With a "turnkey" ordering process, couples choose calligraphy style and paper goods from the gallery (save-the-dates are $300; invitation suites are $400), then Nicole Black will design, print, and hand-address everything for you to stuff, stamp, and mail. (And yes, she really is left-handed.)

MAUREEN MEYER
Los Angeles, CA
maureenmeyerdesign.com

Having worked as a designer for brands like Aveda and Avon, Maureen Meyer takes a highly conceptual approach to wedding invitations. Think of it almost like branding for couples, with ingenious type monograms.

PEEPS PAPER PRODUCTS
Washington, DC
peepspaperproducts.com |
@peepspaperproducts

Laura "LouLou" Baker, who previously worked in fashion for designers such as Narciso Rodriguez, Thakoon, and Givenchy, has created a "fashionable world of luxury paper products" with custom watercolor illustrations to adorn everything from wedding maps to preppy playing cards to give away as favors.

PLUME CALLIGRAPHY
Toronto, Canada
plumecalligraphy.com | @plumecalligraphy

Aileen Fretz has the fine-casual approach to stationery down to a science with delicate, soft, yet readable letters printed on textured handmade paper, silk ribbons, wooden veneer escort cards, and vellum. Choose from a range of semi-custom suites.

RACHEL ROGERS DESIGN
San Francisco, CA
rachelrogersdesign.com | @rachelrogersdesign

Rachel Rogers's process starts with learning about each couple—their interests and passions and the places and things that are important to them—before she makes a sketch for their approval. Once it's approved, she paints the design onto watercolor paper. Playful, custom crests, dozens of which are featured on her site, start at $500, but she can do the whole suite, too.

REFINE
Salt Lake City, UT
refine-studio.com | @refine.studio

Nikkol Christiansen's ultra-pared-down aesthetic and use of negative space feels clean and fresh. Her signature palette is cream, gray, beige, and black, and she also frequently uses blind embossing.

STEPHANIE FISHWICK
Charlottesville, VA
stephaniefishwick.com | @stephaniefishwick

Trained under former White House chief calligrapher Pat Blair, Stephanie Fishwick is highly sought after for her exquisite fine-art approach. Her opulent yet charming botanical collages and wide range of whimsical calligraphic styles are truly frameworthy.

TARA JONES
Dallas, TX
tarajones.com | @tarajonescalligraphy

A skilled calligrapher, Tara Jones offers a range of styles, from embellished Parisian script to modern freehand. Calligraphy for invitation suites starts at $400 (penning the bride and groom's names on the invitations is $125).

TINY BONES
New York, NY
tinybones.com | @tinybonespress

At this company founded by Megan Lorenzo in 2014, all designs are hand-fed through a letterpress on the best quality recycled cotton paper. With an aesthetic that skews clean and simple, the Tiny Bones team can work with an existing logo and/or design that you already have, or they are available to design your project with you.

TINY PINE PRESS
Los Angeles, CA
tinypinepress.com | @tinypinepress

Jennifer Parson's love of handmade craftsmanship began when she was a child in rural Appalachia. Today at her custom print shop, everything is made on vintage Chandler & Prices presses and the aesthetic is organic and artisanal (think pressed flowers, twine wraps, invites printed on wood, and elements connected by a hand-stitched string).

VENAMOUR
New York, NY
venamour.com | @venamour

Under the creative direction of Lisa Hedge, this sophisticated online studio offers three flora-inspired wedding stationery suite collections featuring everything from save-the-dates to table numbers and thank-you cards.

WELL-WRITTEN CALLIGRAPHY
Washington, DC
well-writtencalligraphy.com | @wellwrittencalligraphy

Tim Blair specializes in pointed pen, copperplate, and script calligraphy in classic fonts with beautiful flourishes. Since everything is done by hand, he is also able to match any style and color.

WRITTEN WORD CALLIGRAPHY
Vancouver, Canada
writtenwordcalligraphy.com | @writtenwordcalligraphy

Karla Lim has curated six beautiful and timeless semi-custom suite options (either four pieces or two pieces) for couples to choose from. Clients can then personalize everything from paper stock, calligraphy, and color (flat or shimmery foil), or go the full custom route.

YONDER DESIGN
San Francisco, CA
yonderdesign.com | @yonderdesign

In addition to beautiful paper printing, the husband-and-wife lead team at Yonder is known for their use of exotic and unexpected materials such as leather, glass, acrylic, marble, and mother-of-pearl.

SUPPLIES

CASEY RUBBER STAMPS
New York, NY
caseyrubberstamps.com

This funky East Village establishment where you can design custom stamps for a return address or a name card keeps "artist hours," meaning they are closed in the morning but remain open until 8:00 p.m. (or sometimes later).

CREATIVE CANDLES
Available online and at retailers nationwide
creativecandles.com | @creative.candles

Based out of Kansas City, Missouri, this family-owned business makes hand-dipped, hand-poured, smokeless, dripless candles in just about every shape and shade you could imagine.

FROUFROU CHIC
froufrouchic.com | @froufrouchic

Ginny Au and her France-based stepmother teamed up to create exquisite silk ribbons and styling products (such as crinkled silk table runners). Everything is hand-dyed, hand-torn, hand-frayed, hand-pressed, hand-rolled, and beautifully hand-finished.

GLASSYBABY
Available online and at retailers in California, Oregon, and Washington
glassybaby.com | @glassybaby

Sustainably made by local artisan glassblowers, the vast collection of votives and "drinkers" come in uniquely named hues like the Happily Ever After sets. Glassware is available for purchase and for rent.

IKEA
Locations worldwide
ikea.com | @ikeausa

A trip to the Scandi standby is an economical way to fill out some of the details, and may even be less expensive than renting. Think candles, candleholders, furniture accents, and baskets and boxes to hold welcome gifts.

JAMALI GARDEN
New York, NY
jamaligarden.com | @jamaligarden

This wholesale decor source in Manhattan's Flower District carries everything from fair trade raffia gift totes from Madagascar and exotic seashells from the Philippines to modern zinc planters from Vietnam and hand-thrown pottery from Italy and Tunisia.

SAINT SIGNORA
saintsignora.com | @saintsignora

This online trove features vintage and Italian-inspired procured items that will become instant heirloom pieces. Think Florentine trays (perfect ring boxes), handmade paper, wax seals, and all manner of brooches, pins, lockets, and tiny antique cameos.

SILK & WILLOW

The Hudson Valley, NY

silkandwillow.com | @silkandwillow

From her kitchen, Shellie Pomeroy cooks up old-fashioned plant-dyed silk ribbons and table linens from foraged materials. The results are beautiful colors that are actually found in nature. After tying a bouquet or being wrapped around a flower girl's dress, the high-quality heirloom pieces are meant to be used again and again.

WAX SEALS

wax-works.com | @waxseals

This online company sells custom wax seals with adhesives backs (in addition to the old-fashioned kind) in myriad styles and colors, so all you have to do is peel and stick. Their sister site, WaxSeals.com, has all the design inspiration you'll need.

OTHER CREATIVES & SERVICES

From specialty artists on Etsy to gift-box curators, some wedding vendors don't seem to fit within traditional categories.

CUT ARTS

Southern California

cutarts.com | @cutarts

With a roster of high-profile clients, scissor artist Karl Johnson cuts custom silhouettes to be mounted on card stock, or he can attend your event to create portrait favors.

ETSY

etsy.com

Whether you are looking for ring boxes, charming DIY party favors, or pounds of dried lavender for guests to toss during your recessional, Etsy has a host of creative indie creatives. Some favorite vendors include VerdeStudio and Mail Made Stamps for vintage postage and NatalieStopkaStudio for ribbons.

GREG KALAMAR

Los Angeles, CA

gregkalamar.com | @greg_kalamar

Greg Kalamar will arrive at your wedding with an easel, stretched canvas, and a palette of acrylics and after about four hours will have finished a beautiful in-situ painting of your wedding scene. His services start at around $3,500.

ISHA FOSS DESIGN

Virginia Beach and Richmond, VA

ishafossevents.com | @ishafoss

After planning her own wedding in 2001, Isha Foss launched her planning and design firm. She has since given up the planning aspect to focus on the design of the day, working with couples to create the total look of the wedding with everything from custom draping, furnishings, and flowers to backdrops and linens.

KARINA PUENTE ARTS

Philadelphia, PA

karinapuentearts.com | @karinapuentearts

Karina Puente specializes in white fine-art *papel picado* (like the colorful cutout paper banners, only much higher end) and travels extensively to install her pieces as wedding backdrops, table runners, and installation pieces.

SIMONE LEBLANC

Los Angeles, CA

simoneleblanc.com | @simoneleblanc

Simone LeBlanc specializes in creating expertly curated custom gifts. Couples can collaborate with her on a custom box or they can pick from her portfolio of beautifully edited and assembled welcome boxes, bridesmaid/groomsman gifts, and favors, as well as thank-you gifts for vendors. (*To see examples of her work, visit page 307.*)

THE VENUE REPORT

venuereport.com

Need help finding a wedding venue or unique space for a rehearsal dinner or brunch? This website has one of the most comprehensive lists of spaces for any type of gathering. Think private homes, barns, boutique hotels, wineries, and rooftops. They can also assist with room blocks and securing group rates at hotels.

PHOTOGRAPHERS & VIDEOGRAPHERS

Because choosing your photographer is such a visual decision, the best way to learn about someone's technique and style is by looking at their portfolio. Start by considering the work of photographers closest to your wedding location. If you want to or need to work with an out-of-town photographer (which is pretty common), just be sure to factor in their travel and lodging expenses (and those of their assistants).

AARON DELESIE
New York, NY
aarondelesie.com | @aarondelesie

ALLAN ZEPEDA
New York, NY
allanzepeda.com | @allanzepedaphotography

AMY & STUART PHOTOGRAPHY
Los Angeles, CA
amyandstuart.com | @amyandstuart

APRIL STORY FILMS
Los Angeles, CA
aprilstoryfilms.com | @aprilstoryfilms

BEN BLOOD
Seattle, WA
benblood.com | @benblood

BRAEDON FLYNN
Costa Mesa, CA
braedonphotography.com | @braedonflynn

BRUMLEY & WELLS
Durango, CO
brumleyandwells.com | @brumleyandwells

THE CANA FAMILY
San Luis Obispo, CA
canafamily.com | @canafamily

CHARLOTTE JENKS LEWIS
Brooklyn, NY
charlottejenkslewis.com | @charlottejenkslewis

CHRISTIAN OTH STUDIO
New York, NY
christianothstudio.com | @christianothstudio

CHRISTINA MCNEILL
San Francisco, CA
christinamcneill.com | @christinamcneill

CONNIE WHITLOCK
Denver, CO
conniewhitlockphoto.com | @connie_whitlock

CORBIN GURKIN
Charleston, SC
corbingurkin.com | @corbingurkin

DOCUVITAE
Los Angeles, CA
docuvitae.com | @docuvitae

ELIZABETH MESSINA
Santa Monica, CA
elizabethmessina.com | @elizabethmessina

ERIC KELLEY
Charlottesville, VA
erickelley.com | @erickelley

ERICH MCVEY
Salem, OR
erichmcvey.com | @erichmcvey

GENEVIEVE DE MANIO
Carlisle, MA
demaniophotography.com | @gigidemanio

GIA CANALI
Los Angeles, CA
giacanali.com | @giacanali

GRANT DANIELS
Fort Worth, TX
grantdanielsphotography.com | @grantdaniels

GREER GATTUSO
Gretna, LA
greergattuso.com | @greergattuso

HANNAH THOMSON
Brooklyn, NY
hannahthomson.com | @hannahthomson

HEATHER KINCAID
Los Angeles, CA
heatherkincaid.com | @heatherkincaidphoto

HEATHER NAN
Salt Lake City, UT
heathernanphoto.com | @heathernan

HELENA & LAURENT
Oakland, CA
helenaandlaurent.com | @helenaandlaurent

JAMES AND SCHULZE
Erie, CO
jamesandschulze.com | @jamesandschulze

JAMES MOES
Kansas City, MO
jamesmoes.com | @jamesmoesweddings

JEN HUANG
New York, NY
jenhuangphoto.com | @jenhuangphoto

JILLIAN MITCHELL
Los Angeles, CA, New York, NY, and Sayulita, Mexico
jillianmitchell.net

JOEL SERRATO
Solvang, CA
joelserrato.com | @joelserrato

JOHN DOLAN
New York, NY
johndolan.com | @johndolanphotog

JOSE VILLA
Solvang, CA
josevilla.com | @josevilla

JOSH GRUETZMACHER
San Francisco, CA
joshgruetzmacher.com | @joshgruetz

JUDY PAK STUDIO
The Hamptons and New York, NY
judypak.com | @judypakstudio

KATE OSBORNE
Salt Lake City, UT
kateosbornephotography.com | @kateosborne

KT MERRY
Miami, FL
ktmerry.com | @ktmerry

LARA PORZAK
Los Angeles, CA
laraporzakphotography.com | @laraporzak

LAUREN & ABBY ROSS
Los Angeles and Santa Barbara, CA
laurenandabby.com | @abbyandlauren

LAUREN BALINGIT
Chicago, IL, Nashville, TN, and destination
laurenbalingit.com | @laurenbalingit

LIZ BANFIELD
Minneapolis, MN
lizbanfield.com | @lizbanfield

LOVE + WOLVES CO
Locations worldwide
loveandwolves.co | @ loveandwolvesco

LUCKY MALONE
Denver, CO, and Saratoga, WY
luckymalone.com | @luckymalone

LUCY CUNEO
Charleston, SC
lucycuneoweddings.com | @lucycuneoweddings

MARIA LAMB
Portland, OR
marialamb.co | @maria.lamb

MAX WANGER
Los Angeles, CA
maxwanger.com | @maxwanger

MEG SMITH PHOTOGRAPHY
Napa, CA
megsmith.com | @megsmithphotography

MK SADLER
Los Angeles, CA
mksadlerwed.com | @mksadlerwed

NANCY COHN WEDDINGS
Palm Beach, FL
nancycohnphoto.com | @nancycohnphoto

NANCY NEIL
Los Angeles, CA
nancyneilphotography.com | @lovenancyneil

NICKI SEBASTIAN
Los Angeles, CA
nickisebastian.com | @nickisebastian

OLIVIA RAE JAMES
Charleston, SC
oliviaraejames.com | @oliviaraejameswed

OUR LABOR OF LOVE
Atlanta, GA, Los Angeles, CA, and New York, NY
ourlaboroflove.com | @ourlaboroflove

PAIGE JONES
Portland, OR
paigejones.us | @paigejonesphoto

RYLEE HITCHNER
Tuscaloosa, AL
ryleehitchner.com | @ryleehitchner

SAMUEL LIPPKE STUDIOS
Los Angeles, CA
samuellippkestudios.com | @samuellippkestudios

SARAH FALUGO
Los Angeles, CA
sarahfalugoweddings.com | @sarahfalugoweddings

SASHA GULISH
Larkspur, CA
sashagulish.com | @sashagulish

SCOTT CLARK
Los Angeles, CA
scottclarkphoto.com | @scottclarkphoto

A SEA OF LOVE
Dallas, TX
aseaoflove.com | @aseaoflove

SHARK PIG
Los Angeles, CA
sharkpig.com | @sharkpigweddings

SIDNEY BENSIMON
Los Angeles, CA, and New York, NY
sidneybensimonweddings.com | @ sjbweddings

SYLVIE GIL PHOTOGRAPHY
San Francisco, CA
sylviegilphotography.com | @sylviegil

TARALYNN LAWTON
Mill Valley, CA
taralynnlawton.com | @taralynnlawtonphoto

TANJA LIPPERT
Los Gatos, CA
Tanjalippert.com | @tanjalippert

TEC PETAJA
Nashville, TN
tecpetajaphoto.com | @tecpetaja

TESS COMRIE
Salt Lake City, UT
tesscomrie.com | @tesscomrie

THAYER GOWDY
Bolinas and San Francisco, CA
thayergowdy.com | @thayerandco

THE IMAGE IS FOUND
Kansas City, MO
theimageisfound.com | @imageisfound

**THE WEDDING ARTISTS COLLECTIVE (HEATHER
WARAKSA, NORMAN & BLAKE, SAMM BLAKE)**
Locations worldwide
theweddingartistsco.com | @theweddingartistsco

FEATURED VENDORS

PAGE 210 TOP Designer: Chanel Dror; planner/florist: Mon Plus Beau Jour; stationery: John Derian (place cards), Jennifer Rose Smith (menu); tabletop rentals: Options, Chambord Prestige. BOTTOM Planner: Emily Park; stationery: Tiny Pine Press; rentals: Town & Country Event Rentals.

PAGE 211 TOP LEFT Planner and stationery: Beth Helmstetter Events; florist: Studio Mondine. TOP RIGHT Planner: J. Ben Bourgeois Productions, Inc. BOTTOM LEFT Planner: Bash Please; florist: Soil and Stem; stationery: Rachel Rogers Design. BOTTOM RIGHT Planner: Laurie Arons Special Events; rentals: The Party Store Montana; florist: Sarah Winward (Honey of a Thousand Flowers); stationery: Amber Moon Design, Written Word (calligraphy).

PAGE 213 Planner: Lisa Vorce Co.; florist: Aspen Branch; rentals: Ark.

PAGE 214 LEFT Planner: Callista & Company; designer: Brigit.KH.Studio; florist: Studio Mondine. RIGHT Planner: Jill LaFleur; florist: Flower Wild.

PAGE 215 LEFT Designer: Ginny Au; florist: Mary McLeod (Amy Osaba Events); rentals: 12th Table. RIGHT Planner: Lisa Vorce Co., florist: Saipua.

PAGE 216 LEFT Planner: Emily Park; rentals: Town & Country Event Rentals; florist: Oma Arriola Designs. RIGHT Planner/caterer: Annie Campbell Catering; tabletop rentals: Casa de Perrin; chair and linen rentals: Town & Country Event Rentals; florist: Bloom & Plume.

PAGE 217 LEFT Florist: Studio Mondine. RIGHT Planner: Aaron Hartselle; stationery: Amber Moon Design, Anne Robin Calligraphy (calligraphy); florist: Yasmine Floral Design; rentals: Town & Country Event Rentals, A Rental Connection.

PAGE 219 Planner: Bash Please; florist: Moon Canyon; rentals: Found Vintage Rentals.

PAGE 220 TOP Rentals: Town & Country Event Rentals; stationery: The Paper Bakery. BOTTOM Planner: Ashley Smith Events; stationery: Goods Gang, Jen Kay (graphic design), Tabitha Stoodley (illustrations); rentals: Town & Country Event Rentals, Signature Party Rentals, La Tavola Linens, Hensley Event Resources, FlexibleLove.

PAGE 221 TOP LEFT Designer: Ginny Au; rentals: 12th Table; stationery: Kaela Rawson. TOP RIGHT Planner: Bash Please; florist: Isa Isa Flowers; rentals: Parachute Home and Heather Taylor Home (linens), Casa De Perrin (dinnerware). BOTTOM LEFT Planner: Italia Celebrations. BOTTOM RIGHT Planner: Annie Campbell Catering; rentals: Casa de Perrin.

PAGE 222 TOP Laurie Arons Special Events; rentals: Standard Party Rentals (plates and flatware), La Tavola Linens; florist: Sarah Winward (Honey of a Thousand Flowers). BOTTOM Planner: Bash Please; florist: Soil and Stem.

PAGE 223 TOP Planner: Bash Please; florist: Moon Canyon; rentals: Bright Event Rentals, Found Vintage Rentals. BOTTOM Planner: Lisa Vorce Co.; florist: Saipua.

PAGE 224 TOP Planner: Annie Adair (Tuscan Tour); stationery: Rifle Paper Co. BOTTOM Designer: Joy Thigpen; florist: Studio Mondine; table numbers: Ashley Buzzy.

PAGE 225 TOP LEFT Planner: Oren Co; stationery: Tiny Pine Press; florist: Bloom & Plume. TOP RIGHT Planner: Bash Please; florist: Moon Canyon. BOTTOM LEFT Planner: Lisa Vorce Co.; stationery: Amber Moon Design, Emily Snyder (calligraphy); florist: Aspen Branch. BOTTOM RIGHT Planner: Love & Splendor; stationery: Sue Yang and Esther Lee (The Romance Between).

5 | FOOD & DRINK

PAGES 234–35 Planner/caterer: Annie Campbell Catering; florist: Bloom & Plume; rentals: Casa de Perrin.

PAGE 239 Planner: Shannon Leahy Events; florist: Studio Mondine; rentals: Bright Event Rentals (tables and chairs), Wildflower Linens (chair covers), La Tavola Linens (table linens).

PAGE 240 Planner: Beth Helmstetter Events.

PAGE 241 TOP LEFT Planner: Easton Events; florist: Mindy Rice Design; rentals: Elan Event Rentals. TOP RIGHT Planner: Oren Co; rentals: Found Vintage Rentals. BOTTOM LEFT Planner: Shannon Leahy Events; florist: Studio Mondine. BOTTOM RIGHT Planner: Bash Please; florist: Sarah Winward (Honey of a Thousand Flowers).

PAGE 243 LEFT Planner: Emily Park; catering: Thatcher House; RIGHT Caterer: Ella Freyinger.

PAGE 245 TOP LEFT Planner: Bash Please; furniture: Found Vintage Rentals. TOP RIGHT Planner: Michelle Rago Destinations. BOTTOM LEFT Planner: Maggie Wilson (Shelter Co.). BOTTOM RIGHT Planner: Lisa Vorce Co.; florist: Aspen Branch.

PAGE 246 TOP LEFT Planner: Bash Please; stationery: Rachel Rogers Design. TOP RIGHT Matchbooks: Jonathan Wright. BOTTOM LEFT Planner: Bash Please. BOTTOM RIGHT Illustrations: Kara Strubel.

PAGE 247 TOP LEFT Planner: Beth Helmstetter Events. TOP RIGHT Planner: Laurie Arons Special Events; board: Jill Sassa (PS Paper). BOTTOM LEFT Planner: Bash Please;

flowers: Moon Canyon. BOTTOM RIGHT Planner: Bash Please; florist: Sara Winward (Honey of a Thousand Flowers).

PAGE 249 Planner: Bash Please; catering: Meadowood Napa Valley; plates: Frances Lane.

PAGE 251 TOP RIGHT Planner and stationery: Bash Please. BOTTOM LEFT Planner: Michelle Rago Destinations; stationery: Two Paperdolls. BOTTOM RIGHT Planner: Love & Splendor; stationery: Sue Yang and Esther Lee (The Romance Between).

PAGE 253 Cake: Delicious Arts; florist: Moon Canyon; planner: Bash Please.

PAGE 254 LEFT Cake: Jasmine Rae Cakes. RIGHT Cake: Nine Cakes; florist: Studio Mondine.

PAGE 255 LEFT Cake: Perfect Endings Cakes; florist: Sarah Winward (Honey of a Thousand Flowers); planner: Laurie Arons Special Events. RIGHT Cake: Wicked Island Bakery; planner/florist: Stonekelly Events.

PAGE 256 LEFT Planner: Emily Park; cake: Solvang Bakery; florist: Oma Arriola Designs. RIGHT Planner: Alexandra Kolendrianos; cake: Sherman's Deli.

PAGE 257 LEFT Cake: Branching Out Cakes; florist: Studio Mondine. RIGHT Cake: Amangiri; florist: Sarah Winward (Honey of a Thousand Flowers).

PAGE 258 Cake: Megan Joy Cakes; florist: Aspen Branch.

PAGE 259 Desserts: Lori Stern.

6 | THE PARTY

PAGE 271 Planner: Bash Please; rentals: Bright Event Rentals, Found Vintage Rentals.

PAGE 272 LEFT Planner: Maggie Wilson (Shelter Co.); rentals: Bright Event Rentals (furniture), La Tavola Linens; florist: Brown Paper Design. RIGHT Planner: Oren Co; florist: Waterlily Pond.

PAGE 273 LEFT Planner: Bash Please; florist: Sarah Winward (Honey of a Thousand Flowers); rentals and tent: Bright Event Rentals. RIGHT Planner: 42° North; florist: Lillibet.

PAGE 274 Planner: Beth Helmstetter Events; florist: Camelback Flowers.

PAGE 276 TOP Planner: Oren Co; florist: Mindy Rice Design.

PAGE 277 TOP RIGHT Planner: Beth Helmstetter Events. BOTTOM LEFT Planner: Oren Co; florist: Mindy Rice Designs.

PAGE 278 Planner: Jess Baker.

PAGES 280–81 Planner: Bash Please; rentals: Bright Event Rentals (tent), Hensley Event Resources (chairs), Found Vintage Rentals (furniture); stationery: Stephanie Fishwick, Amber Moon Design; florist: Sarah Winward (Honey of a Thousand Flowers).

PAGES 282–83 Planner: Alexandra Kolendrianos; florist/event designer: Mindy Rice Design; rentals: Planks & Patina (chairs), Elan Event Rentals (lounge seating); cigar roller and entertainment: Bob Gail Events; lighting: Images by Lighting.

PAGES 284–85 Planner: Laurie Arons Special Events; florist: Sarah Winward (Honey of a Thousand Flowers); entertainment: Élan Artists, The Bumbys; lighting: Illusions Lighting Design; custom chandelier: Jacob Wolf.

PAGES 286–87 Planner: Stefanie Cove and Co.; florist: Tinge.

PAGE 291 Planner: Oren Co

PAGE 292 Planner: Joanne Gregoli.

PAGE 294 TOP LEFT Planner: Julia Lake Parties. TOP RIGHT Planner: Maggie Wilson (Shelter Co.). BOTTOM LEFT Planner: Michelle Rago Destinations. BOTTOM RIGHT Planner: Bash Please.

PAGE 295 TOP LEFT AND RIGHT Planner: Maggie Wilson (Shelter Co.). BOTTOM LEFT Planner: Beth Helmstetter Events. BOTTOM RIGHT Planner: Lisa Vorce Co.

PAGE 296 Stationery: Jonathan Wright.

7 | GIFTING

PAGES 304–5 Planner: Bash Please.

PAGE 309 TOP LEFT Planner: Maggie Wilson (Shelter Co.). TOP RIGHT Planner: Shannon Leahy Events. BOTTOM LEFT Planner: Callista & Company; designer: Brigit. KH.Studio. BOTTOM RIGHT Planner: Beth Helmstetter Events.

PAGE 310 TOP Planner: Oren Co.

PAGE 311 TOP LEFT Planner: Bash Please.

PAGES 324–25 Planner: Maggie Wilson (Shelter Co.).

PAGE 339 Planner: Bash Please; florist: Brown Paper Design.

PAGE 382 Dress: Johanna Ortiz.

ACKNOWLEDGMENTS

I am incredibly grateful to friends, family, and colleagues who helped make this book possible. To my family at *C Magazine*, thank you for taking a chance on a young and inexperienced writer all those years ago and for the incredible opportunities and assignments over the years that taught me so much. And, of course, thank you for the introduction to the wedding industry.

Lauren and Abby Ross, the gifted lead photographers on this project, your beautiful images were the inspiration for this book, and it has been such a lovely experience working with you both.

I want to thank members of the wedding community for sharing their experiences and advice. A special thank-you to all the enormously talented photographers who graciously contributed images to make this book complete (see page 383). I am so inspired by the direction this industry is heading in.

Katherine Cowles, I frequently think about how lucky I am that our paths crossed. Thank you for believing in me and for your friendship. You are a true professional.

To the brilliant and tireless team at Artisan who rolled the dice on a first-time author and made me feel like a bona fide New York writer. Lia Ronnen, an incredible listener and teacher, I am beyond grateful. To Bridget Monroe Itkin, a true partner on this project, thank you for your dedication, patience, and for making everything better. A special thank-you to Michelle Ishay-Cohen, Jane Treuhaft, Jennifer K. Beale Davis, Sibylle Kazeroid, Elise Ramsbottom, Nancy Murray, Hanh Le, Allison McGeehon, Theresa Collier, and Amy Kattan. What an absolute privilege and honor it has been working with you all.

Thank you to my family. To my husband, Josh, for the joy of getting to experience our own modern wedding firsthand and for being a wonderful role model for our little boys.

And lastly, to the couples whose beautiful ideas fill the pages of this book: this would not have been possible without your creativity and your willingness to venture off the beaten path. Thank you.

INDEX

PHOTOGRAPHY CREDITS

Most of the images you see in this book were taken by sisters Abby and Lauren Ross. Lauren currently resides in Santa Barbara and Abby in Marina del Rey. They work together and separately (and sometimes with their mother) on weddings, commercial shoots for fashion clients, and fine-art projects. Their work has been published in *Martha Stewart Weddings* and *C Magazine* and on Vogue.com. I am also enormously grateful to the following photographers who contributed their work to this book.

Amy and Stuart Photography: page 83 (bottom left); Sidney Bensimon: page 107 (bottom right); Samm Blake: pages 109, 134 (third and fourth from left), 139 (bottom); Ben Blood: pages 31 (top left), 45 (bottom right), 79 (top right); Jesse Chamberlain, Our Labor of Love: page 108 (left); Lucy Cuneo: pages 85 (top right), 88 (bottom); Sarah Falugo: pages 77 (top left and bottom right), 81 (bottom left and right), 86, 88 (top), 92 (left), 104 (top left), 105 (top and bottom left), 106 (top left), 117 (top right), 121 (top right), 181 (bottom right), 210 (top), 220 (bottom), 313 (left); Braedon Flynn: pages 16, 76, 91, 94, 131 (right), 171, 213, 225 (bottom left), 245 (bottom right), 258, 295 (bottom right); Josh Gruetzmacher: pages 239, 241 (bottom left); Sasha Gulish: pages 100, 106 (bottom left), 175 (bottom left), 186, 203 (bottom right), 260–65, 272 (right), 309 (top right), 313 (right), 382; Rylee Hitchner: pages 7, 14, 99 (bottom left), 104 (bottom right), 116 (bottom right), 148–49, 180, 215 (left), 221 (top left); Kate Holstein: page 224 (bottom); Skip Hopkins: pages 216 (right), 221 (bottom right), 234–35; Olivia Rae James: pages 8, 33 (top left), 99 (top left), 160, 266–67; Emily Michaels King: page 45 (top right); Heather Kincaid: pages 89 (bottom left), 204 (top), 220 (top); Simone LeBlanc: page 315; Tanja Lippert: pages 81 (top left), 107 (bottom left), 131 (left), 165 (left), 204 (top), 256 (right), 282–83; Love + Wolves Co: pages 127, 135; Christina McNeil: pages 89 (top left), 203 (bottom left); Greg Mionske: page 80; Jillian Mitchell: pages 318–23; James Moes: pages 45 (top left), 79 (bottom left), 133 (bottom left), 175 (top right), 181 (top right); Heather Nan: page 165 (right); Shannen Natasha: pages 87, 104 (bottom left), 133 (top right), 161, 169 (bottom right), 203 (top right), 217 (left), 254 (right); Nancy Neil: pages 4–5, 79 (bottom right), 117 (top left), 139 (top), 187, 225 (top right), 181 (top left), 219, 223 (top), 241 (bottom right), 247 (bottom left), 251 (top right), 253, 257 (right), 271, 85 (bottom right); Donna Newman: pages 31 (bottom right), 77 (bottom left), 92 (middle), 115 (top left), 215 (right), 223 (bottom); Sarah Noel: pages 97, 255 (right), 312; Norman & Blake: pages 19, 27, 82, 105 (top right), 121 (bottom left), 202, 221 (top right), 273 (right); Lara Porzak: page 169 (top left); Kaela Rawson: page 50; MK Sadler: pages 2, 12, 89 (top and bottom right), 95 (bottom left), 107 (top right), 108 (right), 132, 134 (second from left), 221 (bottom left), 243 (right), 277 (top left), 297; Joel Serrato: pages 32, 169 (bottom left), 172 (left), 222 (top), 255 (left); The Image Is Found: pages 112 (left), 225 (bottom right), 251 (bottom right); Hannah Thomson: pages 95 (right middle), 99 (bottom right), 105 (bottom right), 115 (bottom right), 167, 179, 225 (top left); Jose Villa: pages 104 (top right), 163, 166 (left), 172 (right), 211 (bottom right), 217 (right), 241 (top left), 284–85; Stephanie Williams, This Modern Romance: page 254 (left).

I would also like to thank the following people and companies for providing images of their products for the featured couples' registries.

PAGE 65 Rachel Rogers painting: Rachel Rogers; Hill House Home Waverly sheet set: Hill House Home; Coyuchi kitchen napkins: Coyuchi; Year & Day flatware set: David William Baum for Year & Day; Royal Copenhagen serving plate: Royal Copenhagen; wooden jar spoons, Richard Brendon crystal barware, and Japanese basket: Ben Kist for March; Antica Farmacista diffuser: Shelley Callaghan for Antica Farmacista.

PAGE 147 Vitamix 780: Vitamix; Heath Ceramics salt and pepper shakers, Edward Wohl cutting board, and David Mellor knife set: Jeffery Cross; Heather Taylor Home napkins: Heather Taylor Home; Le Creuset Dutch oven: Williams Sonoma; Astier de Villatte vase: Astier de Villatte; Dolce Vita Italian flatware and Ichendorf Milano Italian glassware: Joshua Schaedel.

PAGE 195 Hasami porcelain mugs and bowls: tortoise; Amy Dov wall hanging ceramics: Eesome Co; Aleph Geddis sculpture: AJ Ragasa; Kat and Roger ceramics: Tom Piercy/Alpha Shadows; rope incense: Sivana; Poppy and Someday Marfa Moon Mist: Jamie Arrigo; Mystic Mamma desk calendar: Mijanou Montealegre/ Mystic Mamma.

PAGE 233 Atlas pasta machine: Sur La Table; Santa Maria Novella candle: Officina Profumo - Farmaceutica di Santa Maria Novella; Weber Smokey Mountain Cooker smoker: Crate and Barrel; Chemex coffeemaker and Duraclear tumblers: Williams Sonoma; Josef Hoffmann crystal: Neue Galerie New York; Frances Palmer pottery platter: Frances Palmer; Nespresso Aeroccino 4 milk frother: Nespresso; Herend Indian basket china: Herend USA.

PAGE 265 KitchenAid Pro Line stand mixer, Williams Sonoma Professional copper 10-piece cookware set and Global Classic 10-piece wood block set: Williams Sonoma; Lue Brass serving spoon and Heath Ceramics Cloudview dinner set: Jeffery Cross; rose gold flatware: West Elm; Nespresso Citiz espresso maker with Aeroccino: Nespresso; Frette bath towels: Frette; Dyson Pure Hot + Cool Link air purifier: Dyson.

PAGE 303 Sheldon Ceramics Silverlake dinner set and Vermont berry bowl: Sheldon Ceramics; All-Clad Gourmet slow cooker: Williams Sonoma; LSA International Ivalo container and lid: LSA International; Farmhouse Pottery olive oil bottle: Farmhouse Pottery; Match Gabriella place setting: Ellen Silverman for Match; Sol&Luna ice bucket: Sol&luna; JIA ceramic steamer set: JIA; Borosil glass tumblers: Rocky Luten/food52.

ABOUT
THE AUTHOR

Kelsey McKinnon grew up in Chicago and graduated from Boston University with a degree in English. She is a senior contributing editor at *C Magazine*, *C for Men*, and *C Weddings*, where she has led coverage of the wedding industry since the magazine's debut. She lives in New York and Los Angeles with her husband and their children.